PERMANENT
ITALIANS

Also by Judi Culbertson and Tom Randall

Permanent Parisians
Permanent Londoners

PERMANENT ITALIANS

*An Illustrated,
Biographical Guide to the
Cemeteries of Italy*

*Judi Culbertson
and
Tom Randall*

WALKER AND COMPANY
NEW YORK

First published in the United States of America in 1996 by
Walker Publishing Company, Inc.

Published simultaneously in Canada by Thomas Allen & Son
Canada, Limited, Markham, Ontario

Library of Congress Cataloging-in-Publication Data
Culbertson, Judi.
    Permanent Italians: an illustrated, biographical guide to
    the cemeteries of Italy/Judi Culbertson and Tom Randall.
        p.   cm.
    Includes bibliographical references (p.   ) and index.
    ISBN 0-8027-7431-8 (pbk.)
    1. Italy—Biography.   2. Cemeteries—Italy—
Guidebooks.   3. Italy—Guidebooks
    I. Randall, Tom, 1945–   .   II. Title.
CT1125.C85   1996
920.045—dc20   95-41353
                                                         CIP

Series design by Julia Rowe and Summer Hill Books

The photographs on pp. 96 and 100 are by Gayle Simon

Printed in the United States of America

 10   9   8   7   6   5   4   3   2   1

To Andrew and Robin
with love

CONTENTS

	Preface	ix
	Acknowledgments	xi
1	ROME: Antiquities	1
2	ROME: Santa Maria del Popolo and Santa Maria Maggiore	13
3	ROME: Pantheon and Santa Maria sopra Minerva	25
4	ROME: The Protestant Cemetery	43
5	ROME: St. Peter's Basilica	57
6	ROME, NAPLES, and FORMIA: Quick Trips	69
7	UMBRIA and TUSCANY	83
8	FLORENCE: San Lorenzo, the Capelle Medicee, and the Duomo	97
9	FLORENCE: Santa Croce	115
10	FLORENCE: English Cemetery	129
11	FLORENCE: Artists' Churches	137
12	EMILIA-ROMAGNA: Bologna, Ferrara, Ravenna, Predappio, and Rimini	147

Contents

13 NORTHERNERS: Milan, Arqua Petrarca, and Padua 165

14 VENICE: San Zanipolo and Chiesa di San Lorenzo 185

15 VENICE: The Frari, Madonna dell'Orto, and St. Lio 197

16 VENICE: Buried on Water 211

Bibliography 229

Index 233

PREFACE

Italy has long been a land of pilgrims. Natives and foreigners, searching for spiritual, emotional, or physical release, first came to worship at the religious relics and remains of their faith. Centuries of culture have broadened the scope of the pilgrims. They now also come to reconstruct and relive history, and to feast on the art, music, food, and local color. Tourism has boomed and with it books as well as the ubiquitous umbrellas of guides leading flocks of tourists through ruins, across piazzas, and into galleries and cathedrals. And all this for good reason: the history of Italy can be rivaled by very few countries.

From the ancient Etruscans on we can trace the lives and civilizations of its inhabitants. The Roman ruins and the miraculous remains at Pompeii provide a tangible record of daily life from centuries when written records were scarce and in many cases unreliable. "Official" histories were blatantly prejudiced in favor of those in power. The historians Suetonius, Tacitus, and Dio Cassius rectified this to some extent, but they were overly dependent on innuendo, moralizing, superstition, and gossip. But from them, at least, flesh-and-blood characters emerge from the past. Not that the performances of the Caesars, of course, did not provide good reason for shock, scandal, and a winking, lascivious leer.

But the history of Italy covers far more ground than the Caesars. The development of the new religion, Christianity, can be traced in the tombstones of the saints—Cecilia, Francis, Clare, Anthony, and Catherine—as well as in the monuments of early rulers such as Theodoric the Goth and Galla Placidia. History also comes alive in the burial places of the popes, that singular collection of individuals whose personalities light up the walls of St. Peter's.

Another explosion occurs in the fifteenth century. The churches of Rome, Florence, and Venice are suddenly filled with the art and architecture of Raphael, Michelangelo, Botticelli, Titian, Tintoretto, and Brunelleschi. Their bodies are there as well, joined by those of the Medicis and Borgias. Intellectuals such as Machiavelli, Galileo, and Paolo Sarpi are also part of this urban flowering, but in the book we make side trips to the smaller hometowns of Dante, Boccaccio, and Petrarch.

The foreign pilgrims whose graves can be visited in Italy are fascinating and diverse. There is a full complement of poets, from Keats and Shelley to Elizabeth Barrett Browning and Ezra Pound; talented Russians such as Sergei Diaghilev, Igor Stravinsky, and Vladimir Horowitz; and expatriates who fall into no easy category, such as Baron Corvo and Peggy Guggenheim. There is no lack of modern native sons either, from Giuseppe Verdi, Arturo Toscanini, Enrico Caruso, and Giacomo Puccini, to Benito Mussolini and Federico Fellini.

As in Paris and London, there are marvelous monuments. The marble sculptures in Milan are particularly poignant and evocative. They give continuing life to soldiers, doctors, schoolchildren, and brides, reminding us that along with the famous, they too are permanent Italians.

So, pilgrim, we invite you to pick up this book and join us as we explore Italy through the lives and deaths of her most famous permanent inhabitants.

ACKNOWLEDGMENTS

Many people have made significant contributions to the production of this book. First and foremost are Ian and Margo Baldwin, whose interest and enthusiasm were instrumental in bringing the Permanent series to life ten years ago with the publication of *Permanent Parisians.* We also thank George Gibson for his energy and commitment to the series and for bringing it to Walker and Company.

We also thank our editor, Jackie Johnson, for her hard work and valuable suggestions, and our copy editor, Vicki Haire, whose thoroughness with grammar and fact-checking has saved us embarrassment. For the beautiful cover design, we thank John Candell.

Closer to home our appreciation goes out to the staff at Port Jefferson Library and Emma S. Clark Library; Nancy Mullen for her ongoing interest and promotion of the series; Julie McClure for her help with matters photographic; Peggy Bruscia and Bob Christian for Latin translations; Gayle Simon and Sherrie Stehlin for photographic assistance; and Marjorie Freedman for her knowledge of art history.

In Italy we thank John and Adriana Murphy for their assistance and hospitality in Milan; Peter Russell for his time and insight in Florence; Maureen Fant of Rome for her knowledge and interest; the gracious but unknown Neapolitan woman who led us to Caruso and Toto; the Polish choir who sang so beautifully in Assisi; and to Italians in general for their gracious warmth and wonderful food and wine.

Finally we thank Dave and Liz Randall and Gordon and Jean Thomsen for attending, in our absence, to Roark and Helen, who in turn have challenged every book and writing tablet for available lap space.

PERMANENT
ITALIANS

CHAPTER 1

ROME
Antiquities

▲ ▲ ▲

When Brutus proclaimed, "I come to bury Caesar, not to praise him," he was taking on a complicated task. The moment a ruler was pronounced dead, all activity died as well and the world went into mourning. Commoners obediently tore at their hair and wailed, and posthumous honors were debated in the Senate. Out of aristocratic closets came the "wax ancestors," lifelike masks of dead family members that were worn in the funeral procession. With a background dirge of horns, the populace fell into their designated places in the parade and swayed on their way to the Campus Martius.

A thousand wax faces and many more human ones turned to watch as the emperor's body, wrapped in purple and carried on a bier, was hoisted onto the pyre. When the fire was lit, a caged eagle at the top was suddenly released to rise from the smoke, a symbol of the imperial soul breaking free. Because appointment as caesar considerably shortened a man's life expectancy, this elaborate ritual could take place at a moment's notice. More than half the emperors from Augustus to Jovian were murdered, and between A.D. 235 and 285 only one out of 26 died of natural causes.

Although Julius Caesar lay in state on the Campus Martius pyre, a group of magistrates seized the body and carried it into the Forum to decide where he should be cremated. While they debated between the Temple of Capitoline Jupiter and Pompey's Assembly Hall, two divine spirits conveniently appeared and set fire to the bier with their torches. The mourners fostered the flames by throwing on dead branches, court benches, and whatever else was at hand. This cremation site has been traditionally

Opposite: Trajan's Column

identified as the place in the Imperial Forum where the Temple of Julius Caesar stood.

GAIUS JULIUS CAESAR *b. 100 B.C., Rome; d. 44 B.C., Rome. "Veni, vidi, vici."* (I came, I saw, I conquered.) Boasted after one of his last great triumphs, the defeat of King Pharnaces in Asia Minor in 47, the famous phrase would apply equally to Caesar's other military triumphs, his political and administrative reign, and his amorous conquests. His oratory skills were second only to those of Cicero, and his military writings have been read for 2,000 years. His energy, intellect, physical courage, fighting skills, and endurance were legendary. He led by word but more important by example. Often Caesar would march his army twice the normal daily distance.

Caesar was also the ultimate political opportunist. He married for political gain, used intimidation and force against his political foes, and ordered the savage slaughter of hundreds of thousands of the defeated Celtic tribes in Gaul, including the women and children. He was vain and dressed like a dandy. His body hair was plucked with tweezers, and when he grew bald he combed his remaining long wisps forward over his bare head. A notorious womanizer, although such was not unexpected from a man of his stature, he likely also had a homosexual relationship with King Nicomedes of Bithynia in his youth.

Caesar was born to a patrician family of no great wealth but good political connections. His initial marriage to Cornelia, daughter of Marius's successor, Cinna, in 84 seemed politically advantageous until Marius was defeated by Sulla. With an uncharacteristic display of marital devotion, and risking loss of property and even life, Caesar refused Sulla's command to divorce Cornelia. Instead he fled with her to Bithynia and the court of King Nicomedes. There he remained until Sulla's death in 81, at which time he returned to Rome and quickly established himself as a young man of great political promise and acumen.

Nominally a reformer, Caesar easily cozied up to both Pompey and Crassus, the leaders of the opposing parties. He advanced quickly and was elected chief priest in 63. By the year 60, his position was sufficiently strong that he was able to join Crassus and Pompey in the autocratic, informal First Triumvirate, solidifying the arrangement by marrying his 17-year-old daughter, Julia, to Pompey.

But Caesar still lacked the great wealth of his two partners, and for this reason he looked north to Gaul, then under his administration. What he saw was both fame and wealth to be gained through military conquest. From 58 to 51 he pursued this course against the populous but disorganized Gallic tribes with great success, even launching two exploratory invasions into England, the second of which utilized the largest Channel invasion force until D-Day. However, with the death of Julia in 54 and that of Crassus in 53, the ties with Pompey quickly weakened. Civil war became inevitable when Caesar broke Roman law by crossing the Rubicon with his troops in 49. Defeating Pompey at Pharsalus, he pursued him to Egypt only to find that the Egyptians had already killed him.

It was then that the 51-year-old Caesar took up with 21-year-old Cleopatra. Attractive, but not the great beauty of legend, Cleopatra's intellect and drive captured him. In 47 she bore a son, naming him Caesarion. If it was Caesar's child, it was his only known son. Fighting his way through Asia Minor and North Africa, Caesar returned to Rome and was joined there by Cleopatra in 46.

Tending to civil affairs, Caesar instituted long-overdue administrative reforms before returning to the battlefield. He was named perpetual dictator in February 44. This was too much for a large clique of conservative nobility who had hoped for a return of the republic (however corrupt and ill-managed it had been when it was run by them), and his death was plotted by 60 conspirators, 20 or so of whom surrounded Caesar and shared in the attack. According to Suetonius, Caesar fought back until he saw Marcus Brutus, of whom he was very fond, strike him in the groin. With that, Caesar uttered in Greek, "You too, my child?" and gave up the fight, collapsing against the statue of Pompey in the Forum.

THE MAUSOLEUM OF AUGUSTUS

Between the time Augustus succeeded Julius and was consigned to the flames of Campus Martius himself, he created a large mausoleum for his family, though his will excluded his daughter, Julia. When designing the massive round tomb, he no doubt imagined that his line would rest here forever, venerated and undisturbed.

But Romans have a fondness for recycling. During the Middle Ages the Mausoleum of Augustus served as a fortress for the Colonna family, then as a circus, a bull ring in which Goethe watched "beast-baiting," and a concert hall. The family ashes have long since disappeared; the urn of Agrippina, Augustus's granddaughter, was sighted being used to measure grain in the Middle Ages. Between 1926 and 1930 the crypt was cleared of debris. You can look through the main entrance and see something of the interior, but access is no longer permitted.

GAIUS OCTAVIUS (A.K.A. OCTAVIAN, A.K.A. GAIUS JULIUS CAESAR, A.K.A. AUGUSTUS) *b. 63 B.C., Velitrae; d. August 19, A.D. 14, Nola, Campania (NNE of Pompeii).* The seal of Augustus was, appropriately enough, a sphinx. That he remains puzzling to us is no surprise, for the surviving source material is blatantly prejudiced. Prior to the battle of Actium many of the accounts are derogatory, coming from the camp of Antonius (Mark Anthony). After the battle of Actium and his ascension to sole power, there is scarce a mumbling criticism to be found. Indeed, wise patron that he was, he found his praises sung by Virgil, Ovid, and Horace. As a young man he could be ruthless in dealing with opponents, and even though his reputation for clemency greatly improved with age, he still displayed a vengeful nature after Actium, ordering unnecessary executions. Still, it can be argued that much of his savagery was necessary. It was kill or be killed, and given the power he killed first.

Gaius Octavius was the son of a knight and, through his mother, Atia, the great-nephew of Julius Caesar. Impressed by the youth, Caesar, who had no legitimate male sons, adopted Octavian and made him his heir. With Caesar's assassination the will became publicly known, and Octavian took his adopted father's name. But this was not enough to ensure automatic power. As Cicero wrote: "There will be war against Anthony with him as leader. Which are we to follow? Look at his name—but then at his age!" Within a year Cicero's prophecy was borne out. Augustus defeated Anthony, only to then quickly ally with Anthony and Lepidus in the formation of the Second Triumvirate in 42.

For the next 11 years he jockeyed for power. Of invaluable assistance in this regard were his brilliant aides, the diplomat Maecenas and the admiral Agrippa. In the end Lepidus was forced into retirement, and Agrippa defeated Anthony and Cleopatra in the great sea battle off Actium. Anthony fled to Egypt and in the following year joined Cleopatra in the world's most famous double suicide.

Solidifying his hold on Rome was another concern that demanded much of Augustus's attention. Not concerned with further conquest, he downsized the military and rewarded the veteran soldiers with land as Caesar had be-

Rome: Antiquities

fore him. For his immediate protection he established the well-paid Praetorian Guard and hired German bodyguards as a further precaution. To mollify the populace, he restored the institutions of the old republic, but as his enemies alleged, these were toothless bodies. He periodically purged the Senate of his foes, ultimately reducing its size from 1,000 to 600 members, and further undermined its authority by advancing the power of knights as civil servants, thereby empowering a more populist group. Since he feared a replication of Caesar's death, senators were able to address him directly one at a time and only after they had had their togas frisked. And yet, fearful of antagonizing the Senate, Augustus continued to consult with and flatter the senators. To appease the nobles, he ceded the holding of certain consulships while maintaining his power, or *imperium,* over the provinces and military.

Part of Augustus's paradox was that his drive for power and posthumous fame combined with a remarkable modesty in his public and personal dealings. All citizens were allowed to come before him in the mornings with their requests. He ate simply and drank moderately (but aggressively pursued sexual affairs). The Casa di Livia on the Palatine was modest, and he slept in the same room for 40 years. He was an insomniac and a hypochondriac, the latter being either a reason or excuse for missing the action of many battles. Fortuitous illness struck just before the enemy, although in one difficult-to-explain instance Augustus was found hiding in a marsh but not with his toga up. This caused many to believe that he was a coward. To belie this charge, Augustus fought in Dalmatia and then Spain, where he received wounds and injuries and, more important, the realization that he lacked Caesar's fighting skills and military judgment. Rather than push the comparison and risk death or tarnished reputation, he retired permanently from the field.

So while the ego was not unchecked, neither was it asleep. Augustus was always thinking of himself and his position. Even after attributing his gambling losses one night to his generosity in overlooking debts, he allowed that he liked "that better, for my generosity will exalt me to immortal glory." And this handsome, short, blond-haired man had reason for vanity. He governed with a rare acuity, striking a long-lived and delicate balance among the many pressures and groups both within and without Rome. The political machinery he established could not be maintained by his successors, but he controlled it through gifts, promises, or intimidation. The populace

5

were won with "bread and circuses." He staged the most elaborate games yet seen and handed out monetary gifts to as many as 300,000 Roman citizens each year.

Even with all this, the last years of Augustus were troubled. Family problems engulfed him. After marrying off his daughter, Julia, three times for political advantage, he exiled her for immorality. She had sinned less than he and said so: "I never take on a steersman unless the ship is full." (Only when she was pregnant did she take a lover.) Her daughter, Julia, and her son, Agrippa Postumus, were also exiled. Military woes also beset him: first the Illyrian revolt in A.D. 6 and then the disastrous defeat of Varus and three legions by Arminius. Boundaries were shrunk, and Roman prestige was lost. Augustus suffered a nervous breakdown, banging his head against a door and crying: "Quinctilius Varus, give me back my legions." After decades of overwork and questionable health, Augustus wavered in his command. His strength to cope diminished. The empire passed into the hands of his appointed successor, Tiberius, when Augustus died after suffering from a night chill on a sea voyage.

Buried with Augustus is his wife, **LIVIA DRUSILLA** (JULIA AUGUSTA, 58 B.C.–A.D. 29). Livia was first married to Tiberius Claudius Nero and gave birth to the future emperor Tiberius in 42. While she was pregnant with Claudius Drusus in 38 she was forced by Augustus to divorce her husband and marry him. Livia served as a devoted and highly influential counselor to Augustus, and herein lies the controversy. Was she, in her attempts to secure succession of the throne to Tiberius, the murderous conniver as portrayed by Tacitus and by Robert Graves in *I, Claudius*? Most historians now believe this to be a canard. Did she exert her influence on Tiberius's behalf? Most certainly. But rumors that she was responsible for the murders of Lucius and Gaius Caesar and even for hastening the death of Augustus himself are most likely the ancient product of dissatisfied opponents of Tiberius. After the death of Augustus, Livia changed her name to Julia Augusta. She was deified by her grandson, Claudius, in A.D. 42.

Ironically, also buried here are Lucius and Gaius Caesar, and Octavia, sister of Augustus. Nerva, who died in A.D. 98, was the last emperor to be buried here. It has been reported that the ashes of Tiberius, Caligula, and Claudius have also resided in the mausoleum, but there is no firm historical proof of this. Certainly they are not here now. Ashes to ashes. Dust to dust.

TRAJAN'S COLUMN

It is perhaps an indication of some innate sense of respect that Trajan's Column has remained upright and unmolested for almost 2,000 years. Considering that the rest of the Forum lies in ruins and that the mausoleums built by Augustus and Hadrian have been recycled many times over, considering that so much of Italy has been dismantled by the Goths, two world wars, and greedy collectors, it is amazing that this intricately carved column still stands.

The column, 100 feet high, can best be viewed with binoculars or the telephoto lens of your camera. It is made up of 17 marble drums, and the spiraling ribbon that separates the scenes would measure 670 feet if unwound. More than 2,500 figures are seen preparing to leave Rome, crossing the Danube in boats, and battling the Dacians (Romanians). In a kind of backhanded tribute to their tenacious enemy, the scene at the top of the column shows the proud Dacians looking back as they abandon their land to Roman rule.

When the column was dedicated in A.D. 113, it was

topped by a gilded statue of Trajan, replaced by St. Peter in 1588. Although it is no longer open, the staircase inside ascends past 43 windows to the top. Were the ashes of **Trajan** (A.D. 53–117) and his wife, Plotina, ever enclosed in a golden urn inside? Opinion is divided. In any case, little but their memory lingers now.

Did Trajan deserve one of the few lasting memorials in history? As with Antipope John XXIII, who is ensconced in private splendor in the Baptistery of San Giovanni, the question can be debated—except that virtually nothing written about Trajan has survived. His own *Commentaries* on the Dacian Wars have been lost. Except for a few highly laudatory references by Pliny, the record is silent.

THE CASTEL SANT'ANGELO

The Castel Sant'Angelo looks as if it is about to sail off its foundations and down the Tiber, an image enhanced by the angel on top acting as a figurehead, and by the ropes coming down from the tallest mastlike pole. There are several decks that visitors can stand on. When the emperor Hadrian had the tomb built, it was covered by white marble designs and displayed over 60 statues. The burial chamber was down a spiral ramp leading into the heart of the building.

Hadrian's ashes, those of his wife, Sabina, and several successors remained intact until the fifth and sixth centuries when the Goths forced their way in, breaking the urns open in their search for gold. Theodoric used Sant'Angelo as a prison, and it became the refuge of popes who were

hustled along the secret passage from the Vatican during times when the city (or the papacy) was under siege. Later its dark walls housed such prisoners as Beatrice Cenci (buried in San Pietro in Montorio). Today it is a military museum, a function of which Hadrian would surely approve.

PUBLIUS AELIUS HADRIANUS *b. January 24, A.D. 76, Italica, Spain; d. July 10, A.D. 138, Baia.* Hadrian's Spanish grandfather, a tough old farmer who read portents in the stars and animal intestines, woke him one night when he was 11 to tell him he would one day rule the world. Hadrian, familiar with his grandfather's prophecies, went back to sleep. Yet four years later he was summoned to Rome by his guardian and cousin, Trajan.

In 98 Trajan was elected emperor, moving Hadrian unexpectedly closer to succession. The now-ambitious 22-year-old consulted two oracles to see if his grandfather's prophecy still held. He was assured that it did. But for the next 19 years he remained in training, fighting alongside Trajan in two wars in Dacia and then in the Middle East. Between conflicts he served as clerk of the Senate. The large, curly-haired Hadrian was mocked for his Spanish accent and his beard; he corrected his speech but refused to undergo the daily tortures of shaving.

Trajan died in Turkey in 117, unwilling to adopt Hadrian until he was on his deathbed, giving rise to the rumor that the adoption papers were a forgery. The routine plots against Hadrian's life began almost immediately. But the new emperor had the army on his side and soon won over the populace with gladiatorial contests and handouts of gold. He even "commemorated" his mother-in-law's death by sponsoring games and giving away spices.

After his confirmation by the Senate, the 42-year-old turned his attention to Rome. He worked to have the law codified and its worst excesses curbed, such as the killing of all estate slaves, even children, if one of them murdered their master. Under Hadrian's direction the army and the civil service were reformed and revitalized, and the social order tilted to benefit the individual rather than the state. Corrupt financial practices, such as the custom that all citizens had to leave a portion to Caesar in their wills or risk losing the whole estate, were abolished.

When Rome was under control, Hadrian spent the next 11 years touring his provinces of the East. He left behind stone memories of his visit: monuments, arches, and roads in North Africa, Greece, Syria, and Palestine. His extensive travel might have wreaked havoc on his home life if he had had one. But though he had dutifully married Trajan's niece, Sabina, at 24, he avoided his pencil-nosed, grim-lipped wife. Interested only in fashion, she returned her husband's distaste.

Unlike Trajan, Hadrian had as his main goal the binding of Rome and the provinces into a unified empire, a task he felt was complicated by the divisiveness of religion. Of the four competing creeds—the worship of Roman deities, Hellenism, Christianity, and Judaism—he focused his ire on the last. He made circumcision punishable by death and planned his own shrine on the site of the razed Temple of Jerusalem. Naturally it provoked a rebellion, which was unfortunately led by the fanatic Bar Kokhba; the conflict ended in the complete destruction of Jerusalem in 134. More significantly, the actions of both men served to sever Christianity from its predominantly Jewish roots and plant it in the hands of the Gentiles.

Despite Hadrian's popularity in the other provinces, he was not loved at home. By the time he returned to Rome he was already suffering severe nosebleeds, which signaled high blood pressure and hardening of the arteries. The side effects were excesses of rage and ill humor, and there were too many incidents like the afternoon at the races when a jockey performed brilliantly and the crowds clamored for his freedom from slavery. Instead of granting the small favor that would have pleased everyone, Hadrian had a placard carried around the arena that read, "You have no right to demand the freedom of a slave who is not your own property, nor to ask me to secure it for you."

Although possessed of the wonderful estate he had built in Tibur—750 acres of gardens, temples, and terraces—by A.D. 138 he only wanted to die. Unable to convince his servant to stab him in the chest or his doctor to administer poison (the doctor took his own life instead), Hadrian finally succumbed to his illness at 62. He left behind his tangible creations—the Pantheon, Sant'Angelo, and Hadrian's Villa—and a poem addressed to his dying spirit:

> Genial little vagrant sprite,
> Long my body's friend and guest,
> To what place take you your flight?
> Cold and comfortless and white
> Leaving now your play and jest.

Hadrian's fine porphyry tomb was appropriated by Innocent II around 1140 for his own use in San Giovanni in Lateran. It was destroyed by the fire of 1360.

DIRECTIONS AND HOURS: The ancient monuments form a triangle with a healthy walk between them. You may want to start at Castel Sant'Angelo, which can be reached by the no. 28 bus. From Sant'Angelo turn left and follow the Tiber, crossing at the second bridge, Pont Cavour, and walk left to the Mausoleum of Augustus. Trajan's Column is located across from the Monument of Victor Emmanuel II and can be reached by walking south on the Via del Corso or taking one of the buses running down it. All monuments can be viewed anytime from the outside.

ROME
Santa Maria del Popolo and Santa Maria Maggiore

▲   ▲   ▲

SANTA MARIA DEL POPOLO

Santa Maria del Popolo is a tiny church with a lot of visual fireworks. Sculpted angels sit all over the beams, and each chapel has paintings and a decorated dome. According to tradition, the site was originally the burial place of the emperor Nero, distinguished by an enormous oak or walnut tree that drew sustenance from the grave. Witches and demons were alleged to gather under its branches, as well as Nero himself with a few demon crows. In A.D. 1099 Pope Paschal II, following a vision, ordered that the tree be uprooted and incinerated, its ashes thrown in the Tiber, and a small church built here instead. The translation of the church's name is subject to debate. For most, the name translates to "Mary of the People." Another story substitutes a poplar tree for the walnut, and we have "Mary of the Poplars." Finally, the church's guide-book says that it is "Mary of the Parish Community." In their own way they all work, so you can take your pick.

In the 17th century Gian Lorenzo Bernini was given a free hand to "beautify" the church and did so by adding arches, sculpture, and variegated marble. Most of the monuments here belong to long-forgotten bishops and cardinals, and many of the artists whose canvases decorate their chapels are obscure as well. The exception is Caravaggio, whose dark-toned masterpieces, showing the cru-

Opposite: Santa Maria Maggiore

cifixion of St. Peter and the conversion of St. Paul, decorate the Cerasi Chapel, left of the main altar.

On the opposite side of the high altar in the last tiny chapel is buried **Vannozza Cattanei** (1442–1518), the mistress of the Borgia pope, Alexander VI; in his prepapal days she presented him with Cesare, Lucrezia, and Giovanni Borgia. Vannozza Cattanei was married four times, to amazingly compliant men who ignored her relationship with Rodrigo Borgia.

In later years she was a sharp businesswoman, owning considerable real estate, though she was found guilty in 1504 of purloining 1,160 of her neighbor's sheep. But increasingly she turned to good works, and her epitaph in Santa Maria del Popolo described her as "conspicuous for her uprightness, her piety, her discretion and her intelligence and deserving much for what she did for the Lateran Hospital." Unfortunately, anti-Borgia sentiment flared up later on and destroyed most of her tomb.

Buried with his mother is **Giovanni Borgia** (1476–1497), rumored to be Alexander VI's favorite son. The pope made him the duke of Gandía when he was 16 and arranged a suitable marriage when he turned 17. The news from Barcelona to Rome was not good, however. The teenage groom was spending his evenings running with a gang that enjoyed slitting the throats of stray dogs and sleeping with women of uncertain virtue. Furthermore, he was amassing huge gambling debts and not attending to his new wife, Maria Enriquez.

Giovanni denied the stories, replying that he was involved in innocent strolls beside the seashore "in the company of honest men," and was not ignoring Maria. Indeed, within two years he had two children by her. But at a dinner in Rome, a masked man came in, whispered something to Giovanni, and they left together.

The next time he was seen was when his brutally stabbed body was dredged from the Tiber. The pope wept, declaring it was a punishment for his own sins, and vowing to do better. He did, for a little while. The identity of the killers—whether members of a rival political family, a band of outraged husbands, loan sharks, or his brother, Cesare, out of jealousy—was never determined. Giovanni looked beautiful on his bier, and it was said that Michelangelo used his face in the *Pietà*.

The Chigi Chapel is near the back of the church on your left. Designed by Raphael and enhanced by Bernini, it is an interesting mixture of the sacred and the profane. The mosaic cupola shows the planets and their pagan deities as well as the signs of the Zodiac, reflecting Agostino

Chigi's interest in astrology. There are also statues of *Elijah* by Raffaello da Montelupo (ca. 1524) and two later sculptures by Bernini: *Daniel and the Lion* (1655–1657) and *Habakkuk with the Angel* (1655–1661). *Jonah and the Whale* by Lorenzo Lotti (ca. 1520) was created from a design by Raphael; Jonah's face bears a striking resemblance to statues of Antinous—the favorite of Emperor Hadrian—who was tragically drowned when the royal entourage was traveling through Egypt.

If you move all the way to the back of the church, you will come across the startling bust of a skeleton in drapery behind an iron grille. The hands crossed across the chest and the tilt of the head give it an imploring expression. The work was created in 1670 by architect **G. B. Gisleni** (d. 1672) for his own tomb with the words "Neque illic mortiuus" (Neither living here nor dead there). The bronze medallions show a caterpillar changing into a butterfly.

Next to the skeleton is a winged dragon looking fierce, predatory, and unhappy all at the same time. He seems to be struggling to get up out of the foundation and exemplifies a memorial to Nero as well as any here.

LUCIUS DOMITIUS AHENOBARBUS (NERO) *b. December 15, A.D. 37, Antium (Anzio); d. June 9, A.D. 68, Rome.* When baby Nero was born, his father did not pass out cigars. In response to his friends' congratulations, Gnaeus Domitius commented that any child born to him and Agrippina "was bound to have a detestable nature and become a public danger." Perhaps he based his prediction not only on Agrippina II, the scheming sister of Caligula, but on his own moral failures—cheating charioteers out of their prize money and gouging out the eyes of rivals. He died when Nero was only three, too soon to know if his prophecy would come true.

The young ruler began promisingly. When he became emperor at 17 after the death of Claudius, Nero allowed Agrippina to rule until he reached his majority, selecting "the best of mothers" as a military password. He lowered taxes, raised the salaries of impoverished senators, and sponsored entertainments for the masses, even banishing all killing from the gladiatorial contests.

Yet despite his popularity, the ruler with the boyish mouth and carefully arranged curls soon developed the paranoia that came with the office. He had Britannicus, Claudius's son, preemptively poisoned at a banquet. Respected senators were accused of treason and executed, and even his childhood tutor, Seneca, came under suspicion and was forced to commit suicide in A.D. 65. When Agrippina criticized his artistic pursuits, Nero convinced himself that his mother was conspiring to overthrow him and had to be eliminated. Poison, loose ceiling tiles, and a collapsible boat failed to carry her off; he finally had to send two naval officers to stab her to death.

Being part of his present family was just as dangerous. When the pregnant Poppaea complained that he was coming home too late from the games, Nero kicked her to death, then had his stepson drowned on a fishing trip. Taking a fancy to a young boy, Sporus, he had him castrated, dressed him as a bride, and married him in a lavish ceremony.

As his father had predicted, Nero became a public danger. He had young men and women bound to stakes, and then, dressed in wild animal skins, Nero sexually attacked them. When his fortune was depleted, he seized estates and melted down the gold and silver statues in the temples. New magistrates were informed, "You know my needs! See to it that nobody is left with anything." Perhaps the only thing he did not do was start the Great Fire of Rome in 64, though it was rumored that he had burned down the city to make room for his Golden House.

Eventually, Nero was done in by his own ambition—not a thirst to conquer the world but a drive to become an entertainer. He took singing lessons and followed methods of voice improvement such as sleeping with a lead slab on his chest and refraining from eating fruit. Strumming a lyre, he entertained the populace with hours of his own compositions.

When the applause of the dutiful Romans palled, Nero left for Greece, where he made musical competition a part of the Olympic Games. He bribed the best competitors to fail and always managed grateful surprise when he was awarded first place. Ignoring urgent messages from the Senate to return home and tend to official business, Nero tarried in Greece for three years. Finally, after exempting Greece from paying tribute, the victor returned home, his laurel wreaths askew. By then it was too late.

What was left of the Senate had, with the support of the army, declared him a public enemy and condemned him to death by flogging. Provincial governors and the Praetorian Guard joined the revolt, and Nero was forced to flee to a villa in the hills. Hearing the sound of the cavalry coming to take him alive, he gasped, "Dead! And so great an artist!" and managed to stab himself fatally in the throat. He was buried in a white porphyry coffin and placed in the Domitii family tomb.

DIRECTIONS AND HOURS: Take the Metro Line A to the Piazzale Flaminio and walk one block south. The church is open daily 7:00 A.M. to 12:30 P.M. and 4:00 to 7:30 P.M.

SANTA MARIA MAGGIORE

Santa Maria Maggiore, commissioned in the fifth century by Pope Sixtus III, was built to honor the Virgin Mary. The occasion was her elevation as the Mother of God at the Ecumenical Council at Ephesus in 431. The charming legend that Mary caused a patch of snow to appear August 5 on the exact spot where the church was to be built is probably not true, though a yearly mass is celebrated on that date to commemorate the miracle.

Our interest is in the two chapels at the front of the church, the Borghese Chapel and the Sistine Chapel. To the left is the Borghese Chapel, where Pope **Paul V** (1550–1621) is interred. His statue shows a hatless Paul kneeling in prayer. It is flanked by two large bas-reliefs: The relief on the left shows Emperor Rudolf II battling the Turks for Hungary; the other is of Paul himself, overseeing construction of fortifications in Ferrara.

In an indirect way, both visitors and Roman residents owe a debt to Paul V. Born Camillo Borghese, he greatly enriched his family's coffers when he was pope, thus leaving the city the beautiful Villa Borghese. Paul had less success in keeping his subjects in line. When Venice ignored his complaints about bringing priests to trial in secular courts, he took the ultimate remedy of placing the city under an interdict and excommunicating its doge and Senate. The Venetians, led by Fra Paolo Sarpi, thumbed their collective noses. Unable to raise military support from England or Holland to punish the rogue city, Paul finally allowed France to mediate a compromise. But it was a moral defeat.

Also interred in the Borghese Chapel is Pope **Clement VIII** (1536–1605). His monument shows him wearing a very high papal crown and holding out his hand in benediction. Clement's strengths were his piety and humility. Unfortunately, he was indecisive and a procrastinator, and moved between expensive households in an attempt to cure his gout. He banned books by Jews, put teeth into the Inquisition, and raised nepotism to a fine art.

On the wall is the stone of historian **Bartolomeo Platina,** who chronicled all these papal deeds and misdeeds. His inscription, in Greek and Latin, reads, "Do not disturb Platina and his family, they are close and want to remain alone. Console yourself, brother; whoever dies well shall live again."

Finally, in an unmarked coffin in the Borghese vault is the fascinating **Pauline Bonaparte Borghese** (1780–1825). Many people know her as the reclining marble nude done by Antonio Canova in the museum in the Borghese Gardens. The statue was commissioned by Pauline as a wedding gift for Prince Camillo Borghese, probably the only thing he ever got from his spoiled young wife besides temper tantrums and infidelity.

If she had little regard for the Borghese clan (who returned the favor by not bothering to label her coffin in the family vault), she adored her brother Napoleon. When he was exiled to Elba, she went to live with him, liquidating her jewelry for his financial support. After his death in 1821, she returned to Rome. Although she had always used poor health to manipulate those around her, when she developed cancer she faced her fate bravely, dying at 45.

In the Sistine Chapel, directly across from the Borghese, are buried a saint and two popes. Under the small altar to your left, which shows two stylized figures in bas-relief, are the remains of **St. Jerome** (ca. 347–420). After a dream in which Jerome, a Latin scholar, was denied entrance into heaven on Judgment Day, he became a hermit. After learning Hebrew, he was ordained a priest.

Conversion did not improve his caustic wit and consequent unpopularity, however. One of his favorite targets was fashionable priests who had their hair styled and "walked on tip-toe lest they should soil their feet." In 386 the saint retreated to Bethlehem with St. Paula and established a monastic settlement.

The monument to **Pius V** (1504–1572) is similar in pose to Clement VIII's except for the golden halo behind his head. The halo is not accidental. Pius was beatified in 1672, and his remains were placed in the sarcophagus below his statue. Every year on his feast day, April 30, a panel is slid open and Pius, clad in a lace surplice, can be viewed.

Pius had a variety of careers, from shepherd to Dominican monk to head inquisitor, before becoming pope in 1566. He continued to wear his rough monk's garments under his robes and condemned prostitution and bullfighting. He also cut down on the use of indulgences,

which, under Leo X, had become one-way tickets to heaven. Perhaps he went a little too far in his zeal to stamp out Protestantism, excommunicating England's Queen Elizabeth in 1570 and releasing her subjects from allegiance to her.

From the looks of his statue, **Sixtus V** (1520–1590) was a huge, good-natured saint. A small halo illuminates his head; he is kneeling humbly, hands clasped, his hat beside him. But in this instance appearances are misleading. Sixtus burst onto the papal stage with violent energy, earning the nickname Iron Pope.

His first act was to control widespread banditry by tracking down and executing thousands of offenders and punishing the nobles who had sheltered them. He then raised taxes, instituted economic reforms, and lived so frugally himself that the treasury was quickly packed with gold. Despite his reforms of church administration and his building projects throughout Rome, Sixtus was not much loved. When he died of malaria, they tore down his statue on the Capitoline Hill.

In a small chapel to your left is a famous tomb, that of

Cardinal **Gonsalvo Rodriguez** (d. 1299). The cardinal is shown in marble, reclining on his deathbed with two angels getting ready to close his mortal curtains. Above him in mosaic is the 13th-century equivalent of a cartoon. St. Matthew and St. Jerome are arguing over who has the best burial spot in the basilica, while Cardinal Rodriguez is thinking, with a smile, that it is his.

Outside the chapel on the steps and pavement to your left is the small slab tomb of the Bernini family. It has a crown design at the top.

GIAN LORENZO BERNINI *b. December 7, 1598, Naples; d. November 28, 1680, Rome.* Perhaps because so much of his work was functional—tombs, fountains, and stage scenery—Bernini believed that his reputation would decline after his death. And it did, helped along by John Ruskin, who labeled Bernini "the epitome of bad taste." Other critics have since deplored baroque art; yet there is something wonderful about Bernini's ability to capture the most dramatic moment in a person's life in marble, whether it be St. Theresa, eyes rolling in ecstasy at being stabbed, or St. Lawrence about to be immolated on a gargantuan grill.

Bernini, the son of a Mannerist sculptor, carved his first marble head when he was eight. At 10 he was presented to Pope Paul V, who asked him to sketch a head. "What head does Your Holiness wish? A man or a woman, old or young, and with what expression—sad or cheerful, scornful or agreeable?" The delighted pontiff prophesied that Bernini would be the Michelangelo of his day. When Bernini was leaving, Paul offered him a chest of gold medals, telling him to help himself and laughing when the child grabbed as many as his pudgy hands could hold.

By 19, Bernini had already done a bust of his early admirer and other work for the Borghese family. He was moving away from the elongated figures and awkward groupings of his father's style and into the naturalism of the baroque. He also subscribed to the theory that there was only one "correct" position from which to view a work of art.

Bernini's early subjects were largely mythic, including the horrifying sight of Daphne metamorphosing into a tree in Apollo's arms. Then in 1623 the new Barberini pope, Urban VIII, called Bernini in and told him how lucky they were to have each other. The sculptor thus began a lifelong association with St. Peter's. Between 1624 and 1633 he created the Baldacchino, the eight-story bronze and gilt canopy over St. Peter's tomb. Its soaring columns included the crawling bees of the Barberini family. Between 1627 and 1647 he created the monument of Urban VIII and worked on that of Alexander VII between 1672 and 1678.

The boy who grabbed the medals was alive in the 40-year-old man who grabbed his assistant's wife, Costanza Bonarelli. Their affair was stormy and public, though it resulted in a wonderful bust of Costanza. But after Bernini openly insulted her husband and then chased his own brother, Luigi, with a sword, his mother begged Urban VIII to restrain her impetuous son. The pope decided it was time Bernini marry. Doing nothing by halves, he did so and produced 11 children.

Bernini never abandoned his work in marble but looked to other arts for amusement. He wrote and directed witty comedies in which he was also responsible for composing the music, painting the sets, and sometimes acting as his own leading man. His special effects were wonderful. In *The Fair,* a walk-on "accidentally" set fire to the backdrop with his torch, ignoring the alarmed cries of the audience. As they began to stampede out, the fire turned into a beautiful garden. In *The Flooding of the Tiber* a large quantity of real water rushed onto the stage and toward another gullible and panicked audience. At the last moment a sluice gate opened and the water disappeared.

Building the Four Rivers and Moro fountains must have been child's play by comparison, but Bernini was not as fortunate with the bell tower he designed for St. Peter's. After it started causing cracks in the basilica in 1645, he had to pay for its demolition. Temporarily in disgrace, the miffed sculptor created *Truth Unveiled* (ca. 1646) and the

Ecstasy of St. Theresa (1645–1652). But by the time he died at 82 after a stroke, he had long been back in favor, prompting his generous comment "Rome sometimes sees poorly but never goes blind."

DIRECTIONS AND HOURS: Take the metro to Termini and walk four blocks on Via Cavour to Piazza dell'Esquiline. The church is open daily 9:30 A.M. to 6:30 P.M.

ROME
Pantheon and Santa Maria sopra Minerva

▲ ▲ ▲

PANTHEON

The Pantheon, which began as a tribute to all gods, has narrowed its focus over the centuries to a handful of mortals. Nevertheless, it remains a wonder of design; the harmony you feel inside the rotunda may be because it is exactly as high as it is wide (142 feet). On a sunny day light streams in from the cupola opening, illuminating the seven chapels and eight smaller niches that ring the hall.

Although Hadrian completely rebuilt the temple in A.D. 120 after it had been destroyed by fire, he placed the inscription of the original builder in 27 B.C. on the portico: "M. Agrippa L. F. cos tertium fecit" (Erected by Marcus Agrippa, son of Lucio and three-time consul). The Pantheon has been stripped, remodeled, and replated through the ages, the most notorious activity occurring in the time of Urban VIII when he not only melted down the bronze portico ceiling for the Baldacchino in St. Peter's but used what was left over for 80 cannons. He also commissioned Bernini to replace the second triangular pediment with a rectangle sporting two rather silly turrets on the ends—known to the Romans as the "ass-ears of Bernini." These were finally removed in 1883.

As you enter, go around to your left. In the second chapel is the vermilion porphyry monument to King **Humbert I** (1844–1900) and Queen **Margherita** (1851–1926). It is decorated simply with four carved lions' heads

and topped by a metal cushion, diadem, and crown. The tomb behind is a rectangle of alabaster surrounded by bronze friezes representing Generosity and Munificence. To the right is a smaller monument to Humbert with an ancient warrior in bas-relief on one side and a modern soldier with a plumed hat on the other.

Humbert I, the son of Victor Emmanuel II, and Margherita were first cousins, whose arranged marriage took place when she was 17. Humbert had a placid childhood; his education was supervised by the military and left him with wide cultural gaps, not helped by his proclivity to hunt pheasant and hare rather than knowledge. Margherita, by contrast, was well-schooled by an Austrian governess in music, art, and the classics. With her tall blond beauty and her knowledge of poetry, Margherita quite captivated Carducci, who rewarded her with his famous "Ode to the Queen of Italy."

Humbert and Margherita clung anxiously to their monarchy, looking to other royal houses for support. The king and queen were relieved when Franz Joseph of Austria and Prince Bismarck of Germany formed a Triple Alliance with them in 1882. Yet it could not stop the effects of a skirmish with France in which a boycott of Italian wines, olive oil, and produce brought on a depression and then revolution.

In 1898 workers at the Pirelli rubber factory in Milan walked out in sympathy with workers in other cities protesting the high price of bread. Humbert received a garbled report that Milan was under siege, and declared martial law in half of Italy's cities. Socialists were killed or imprisoned, and Humbert sent a congratulatory telegram to the most repressive of the generals—a message which was to have fatal consequences for him.

Back in Paterson, New Jersey, an immigrant named Gaetano Bresci read the text of the telegram in the papers and seethed. Saving whatever money he could from his job in a silk factory, he sailed for home in May 1890. On July 29, 1900, the tall white-haired king with the drooping mustache and inscrutable expression was awarding the prizes in a gymnastics competition in Monza. After the ceremony, as he sat in his carriage receiving the cheers of the crowds, Bresci stepped forward and shot him three times.

Margherita declared it the crime of the century. (Certainly it was one of the first. . . .) Because of the heat, a prompt burial was urged, but the queen insisted on packing Humbert in ice and using fans to blow the cold air around the room. Graciously she allowed his longtime mistress to have a few moments alone with the body. Bresci was tried, convicted in nine minutes, and sentenced to life imprisonment.

Margherita lived on as the queen mother for another 26 years, continuing her intellectual salons and charitable works. During World War I she turned her home into a hospital and helped nurse the injured herself. When she died of a cerebral thrombosis after being weakened by influenza, she was sincerely mourned by the populace. Calvin Coolidge sent his regrets.

In the next chapel, under glass, is the tomb of Raphael. He lies in a carved stone sarcophagus with two bronze birds hovering overhead. The sarcophagus, which predates the artist by centuries, was the gift of Pope Gregory XVI in 1833. Before the transfer, Raphael's original tomb was opened to verify whether the artist's remains were actually there. They were, though mired in mud from earlier river flooding.

RAPHAEL (RAFFAELLO SANZIO or SANTI) *b. 1483, Urbino; d. 1520, Rome.* Raphael was born on Good Friday and died on Good Friday, and in the 37 years in between he made the world adore him. Like many Italian artists, he was the son of a minor painter. Orphaned early, he endured unpleasant quarrels over his father's estate between his uncle and stepmother, until he apprenticed himself to Perugino's workshop. He quickly absorbed the artist's sunny style and improved on it. One of his earliest paintings, *Vision of a Knight* (ca. 1504), shows a sleeping youth caught between two women: Industry holds a book and a staff; sensuous Love proffers a primrose, ready to lead him down that path.

Raphael chose both. But first he worked hard to establish himself as an artist. At 20, he went to Florence and spent three years touring studios and learning from other painters. A self-portrait from those days shows him doe-eyed and wistful, still looking for his place in the world. Returning to Perugia, he painted the *Madonna of the Grand Duke* (ca. 1505) in the style of Leonardo da Vinci. Either because people began to believe that the painting could do miracles or because a near-Leonardo was better than none at all, commissions started to come in.

In three years Raphael painted 17 Madonnas and Holy Families for Florentine patrons, paintings with bucolic settings and often a third figure such as Joseph or young John the Baptist. His portraits, also popular, were infused with the personality of the sitter, though idealized for posterity.

In 1509 he was called to Rome by Pope Julius II to decorate the walls of the papal apartments. Michelangelo was at work nearby, painting the ceiling of the Sistine Chapel. Though Raphael admired the older artist, honoring him by painting Michelangelo as Heraclitus in *The School of Athens* (1510), the feeling was not mutual. Perhaps Michelangelo saw him as a rival for commissions; perhaps he had noticed that the musculature of his own figures was showing up in Raphael's papal frescoes.

Michelangeo, often caustic, came upon the popular Raphael with his entourage and sneered, "You look like a prince instead of a painter."

"And you, walking alone, look like a hangman." So ended any hero worship.

Years later, when Giuliano de' Medici commissioned Raphael to paint an altarpiece for a French church and gave a similar commission to Sebastian del Piombo, Michelangelo offered to "help" Piombo to make his the better.

By then there may have been genuine reason for resentment. Julius II had died in 1513 and been succeeded by the amiable Medici pope Leo X. But Leo had grown up with Michelangelo, and his feelings about him— "He is too violent; one can't deal with him"—caused him to favor Raphael in commissions. In 1514 Raphael was made the architect of St. Peter's and the Vatican and put in charge of archaeological excavations for Rome.

What was so appealing in Raphael's art was his idealism, the world he created of calmness and grace. His figures moved in mysterious harmony. Too much of its execution was left to his assistants, causing headaches for art historians, but his own touch was unmistakable: glowing reds and blues, the individualistic preoccupations of the characters in group scenes such as *Parnassus* (1510–1511) and the *Large Holy Family* (1518), the diversity of his Madonnas.

Uninterested in the standard expressions of maternal devotion, he painted *Loreto Madonna* (ca. 1510) with the Madonna holding up a veil and looking down at Baby Jesus appraisingly, as if trying to gauge his intelligence. The *Madonna della Sedia* (ca. 1512), based on a Roman peasant, stares at the artist with defensive protectiveness while the Babe gropes for her breast. His most famous, the *Sistine Madonna* (1514), includes Pope Julius II, St. Barbara, patron saint of "the hour of our death," and the two putti, elbows resting on the wood of his coffin lid, that are reproduced everywhere.

Despite his busyness, Raphael never passed up romance. His patient fiancée, Maria Bibbiena, died before the marriage could take place, and Raphael had to console himself with a bevy of other young women. Giorgio Vasari, the *National Enquirer* of his day, explained the cause of Raphael's death as his becoming overheated by amorous pursuits and failing to tell the doctors the reason for his feverishness—causing them to bleed him fatally.

Certainly his death was unexpected, sending shock waves through Rome. There was just enough time for Raphael to ask to be buried in the Pantheon with Maria Bibbiena, and for his current lover to be ordered, weeping, out of the room so that the pope's emissaries could enter and give the papal blessing. At the foot of the artist's bed was the unfinished *Transfiguration,* the commission Michelangelo had promised Piombo they would upstage. The painting was carried in the funeral procession like a banner and was so powerful that Giulio de' Medici kept it in San Pietro in Montorio rather than send it to France.

High on the left is a dusty bust of Raphael done by Giuseppe Fabris in 1833.

The real hero of the Pantheon is Victor Emmanuel II, directly across the way. His large sarcophagus is flanked by a male and female color guard, numerous live floral arrangements, and metal wreaths. The black metal tomb says simply "Father of the Country" and is topped by a large eagle with its wings spread. Below is a shield showing the arms of the House of Savoy. The initial plan was for him to be buried in La Superga, the family mausoleum outside Turin, but he was considered too much of a treasure to be allowed to leave the capital.

VICTOR EMMANUEL II *b. March 14, 1820, Turin; d. January 10, 1878, Rome.* Sardinia, the early home of Victor Emmanuel, seems like an exotic afterthought. Visitors to Italy seldom venture farther south than Capri or the Amalfi Coast, and rarely think of taking a boat to the island. Yet in 1848 the Kingdom of Sardinia, whose elastic boundaries often stretched to include Nice and Turin, was enough of a power to be engaged in war with Austria. Though Victor Emmanuel was married to the archduchess of Austria, Adelaide, he was also the son of King Charles Albert of Sardinia. Opting for filial loyalty, he fought energetically, but Sardinia was defeated. In 1849 his father abdicated to Victor in the interests of peace.

The next time the two countries fought, in 1860, Sardinia had Napoleon III and his forces on its side. When the battle dust cleared, Austria was clutching Lombardy and Victor Emmanuel had been proclaimed king of a United Italy, which included Tuscany, Parma, Modena, and Romagna. He was aided by such valuable advisers as Giuseppe Garibaldi and Camillo Cavour.

More enthusiastic than introspective, Victor Emmanuel enjoyed the good life. His favorite pastime was hunting with a few trusted friends and collecting horses, which he stabled in the Bóboli Gardens. Stocky and blond with an elaborate mustache, he had married at 14 and fathered six children. The attentions of women always pleased him. After Adelaide died in childbirth in 1855, he settled down, without benefit of the pope's blessing, with a beautiful young seller of provisions to the army, Rosa Vercellana.

Perhaps because he considered himself a good Catholic nevertheless, it took King Victor 10 years to develop the stomach to march on Rome, where Pope Pius IX ruled politically and spiritually. At that time Pius had been pope for almost 25 years. A dramatic preacher who as a young man had once doused a human thighbone with alcohol and set it ablaze to illustrate hellfire, he had been greeted with wild enthusiasm at his election. He had planned such reforms as introducing the railroad and permitting newspapers but was chased from the city by the revolutions of 1848–1850. When he returned, accompanied by the French, his popularity had waned.

But although Pius became used to the French occupation, he was not ready to give up his throne in 1870. After Victor Emmanuel marched in and conquered Rome, making it the capital of Young Italy, a steady stream of anathemas issued from the Vatican, dubbing King Victor the "robber-king" and Antichrist. As the final insult, Victor Emmanuel had taken up residence in the Palazzo del Quirinale, the traditional summer and ceremonial home of the papacy.

King Victor generously made sure that nothing in Pius's room in the Quirinale was disturbed. Oddly, during these years of public feuding, Pius and the excommunicated monarch exchanged gentle private letters. When the king was on his deathbed, boils covering his body and in respiratory distress, the pope, who could not bear to consign anyone to the hell he had so graphically preached about, sent two prelates to administer last rites. Three weeks later Pius IX followed Victor Emmanuel into eternity.

The gold lamp hanging above the tomb commemorates **Victor Emmanuel III** (1869–1947), who died in exile in Alexandria. King of Italy between 1900 and 1946, he joined the Allied forces in World War I but in the turmoil afterward focused on Mussolini and was active in bringing him to power. Under the Fascists, Victor was king in name only; in 1943, bending to the party's will, he dismissed and imprisoned the dictator. In 1946, to save the monarchy, he abdicated to his son. But Humbert II reigned for only a month before Italy voted in a republic and both kings were exiled.

Victor Emmanuel headed for Egypt. When he died of lung congestion, the inevitable question was whether or not his body would be returned to the Pantheon. But because the Constituent Assembly had banned the monarchs from Italy, this lamp was substituted instead.

DIRECTIONS AND HOURS: Take the no. 64 bus to Piazza del Gesu and walk several blocks north to the Piazza Minerva. Between July and September, the Pantheon is open daily 9:00 A.M. to 5:00 P.M., Sundays 9:00 A.M. to 1:00 P.M. Between October and June, daily closing (except Sunday) is at 2:00 P.M.

SANTA MARIA SOPRA MINERVA

Santa Maria sopra Minerva was so named because it was believed to have been built over a temple to the goddess. Its tan baroque facade is enhanced by the statue of a small elephant sculpted by Bernini; on its back the animal stoically balances an obelisk from the Temple of Isis that was found in the garden of the church's monastery.

Inside, Santa Maria sopra Minerva seems to be all faces and skulls, pressed against columns and hanging out from walls. A particularly macabre skeleton is halfway down on your right, opposite a large plan of the church. Death wraps its skeletal arms around a distinctly disconcerted **Alexandro VII** (d. 1661)—a decent-looking man with a neat Elizabethan goatee. Below them is a howling, snake-haired Medusa. It is speculated that it may be a monument to Pope Alexander VII, who is buried in St. Peter's.

Directly opposite on the left-hand wall, the skull on the tomb of **John Vigevano** (d. 1630) appears particularly vicious. Vigevano, shown above it, appears uneasy and a little embarrassed. The monument is the work of Bernini, whose arresting skeletons have taken up residence in churches all over Rome.

If you stay on the left and move up to the front, you will reach the Chapel of St. Dominic, which holds the remains of **Pope Benedict XIII** (1649–1730). He is buried in a marble sarcophagus with a bas-relief that shows him presiding over the Roman council. The matronly women flanking his elevated statue represent Religion and Purity.

The story of Pope Benedict is that of a good man with bad advisers. Refusing to move into the luxurious Vatican apartments, Benedict kept the simple lifestyle of a monk, which included administering the sacraments, ministering to the sick, and giving religious instruction. But he put his trust in a homeboy from Benevento, Niccolò Coscia, who, in turn, appointed other Beneventans. This clique accepted bribes from rulers, sold offices, and gave Benedict bad advice. When the pope died, they barely escaped with their lives.

In the diagonal chapel, situated behind a metal fence simulating a flowering hedge, is the slab tomb of Fra Angelico. The artist is shown in bas-relief lying in a pillared archway, his large hands crossing each other flatly like a pair of empty gloves. He is cowled, his round eyes appearing sightless. The epitaph beneath his feet, written by humanist Lorenzo Valla, translates to "Here lies the venerable painter Fra Giovanni of the Order of Preachers. Let me not be praised because I seemed another Apelles, but because I gave all my riches, O Christ, to Thee. For some works survive on earth and others in heaven. The city of Florence, flower of Etruria, gave me, Giovanni, birth."

FRA ANGELICO *b. ca. 1395, Vicchio; d. February 1455, Rome.* The paintings of Fra Angelico come down through the centuries vibrant with goodness and charm. Their colors are the reds, golds, and blues of illuminated manuscripts, and the expressions on the faces are uniformly thoughtful. Even the damned, shown in compartments in hell in *The Last Judgment* (ca. 1430s), look only mildly annoyed, as if the kindhearted friar could not bear to make anyone truly suffer.

Except for his saintliness, few facts about Fra Angelico exist. His date of birth has been guessed as being anywhere between 1387 and 1400; his ordination as a Dominican monk is put at about 1420. The religious life allowed

him the "quiet and freedom from care" that he felt necessary for any artist, but it was more than a safe haven. According to Giorgio Vasari, Fra Angelico prayed over his
brushes, wept when he painted a crucifixion, and never
retouched a work, feeling that what was put down first
was God's will.

When the monk began painting in Fiesole around 1428,
his work consisted of altarpieces, triptychs, and illuminated pages. Then in 1436 Cosimo de' Medici gave the
Fiesole Dominicans the ruined monastery of San Marco in
Florence. "Ruined" was no romantic phrase; the friars
lived in makeshift huts or damp cells with rats for two
years before reconstruction could begin. When it did, it
was Fra Angelico's task, working with the architect Michel-
ozzo, to fresco the walls.

Perhaps because of the materials and the aging process,
the colors in San Marco are richly muted into pale or-
anges, soft blues, and creams. The more than 40 frescoes
illustrate scenes from the life of Jesus, from a wonderful
Annunciation to Jesus crowning Mary somewhere in the
clouds. The exception in style is the altarpiece showing
scenes from the lives of the martyred saints, Cosmas and
Damian. These saints are depicted in bright colors, their
halos rolling down the road like wheels, their decapitated
heads at the center.

In 1445 Fra Angelico was summoned to Rome to decorate the Chapel of Nicholas V in the Vatican; he chose
scenes from the lives of St. Stephen and St. Lawrence. It

was inevitable that his art would become more skilled and sophisticated and perhaps less appealing. Yet there are still some wonderful surprises. In the *Annunciation* panel of the Annunziata Silver Chest (1451–1453), the angel breaking the news to Mary has graceful wings with red, yellow, and blue stripes and a large black dot in the middle like an exotic butterfly.

Until his death 10 years later, Fra Angelico traveled back and forth between Rome and Fiesole, where he was prior of the monastery between 1448 and 1450. He passed away peacefully in Rome.

The main altar is a tomb to St. Catherine of Siena. Her life-sized painted wooden carving shows her wearing a dark blue and white habit, the work attributed to Isaia da Pisa. Two marble cherubs hold a banner with her name. Note the lovely stained-glass windows behind her altar.

ST. CATHERINE OF SIENA *b. 1347, Siena; d. April 29, 1380, Rome.*

> I went to Siena to Saint Catherine's own
>   church . . .
> To pray to her to cure me of my heartache and
>   shyness . . .
> Make the person that sings this song less shy than
>   that person is,
> And give that person some joy in that person's
>   heart.

Kenneth Koch's poem, movingly set to music by Virgil Thomson, depicts a penitent who, drawn by the legend of her strength, love, devotion, and sympathy, has come to St. Catherine so that her heart might be made open and receptive. It is a clear demonstration of St. Catherine's presence even in the twentieth century. In her own time everyone who knew her called her "Mama." Even those who initially preferred the more formal "Madame" soon gave way to her maternal nature, for she was an Italian mother: strong, protective, assertive, wheedling, insistent, and comforting. On one occasion she even addressed Pope Urban V as "Babba mio." Childless and unwed to anyone but Christ, she was a mother to the world at large.

There were 25 Benincasa children. Accounts differ as to whether Catherine was number 23, 24, or 25. Her father, Giacomo, was a well-to-do dyer. Her mother, the fertile Lapa, has often been portrayed as being pinched and cross by historians who never had to give birth to and raise 25 children, including a precocious mystic. Catherine's first vision came to her at age six. When out walking with her brother, she was visited by Christ and two saints, Paul and John. The following year she pledged her virginity to God. As she grew older, Catherine's devout practices interfered with her mother's goal of finding a suitable husband for her daughter. In defiance Catherine cut off her long blond hair. To break her rebelliousness, Lapa deprived Catherine of her bedroom and assigned her the most menial tasks at home. These Catherine performed with grace and aplomb. Her parents, impressed, were grudgingly won over.

Catherine was given a small room at the top of the family home, where she devoted herself to fasting, meditation, prayer, and self-flagellation. She secluded herself for three years. At 20 she ventured out to mass and experienced a vision of Christ directing her "to love her neighbor as herself and to serve Christ in the neighbor."

Catherine undertook that mission by tending those sick with the plague. With her goodness, directness (she always looked her listeners in the eye), and exuberance, she attracted a prestigious following which came to be called the Caterinati and was composed of "old and young, priests and laymen, poets and politicians" whom she had rescued from their dissolute ways.

Soon the scope of her mission expanded to include moral attacks on the clergy for their worldly concerns with money and status. She urged the pope to address these problems which were corrupting the "bride of Christ." From here she extended her influence directly into the political realm by urging Pisa, Lucca, and the British mercenary Sir John Hawkwood to join in a crusade to regain the Holy Land from the infidels. But a short time later her attitude toward the Moslems had turned about. No longer demonizing them, she declared them to be "our brothers, redeemed by the blood of Christ, just as we are." It was a remarkable and courageous public stance.

To other leaders of Europe, Catherine addressed appeals and treaties for peace. These efforts at moral suasion were unsuccessful. Success did arrive through her visit to Pope Gregory in Avignon. While there, it was she who convinced the timorous pope to return the papacy to Rome.

These efforts are more remarkable yet when we realize that Catherine remained illiterate throughout her life. This did not stop her from dictating any number of

SANTA MARIA SOPRA MINERVA

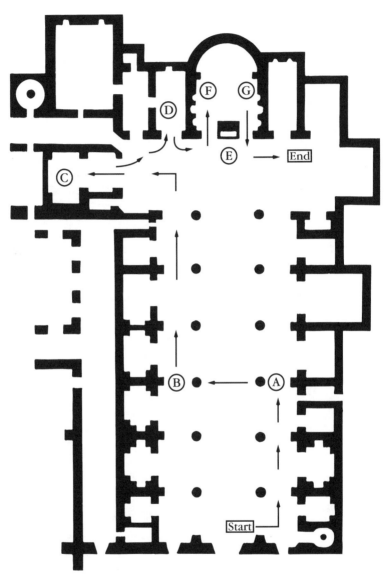

A Alexandro VII
B John Vigevano
C Pope Benedict XIII
D Fra Angelico

E St. Catherine of Siena
F Pope Leo X
G Pope Clement VII

letters and two books, *The Dialogues of Catherine* (ca. 1377) and *A Treatise of Divine Providence* (1378), which were widely read and discussed within the church for years.

Catherine's continuing visions over the years strengthened her belief and sense of purpose. In one vision she was wedded with Christ as the Virgin Mary looked on. She received the stigmata, but this became visible to others only at the time of her death. Self-denial was constant. Although she was a wonderful cook for others, she herself ate only bread, water, and bitter herbs. At all times she wore a hair shirt, and when this needed cleaning she wore iron chains.

Such a regimen took its toll. A staunch supporter of Urban VI over Clement VII during the Great Schism, Catherine was summoned to Rome by Urban to lend her moral standing to his defense. There, physically exhausted and spiritually discouraged by the corruption of the papal court, she collapsed at St. Peter's. Her death was painful as she wrestled violently with her demons.

Her message of activism remains a strong one. "It is through silence that the world is lost"—a silence she broke for individuals, governments, and popes alike.

Finally, in the first main chapel to your right, are the twin tombs of the two Medici popes, Leo X and Clement VII, which owe a certain debt to Michelangelo. Both popes are shown seated on raised thrones, flanked by a pair of prophets. The bas-reliefs above them contain some revisionist history, particularly Clement's. It shows Charles V clasping the pope around the waist in submission—not exactly an accurate image, as his biography indicates.

POPE LEO X (GIOVANNI DI LORENZO DE' MEDICI) *b. December 11, 1475, Florence; d. December 1, 1521, Rome.* When the College of Cardinals met in 1513 after the death of Pope Julius II, they were looking to elect his exact opposite—someone who would *not* march them all over Italy, harangue the faithful, and keep the papal treasury locked up tight. They settled on easygoing Giovanni de' Medici after they were assured by his doctors that the young cardinal, who suffered from an open stomach ulcer and a leaking anal fistula, did not have long to live. His early death would allow them all another shot at the papacy.

Giovanni's father, Lorenzo the Magnificent, had bought a cardinal's hat for his son when the boy was only 14. Giovanni had not changed much since then. Sunny-natured, nearsighted, intelligent, and addicted to good food and drink, he was, at the time of his coronation, only slightly more massive. But he was enchanted by the hoopla, and his pleasure was enchanting to watch. Only the traditional warning, "Thou shalt never see the years of Peter"—no pope was supposed to reign as long as St. Peter's 25 years—may have given him a moment's pause.

In the meantime, as he pointed out to his brother, "God has given us the papacy. Let us enjoy it!" Enjoyment showed itself as dinners with delicacies such as parrots' tongues, nightingales flying out of pies, and naked toddlers emerging from puddings. Leo X commissioned Raphael to paint the other great Leos—Leo I, Leo III, and Leo IV—but with his own features. He turned out small poems and epigrams, though he did not give much support to fellow writers Machiavelli, Ariosto, and Erasmus.

Leo's goal was for the world to be happy. Tossing gold coins to the peasantry when he traveled, he signed petitions for grants, pensions, and dowries whenever he could. He spent a fortune trying to establish a dynasty by promoting his remaining brother and his only legitimate nephew to positions of power; ungratefully, they soon died.

Despite his generosity, and the educational and physical improvements he made to Rome, there was a failed plot among several College of Cardinals members to assassinate him by poisoning the bandage applied to his rectal fistula. And then there was Martin Luther. "Leo laid the egg which Luther hatched," went the saying that referred to Leo's reintroduction of indulgences to reduce an individual's time in purgatory. Or, as a derisive couplet went, "As soon as the coin in the coffer rings/The soul from out the fire springs."

Everyone agreed that Leo, if he had to die, timed it beautifully. When he succumbed to the complications of a cold at 45, Luther was still an obscure monk, the armies of France were in retreat, and his rule was designated as the Golden Age. The people mourned him loudly. The bankers were even more inconsolable; when they went to call in the enormous loans that had funded the young pope's generosity, they found the papal treasury bare.

The monument of Pope Clement VII shows him in marble as long-bearded and seated, blessing the crowd. In separate niches are statues of two prophets, with bas-reliefs of scenes from his papacy above. Surmounting everything is the Medici shield with the family balls.

POPE CLEMENT VII (GIULIO DE' MEDICI) *b. May 26, 1478, Florence; d. September 25, 1534, Rome.* Born on the wrong side of the blanket, Giulio de' Medici would have spent his early years in a Florentine slum had his father, Giuliano, not been assassinated. Giuliano's grieving brother, Lorenzo, sought out the illegitimate baby and raised him in the Medici palace. Dark, handsome, and witty, Giulio displayed much of his late father's charm, though a certain need to please and to be seen to be in the right earned him the nickname of the Chameleon.

His cousin, Leo X, cleverly had him legitimized by rewriting family history so that Giulio could be made a cardinal. He performed that office beautifully, and when he was elected pope in 1523, it was with the happy expectation that he would continue Leo's Golden Age.

Insofar as the arts and learning were concerned, he was able to, continuing his family's patronage of Raphael and Michelangelo, and arranging private apartments for Leonardo da Vinci. He also supported the work of the Polish astronomer Copernicus. But the joie de vivre of Leo's reign was gone. Partly by nature and partly because of the bankrupt treasury he had inherited from his cousin, Clement quickly developed a reputation for stinginess. But it was his foreign policy that proved his undoing.

Two feisty young rulers, King Charles of Spain and King Francis of France, were eyeing Italy and each other. Clement, still needing to placate everyone, secretly signed treaties with both kings. The secret did not remain one for long. An angry Charles, aided by Germans and other Italians, sacked Rome, holding Clement a prisoner in Sant'-Angelo. The Swiss Guard was obliterated, innocent citizens were murdered, and sacred relics destroyed. It took the payment of a huge ransom and the promise that the pope would crown Charles emperor to get Clement released to his ruined city.

In his last five years as pope, he jumped back and forth on the issue of Henry VIII's divorce from Catherine of Aragon and skillfully avoided the convening of a council to address the growing threat of Martin Luther and his followers. It was not an issue Clement wanted to face. Emaciated, his skin yellowed from liver disease, he died at 55. This time the populace rejoiced. As a contemporary, Francesco Vettori, pointed out, "Clement had gone to a good deal of trouble to develop from a great and respected cardinal into a small and despised pope."

DIRECTIONS AND HOURS: Take the no. 64 bus to Piazza del Gesu and walk several blocks north to the Piazza Minerva. The church is open daily 7:00 A.M. to noon and 4:00 to 7:00 P.M.

CHAPTER 4

ROME
The Protestant Cemetery

▲ ▲ ▲

Seldom has a cemetery, large or small, attracted so much literary comment. "The most beautiful thing in Italy," wrote Henry James, who was a frequent visitor to the grave of Constance Woolson. "It might make one in love with death to be buried in so sweet a place," enthused Shelley—whose chance to find out came all too soon. Joseph Severn, mourning Keats, felt that such a place could not exist in England. "I visit it with a delicious melancholy which relieves my sadness."

Yet in the beginning the cemetery was considered no more than a necessary evil, a utilitarian concession to foreigners. Until 1738 only Roman Catholics were allowed to be buried in Rome. Protestants and other infidels had to be either transported to Leghorn, about 160 miles away, or interred with the prostitutes of the Piazza Flaminia below the Pincian Hill.

Once the Cimitero Acattolico (non-Catholic) was established, the rules were strict. Burials had to be at night by torchlight, crosses could not be used to decorate the graves, and until 1870 a papal commission ruled on every proposed inscription—rejecting even a modest "She rests in God," on the basis that there *was* no rest in God outside the Catholic Church. Plantings were forbidden because they might interfere with the view of the Pyramid of Gaius Cestius. The populace showed its opinion by dropping dead cats and dogs in the moat around the cemetery.

It is a tribute to the growth of religious tolerance that the entrance gate now has engraved over it: "Resurrecturis" (dedicated to those who shall rise again).

To enter the cemetery, you will need to ring the bell and have the gate unlocked for you. When you are inside, walk past the office and into the oldest section. At the end of the path near the wall are two upright monuments. The one on your left has a lyre missing strings and the words "This Grave contains all that was Mortal of a Young English Poet Who, on his Death Bed, in the bitterness of his Heart, at the Malicious Power of his Enemies, Desired these Words to be engraved on his Tomb Stone. 'Here lies One Whose Name was writ in Water.' February 24th 1821."

JOHN KEATS *b. October 31, 1795, London; d. February 23, 1821, Rome.* Never has an epitaph proved so wrong, for this is no watery grave. The poetry of John Keats will certainly outlive the chiseled stone that marks his remains. Along with Byron and Shelley, Keats is considered to be one of the three great romantic poets. They all died young, but Keats, best fulfilling the romantic stereotype, died the youngest. His major output was accomplished in

a mere four years (1816–1820) and represents an astonishing and sudden maturity.

Keats was born into a family of comfortable means. His father, Thomas, was an ostler for his future father-in-law. His mother, Frances, was pretty, sensuous, and well educated. Three boys and a girl followed before Thomas died in 1804 after falling from his horse. In 1810 Frances, giving way to consumption, followed her husband. The children's estate was left in the hands of a tightfisted executor, Richard Abbey.

Up to this time Keats had received a good education at a school run by John Clarke, whose son, Charles Cowden Clarke, helped with the teaching and formed a close relationship with the young Keats. A good student, the diminutive Keats (not an inch over five feet in adulthood) was rambunctious and aggressive, but his schooling ended when Abbey apprenticed him to a surgeon and apothecary. Fortunately, while studying this trade at Guy's Hospital in London for the next five years, Keats was also able to visit and continue his studies and friendship with the younger Clarke.

Attempting his first poetry at the age of 18, Keats tried to mimic the style of Spenser, the imagery of his "sea-shouldering whales." He had a visceral response to Spenser, a swooning obliviousness which characterized the romantics. Three years later, in 1816, Leigh Hunt published "To Solitude" in the *Examiner*. It was Keats's first poem in print, and the proud poet began affecting a Byronic style of dress. Later that year Clarke took the young poet to meet Hunt.

Keats began to show glimmers of true talent with the writing of "On First Looking into Chapman's Homer" (1817) and quickly became a mainstay of Hunt's cottage in Hampstead. There he met Benjamin Haydon, the artist, as well as William Hazlitt, Charles Lamb, and his future close friends John Hamilton Reynolds, John Severn, Charles Dilke, and Charles Brown. Keats's intelligence, vivacity, and sincerity attracted people to him; his friendships were enduring and marked by loyalty and admiration. They served him well during his last years. Keats's letters to his friends, siblings, and his love, Fanny Brawne, are considered to be among his finest achievements.

When Keats forsook medicine for poetry, his decision drew the ire and scorn of Abbey. Throwing himself into the epic romance poem *Endymion*, which would occupy him until 1818, Keats underwent a profound learning experience. What emerged was not great poetry but rather a thorough understanding of structure and line. Knowledge of critics also came his way, but in general this seemed not to faze him. The book was viciously criticized by *Blackwood's Magazine* and *The Quarterly Review.* Such was to be expected, but Keats was less affected than most, for his learning experience proved to be his harshest and yet most valuable critic.

Moving about as he wrote, Keats settled in at the end of 1818 to nurse his brother, Tom, who was dying from tuberculosis. At the same time he fell in love with Fanny, then only 18. She was pretty and vivacious but still flighty and immature. They were nevertheless soon engaged. This death and love combined with Keats's poetic growth and set the stage for the dramatic outpouring of his greatest poetry. In nine astonishing months, from January to September of 1819, Keats wrote "The Eve of St. Agnes," "La belle dame sans merci," "Lamia," his six odes, and a number of his sonnets. Here we see not only the maturation of style and form but also the best expression of his ideas like that of "negative capability," by which he meant man's capability of "being in uncertainties, Mysteries, doubts, without any irritable reaching after fact & reason"—in other words, an artistic or aesthetic detachment.

One evening in February 1820, Keats, who had long had a premonition of early death, became ill and coughed up blood. Bidding Charles Brown to bring the candle closer to the sheet, Keats stared at the blood and declared, "I know the colour of that blood; it is arterial blood;—I cannot be deceived in that colour;—that drop of blood is my death-warrant;—I must die." Though he worked on *Hyperion,* Keats would not complete another poem. He wandered about experiencing occasional respite and rejuvenation, and for a period he was nursed by Fanny. The experience quickly matured Fanny, and the relationship deepened. But the passions of love were too much for the ill and sensitive Keats. They drained him, and he felt the love would kill him.

With Severn, Keats sought health in the warmer climate of Italy. Settling in Rome, Keats spent his last months in an apartment by the Spanish Steps. He experienced the bitterness and resentment that prompted, as perhaps did the waters of the fountain on the Piazza di Spagna, his choice of epitaph. But his good moods prevailed. In his last letter, written to Charles Brown, Keats signed off: "I can scarcely bid you good-bye, even in a letter. I always made an awkward bow." On Friday, February 23, 1821, his burial plans in place and content in knowing that Fanny's

THE PROTESTANT CEMETERY IN ROME

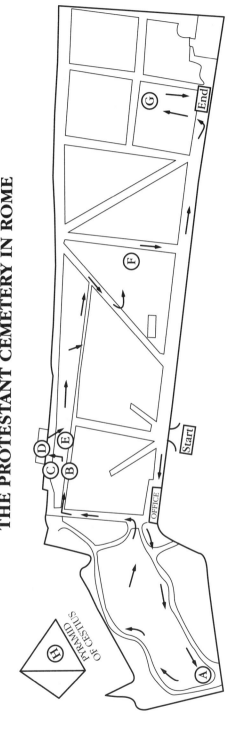

A John Keats, Joseph Severn
B Constance Woolson
C William W. Story
D Percy Bysshe Shelley, Edward Trelawney
E Rosa Bathhurst
F William Stanley Haseltine
G Antonio Gramsci
H Gaius Cestius

47

last and unopened letters would be placed in his coffin, Keats called, "Severn—Severn—lift me up for I am dying—I shall die easy—don't be frightened—thank God it has come." For the next seven hours Severn cradled Keats in his arms. Febrilely sensitive, Keats whispered, "Don't breathe on me—it comes like ice." He died peacefully, as if falling asleep.

The companion monument of Keats's friend **Joseph Severn** (1793–1879) has an artist's palette and down-turned paintbrushes. He identifies himself foremost as the "devoted friend and death-bed companion of JOHN KEATS." The pair met in 1816 through a mutual school friend. At that time Severn, the son of an overbearing music master, was struggling, against his father's wishes, to become a painter.

The blond and lighthearted Severn was an optimistic counterpoint to the darkening poet. If anything, he was too ready to believe the world's assurances that Keats would recover his strength in Rome, and bounded around the city, sketching the ruins and presenting letters of introduction to the prominent. Yet when Keats's hemorrhages and depression gave way to the final fever and constant dry coughing, Severn finally had to admit that there would be no recovery.

He was crushed by his friend's death but stayed on in Italy, eventually marrying and producing a large and happy family. Though he developed into an undistinguished painter, his true gift was the charm that led to his appointment in 1860 as British consul to Rome.

Also buried here is Severn's infant son, who died tragically in 1837 when, taking an afternoon nap, he slipped between his crib railings and broke his neck. The baby's stone mentions that the "poet Wordsworth was present at his baptism in Rome."

The Celtic cross nearby commemorates **John Bell** (1762–1820), a distinguished Scottish surgeon who became a friend of the Shelleys. The doctor treated the poet for symptoms of consumption and attempted unsuccessfully to save the life of little William Shelley.

Exit the Parte Antica and walk all the way back to the rear of the cemetery, then turn right onto the next to last path. A little way down is the flat marble slab, decorated with a cross, of **Constance Fenimore Woolson** (1840–1894). Constance, whose writing supported her family, wrote for the *Atlantic Monthly* and *Harper's*. The magazines begged her for more stories than she could write, and her novels, including *East Angels* (1886) and *Juniper Lights* (1889), were eagerly received.

After her mother's death she settled in Europe, becoming a close friend of Henry James and sharing a villa with him. Although she worshiped his writing, she found the author self-centered and afraid to commit himself—at least to her. An entry in one of her journals was the basis for his story "The Beast in the Jungle" (1902). The climax of the story is set at Woolson's grave.

How she died remains a mystery. Suffering from typhoid fever, she fell or jumped from her balcony in Venice.

In the last row are **William Wetmore Story** (1819–1895) and his wife, **Emelyn** (1820–1895). Their tomb is decorated by his sculpture *Angel of Grief,* a copy of which was erected at Stanford University in California, in memory of the earthquake victims of 1906.

Story, the son of a Supreme Court justice, studied law himself and entered a Boston firm. When his father died in 1845, the younger Story was chosen to make his memorial bust and went off to Italy to study sculpture. Here he found a dazzling sunlit landscape of pageantry and picturesque ruins, far different from his New England world. The Storys made several trips and eventually settled in Rome, renting the second story of the Palazzo Barberini. They entertained lavishly; one room was fitted out as a theater where the expatriates could put on plays.

Like other American sculptors in Rome, Story drew uncritically on Greek and Roman art, borrowing bits and pieces for his *Medea*s and *Salome*s. Yet though he was considered successful, he was ready to give up sculpture in 1862; then two of his works, *Cleopatra* and *Libyan Sybil,* caused a sensation at the London International Exposition. Hawthorne helped further by praising *Cleopatra* in his story *The Marble Faun* as "fierce, voluptuous, passionate, tender . . . one of the images that men keep forever, finding a heat in them that does not cool down through the centuries."

The Storys' young son, **Joseph** (1847–1853), is buried here also. A playmate of the Brownings' son, Pen, Joe was struck suddenly with a mysterious fever and perished in a week. Elizabeth Barrett Browning was terrified that Pen would fall ill and was upset with her husband, Robert, for helping to nurse Joe's sister, but no one else died.

Walk up the steps to the right of the Story monument.

To your left in the ground is another poet accompanied by a friend, Percy Bysshe Shelley and Edward J. Trelawny. Trelawny's grave gives this explanation: "These are two friends whose lives were undivided; So let their memory be now they have glided under the grave; Let not their bones be parted, For their two hearts in life were single-hearted." It is a surprising epitaph, considering that Trelawny knew Shelley for less than six months before he died and had little in common with him.

Shelley's grave notes simply "Cor cordium" (Heart of all hearts) and a quote from *The Tempest* by Shakespeare: "Nothing of him that doth fade, / But doth suffer a sea-change / Into something rich and strange."

PERCY BYSSHE SHELLEY *b. August 4, 1792, Field Place, Sussex; d. July 8, 1822, the Gulf of Spezia, Italy.* Timothy Shelley, father of the poet, was the most stolid and conventional of gentry. But by allowing his oldest son to roam free, indulging his imagination and dominating his admiring younger sisters by ghost stories and fanciful expeditions, he inadvertently created a proto-

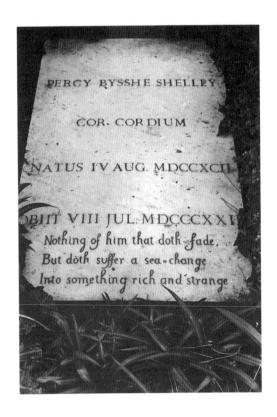

Frankenstein: a creature unable to live within normal social limits.

Shelley, sent to Eton at 12, refused to "fag" (wait on upperclassmen) and was thus made a scapegoat—a scapegoat who, on occasion, struck back viciously. By graduation he was tolerated as an eccentric and even admired as the author of a published Gothic novel, *Zastrozzi: A Romance* (1810). His career at Oxford ended after six months, however, when he and a friend published *The Necessity of Atheism* (1811). The pamphlet set out to show that God's existence could not be proved empirically. Typically, Shelley sent the "anonymous" invective to all the bishops and heads of the colleges and was expelled on the technicality of refusing to admit to its authorship.

Cut loose and increasingly estranged from his father, Shelley gave himself over to independent reading and writing. He set out to rescue 16-year-old Harriet Westbrook, whose father had "persecuted her in a most horrible way by endeavoring to compel her to go to school." He believed in free love, but Harriet held out for a ring, and they were married in Edinburgh in 1811.

By the time their second child, Charles, was born in 1815, Shelley had already defected to the Wollstonecraft-Godwin camp. Long an admirer of William Godwin, author of *Political Justice*, Shelley's first major work, *Queen Mab* (1813), reflected many of his theories. The long poem attacked organized religion, war, and the tyranny of social and political institutions; it also preached free love, intellectual independence, and vegetarianism.

Godwin was delighted to have the young poet warming himself at the family hearth and accepted financial support from Shelley, but was outraged when he also appropriated Mary, Godwin's beautiful, blazingly intelligent 16-year-old daughter and Mary's stepsister, Claire Clairmont. No longer welcome in the Godwin home, the trio began the odyssey that would bring them to Italy.

Before then, Shelley had to deal with Harriet's suicide in 1816. Despairing and very pregnant, she gave her children to her parents and sister and drowned herself in the Thames. Shelley fought unsuccessfully for custody, going so far as to wed Mary to demonstrate his respectability. It didn't help, and he took the loss of his children as proof that he was an outcast in British society.

But Italy was no utopia. Shelley suffered from poor health there, appearing to strangers as gaunt as a madman. Although he had finally inherited money, his generous support of William Godwin, Leigh Hunt, and others left him financially strapped. Mary was unhappy over Shelley's emotional attachment to Claire, and Claire was miserable because Lord Byron had claimed custody of Allegra, the daughter they had had together. The crushing blow came between September 1818 and June 1819 when Clara and William, the Shelleys' two beloved children, both sickened and died.

It was out of this despair that Shelley's greatest works came: *The Cenci* (1819), a tragedy based on the story of Beatrice Cenci, whose father's extreme cruelty led her to have him murdered; *Prometheus Unbound* (1820); and a number of lyric poems, including "The Cloud" (1820) and "To a Skylark" (1820). "Adonais," an elegy for Keats, was published in 1821, as was *Epipsychidion*, an interestingly autobiographical long poem.

Ranked as one of the great romantic poets, Shelley moved dizzyingly from despair to ecstasy, scorning the ugliness of daily life for the hope of a Platonic world in the future. (His ring bore the motto *Il buon tempo verra*—"The good times will come.") Sometimes satiric, his poetry is more of mood than tangible objects. Who can forget such lines as "Best and brightest, come away!" and "If Winter comes, can Spring be far behind?"

Searching for happiness, Shelley worked to set up a literary community at Pisa with Lord Byron, Leigh Hunt, and Jane and Edward Williams. Williams, a retired army officer from India, was Shelley's sailing companion on the craft they owned together, the *Don Juan*. He was with Shelley the day they left Leghorn and got into a sudden squall with cliff-high waves. According to an Italian captain who tried to rescue them, it was Shelley who refused help. When they were told to at least lower their sails, it appears to have been Shelley who prevented Williams from doing so.

The bodies washed up 10 days later and were temporarily buried in sand with quicklime. Then Trelawny provided a portable furnace and the remains were cremated on the beach. Shelley's ashes waited several months in the wine cellar of the British consul before they were buried in the Protestant cemetery. As he himself wrote, "Death will come when thou art dead, / Soon, too soon."

Edward John Trelawny (1792–1881), born in Cornwall, had the appearance of a pirate: muscular and swarthy, with glittering white teeth and a thick black beard. He cultivated his image by wearing open-necked shirts and kerchiefs and living the life of an adventurer. Invited to Pisa by his friend Edward Williams, he entertained Shelley's literary community with anecdotes of narrow escapes.

Trelawny also provided the model and the drawings for the *Don Juan* and planned to sail alongside Shelley and Williams that last day in Byron's schooner, the *Bolivar*. Difficulty in getting port clearance papers prevented him. Trelawny designed Shelley's tomb, then accompanied Byron to Greece where he hired himself out in the Greek War of Independence. Still seeking adventure, he swam the Niagara River just above the Falls, then returned to England where he published *The Adventures of a Younger Son* (1830) and *Recollections of the Last Days of Shelley and Byron* (1858). Trelawny can be seen as the ancient seaman in Sir John Millais's *The Northwest Passage*.

When you have finished viewing Trelawny's grave, drop down two rows to one of the most cautionary monuments in the cemetery. It belongs to **Rosa Bathhurst** (d. 1924), who drowned in the Tiber at 16, "owing to the swollen state of the river and her spirited horse taking fright." The memorial, erected by Mrs. Bathhurst, explains how Rosa's father had disappeared some years earlier on a secret mission to Vienna. The epitaph warns viewers that no matter how happy they think they are now, their joy can be swept away in a matter of moments. The bas-relief on Rosa's monument shows an angel pointing the young girl upward.

Another poignant epitaph is on the more recent grave of **Jean-Louis Cattani** (1931–1968) near the Parte Antica. It advises visitors to "pity those men who from the start/ Were martyrs to some dream of art."

Near the front is the full-sized sculpture of **Devereux Plantagenet**, who died at 21. He is shown reclining, perhaps already in ill health. The book he was reading is cast aside, and his small dog is snuggled close to him.

Walk back up the path and to your right. Move down another two rows to the large monument of Commodore **Thomas Jefferson Page** (1808–1899), grandson of the signer of the Declaration of Independence, Thomas Nelson, Jr. Tending the grave is a beautiful young woman holding a bouquet and looking skyward.

Nearby is the wistful statue of **Georges Volkoff** perched on his grave; he died in 1936 at the age of 11. Young Georges, dressed in school clothes, sits on a rough-cut stone holding a book in his hand and staring off to his left.

Return to the very center of the cemetery and walk up the main aisle. Six rows up on your left is the simple classical column of **William Stanley Haseltine** (1835–1900), an artist who specialized in scenes of rocky coastlines and classical ruins.

Across the way, near the angel of Finnish art patron **Carl Isak Victor Hoving** (1846–1876), are two monuments that are touching in their own right. That to **Gerda Salzman** (1897–1908) shows her favorite things: her music bag, a jump rope, an open book, and a basket of flowers.

More upbeat is the stone of **Lewis Charles Harold Geoghegan**, or, as he used to call himself, *Il Bardo Errante* (the Wayward Bard). It shows his portrait as long-nosed and large-eared, with hair like a poor man's Jesus. The monument was erected "by his friends at the Caffe Greco." During expatriate days the Caffe Greco, near the Spanish Steps, was a large, dingy coffeehouse with a noisy and artistic clientele. Each room was dominated by a different nationality, and even Buffalo Bill stopped by during his travels.

Finally, down at the far end of the cemetery is the plain marker of **Antonio Gramsci** (1891–1937), the philosopher of humane socialism. A passionate fighter against Fascism, he was arrested in 1926 when the Fascists outlawed the Communist party, and died in one of Mussolini's prisons. His *Prison Notebook* and *Letters from Prison* were published posthumously.

After leaving the cemetery, you may want to walk around to the pyramid. **Gaius Cestius** is known to history for his monument, not for his achievements while alive. He lived as a praetor, tribune, and member of the High Priest Collegium, which prepared sacred feasts in honor of the gods. When he died in 12 B.C., his will stipulated that an Egyptian-style tomb be erected within the year. Over the centuries it has become a convenient landmark.

DIRECTIONS AND HOURS: Take the metro to the Porta San Paolo stop (Piramide) and cross the square to the Via Caio Cestio. Follow the wall around to the entrance. The cemetery is open 8:00 to 11:30 A.M. and 2:30 to 4:30 P.M. and closed Wednesdays.

C H A P T E R   5

ROME
St. Peter's Basilica

▲   ▲   ▲

Standing in St. Peter's Square, looking up at Bernini's statues lining the roof, you realize just how extensive Roman Catholic history is. Of the 140 saints in biblical robes, Roman tunics, and bishops' bonnets, not all are the people you might expect to find. A surprising 33 of them are women, and there are also characters as offbeat as St. Genesius, the patron saint of comedians; this Roman actor was converted to Christianity midjoke and refused to go on with a play that satirized baptism. He was subsequently beheaded by Diocletian.

Only a handful of the statues are popes, but popes are what we are concerned with at St. Peter's. Their descriptions should not be taken as either a criticism or a defense of the papacy, but simply as an attempt to locate the personality under the crown.

The basilica has existed in some form since the second century, when Pope Anicetus built an oratory over the tomb of St. Peter. Constantine built a basilica on the site, which was consecrated in 326. (As penance, the emperor filled and carried away 12 buckets of earth from the building site and was very pleased with himself.) Between 1452, when serious interior damage was discovered, and 1626, when the new St. Peter's was consecrated, numerous artists/architects, including Rossellino, Bramante, Raphael, and Michelangelo, all worked on designs; it was Carlo Maderno who finally brought the project to completion. Bernini did much of the interior work and, of course, the colonnade.

After you enter the basilica and stop to admire Michelangelo's *Pietà,* continue down the right side to the monument of Sweden's Queen **Christina** (1626–1689). The bas-relief on her sarcophagus illustrates the moment of

57

her conversion to Roman Catholicism in 1655. Her bronze likeness, which shows her in profile with elaborately arranged hair, is at the top.

Under the direction of her father, Christina was given a strongly masculine upbringing. Except for the two years right after his death in 1632, when her emotional German mother claimed possession of her, his command that she be raised neither by foreigners nor by women was obeyed. In any case, Christina was repelled by her mother's "feminine morbidity," which included keeping their bedroom draped in black velvet and placing the late king's embalmed heart in a gold case over the bed.

By the time Christina took the oath of "King" at 18, she was an expert horsewoman and fluent in six languages. She was successful in bringing about the Treaty of Westphalia to end the war in Germany in 1648 and worked to make Stockholm a cultural center. Along with rare books, manuscripts, and new dances, she imported mathematician and philosopher René Descartes over his protests. Perhaps in retaliation, he soon died.

Christina realized that she did not enjoy the responsibilities of the crown and wanted to abdicate. In 1651 her ministers accepted her decision. Leaving the country incognito, she chopped off her hair and changed into men's clothes. At the border she gave the exultant cry, "At last I am free!"

Besides being freed from responsibility, she was also free of her father's Lutheranism and the hellfire warnings that had upset her as a child. Her formal conversion to Catholicism came soon after, and the following year found her in Rome. Richly rewarded by Alexander VII, Christina was delighted by the rare books and art treasures of the Vatican, as well as the mild climate.

On the left-hand side of the next chapel is the monument to **Pius XII** (1876–1958) by Francesco Messina, a simple sarcophagus of white stone with a depiction of the Madonna and Child on the wall in back. The first pope from Rome since 1730, Pius was also the first to fly in a plane, descend into a mine, or visit a submarine. Thin, aristocratic, and saintly, after World War II he was criticized for not doing more to protect the Jews. By then he had a new enemy. He excommunicated Italian Catholics who joined the Communist party, as well as the leaders of the Eastern bloc countries.

Matilda of Canossa (1046–1115) is honored under the next arch. Although she died in 1115, her remains were not brought here from Mantua until 1635, when they were placed under an uninspired monument by Bernini. The

ST. PETER'S BASILICA

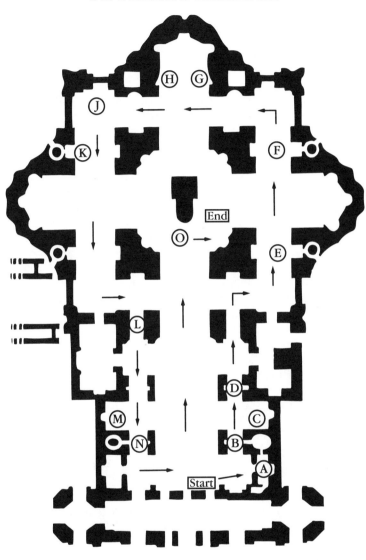

A	Michelangelo's *Pietà*	**H** Paul III
B	Queen Christina	**J** Leo III
C	Pius XII	**K** Alexander VII
D	Matilda of Canossa	**L** Leo XI, Innocent XI
E	Benedict XIV	**M** Pius X, Innocent VIII
F	Clement XIII	**N** The Stuarts
G	Urban VIII	**O** St. Peter

bas-relief on her sarcophagus shows the humiliation of Emperor Henry IV by Pope Gregory VII outside her castle in 1077; the emperor was alleged to have waited barefoot in the snow for three days, trying to get his excommunication lifted. The incident gave rise to the expression "going to Canossa," meaning to give in to the demands of the Catholic Church.

Continue on your right to the monument of **Benedict XIV** (1675–1758). He has one arm raised to proclaim the Jubilee Year of 1750; the other hand looks as if he is pushing a child's head down.

Wisdom and Impartiality flank his figure, but it appears that Wit and Good Nature would be just as appropriate. Benedict was elected pope after a painfully drawn-out conclave in 1740, during which he pointed out that if they wanted a saint or a statesman they should elect one of the other two candidates, "But if you want a good fellow, take me." They opted for bonhomie—and got a good dose of saintliness and political shrewdness as well. Voltaire dedicated his play *Mahomet* to Benedict, and the pope was praised by the English novelist Hugh Walpole as "a prince without favorites, *a pope without nephews,*" "nephew" being a euphemism for an illegitimate son.

The tomb of **Clement XIII** (1693–1796) by Antonio Canova is quite beautiful, though the pope, kneeling in prayer on the top, is the least interesting figure. To his right stands Religion with a spiky headdress resembling that of the Statue of Liberty. To the left is a languorous male nude, the Genius of Death, with his horn lying beside him. His sensuality disturbed conservative elements, and during late Victorian times his critical elements were shielded by a white-painted tin drapery. At the bottom of the sculpture are two lions; the one on the right would appeal to any pet lover.

A compromise candidate, Clement XIII accepted his election to the papacy with reluctance. Mild-mannered and gentle, he spent most of his 11 years in office defending the Jesuits but took time out to fig-leaf the nude statues and paintings of Rome; not even the Sistine Chapel escaped his campaign for modesty in art. He surely would have approved the adjustments made to his own monument.

The twin monuments to **Urban VIII** (1568–1644) and **Paul III** (1468–1549), flanking the Throne of St. Peter in the front, are of such dark bronze that it is difficult to make out their details. If you have binoculars, you will find the figures intriguing. On Pope Urban's, a marble Charity suckles an infant and smiles down fondly on a child who is crying inconsolably. Justice, sword in hand, is looking heavenward with boredom. This is vintage Bernini.

Although Urban VIII, born Maffeo Barberini, made some positive changes to ecclesiastical procedures and nurtured Bernini, he also made some bad mistakes. He was involved in condemning Galileo, forcing the scientist under threat of torture to renounce the Copernican system. To decorate the interior of Saint Peter's, Urban helped himself to bronze from the Pantheon, inspiring a local wit, Pasquino, to comment, "What the barbarians spared, the Barberini destroyed." And he had a whole family of nephews. The Roman populace, a critical crowd, celebrated when he died.

The tomb of Paul III, done by Guglielmo della Porta under Michelangelo's direction, is choppier in design but has more intriguing female statuary. The younger woman on the left has her dress drawn up to show her knees and thighs in a way that would get her barred by the dress-code police at St. Peter's entrance. She is gazing at a very old woman who is looking into a hand mirror and appearing unhappy at what she sees.

Unlike Urban VIII, Paul III is mostly remembered for beneficial actions. He commissioned Michelangelo to paint the ceiling of the Sistine Chapel. In the face of Protestantism, he convened the Council of Trent. And he excommunicated Henry VIII.

The next chapel holds a pride of lions. Leo II (d. 683), Leo III (d. 816), and Leo IV (d. 855) are buried together in a richly inlaid marble tomb beneath a painting of the Madonna and Child. The sarcophagus is under an exquisite mosaic floral altar. Leo XII (d. 1829) is interred under the pavement, and the altar on the left holds the remains of Leo the Great (Leo I, d. 461). The bas-relief portrays him stopping Attila the Hun in battle.

In the days when the papacy was vied over by wealthy Roman families, **Leo III** was attacked on his way to mass by family members of his predecessor, Hadrian. By trying to cut out his eyes and tongue, they hoped to render him unfit for office and return the throne to their family. When the attack failed, they denounced Leo for perjury and adultery, charges which were probably true. He fled to the protection of Charlemagne in Paderborn, Germany, where his wounds healed, and returned the favor by crowning Charlemagne "emperor of the West" on Christmas day, A.D. 800. This is traditionally considered the beginning of the Holy Roman Empire.

The monument to **Alexander VII** (1599–1667) is amazing and complex. From a distance the mottled brown mar-

ble drape truly resembles fabric. Flying out from beneath the shroud and waving a time's-up hourglass is a gilt skeleton. Because the door was already there, Bernini skillfully incorporated it into the design, making it appear to lead to a crypt. Above, one of the marble women is holding a fat baby that looks unconscious. The other, entwined in the drapery on the right side, is as beautiful as a Botticelli heroine. At the top, fingers tented, Pope Alexander looks uncertain about the attention he is getting.

Leo XI and Innocent XI face off across a dim archway. On the monument to **Leo XI** (1535–1605), the rosebuds and the inscription "Sic floruit" (So fades the flower) allude to his brief 27 days as pontiff; already in frail health, Pope Leo Medici caught a chill in St. Giovanni in Laterano and died soon afterward. The bas-relief on his sarcophagus shows his part in the conversion of Henry IV of France, about which the king allegedly made the cheerful comment "Paris is well worth a mass."

Innocent XI (1611–1689) is joined by Justice and Religion, attributes of which he had plenty. He is sculpted holding the keys to the kingdom and wearing a simple cap. Modest, pious, and charitable, Benedetto Odescalchi stated that he would accept the papacy only if the cardinals electing him subscribed to his program of reforms. Out went nepotism and Simony; in came strict adherence to monastic vows and the selection of priests and bishops based on their spiritual qualifications. When he attempted to ban carnivals, however, the public decided he had gone too far.

Pius X (1835–1914), head sinking under an ornate crown, looks stern, almost disgruntled. His arms are raised in a "Look—don't blame *me*" gesture. What he was both blamed and praised for was spiritual intransigence. He alienated the Russian and British governments by championing Catholic minorities in their countries and offended the United States by refusing to receive Theodore Roosevelt after he had lectured at the Methodist church in Rome. Yet Pius's insistence on the spiritual led to its inclusion in daily life, and a revitalization of church music and the liturgy. Even during his lifetime he was credited with various miracles, and by 1954 had been canonized as a saint.

Across the way from Pius X is the interesting bronze memorial to **Innocent VIII** (1432–1492). Perhaps it is the coloring and delicate details that give it a Byzantine look. Done by Antonio del Pollaiolo, the memorial shows the pope both lying on his sarcophagus and sitting on his throne. The spearhead he is holding in his left hand represents the spear he received from Sultan Bayezid II in 1492, which was said to have pierced the side of Christ during his crucifixion.

You might wonder what would induce the Ottoman Empire, Italy's longtime enemy, to give up such a treasure. But Bayezid was interested in keeping his brother and political rival, Djem, imprisoned in Rome, and offered a large yearly cash payment as well. The unfortunate Djem had fled to the island of Rhodes, where the sultan had been paying an official a modest sum to keep him there. But the official was persuaded to turn Djem over to the wily pope in return for a cardinal's hat. The sultan, annoyed that it would now cost him more, tried to have the pope's drinking water poisoned. When that failed, Bayezid capitulated and offered the spear—a relic whose authenticity has always been in doubt.

In short, Innocent was no Pius X. Although personally likable, he fell into the practice of selling curial offices to the highest bidders and passed out cardinals' hats as if at a New Year's Eve party. One cardinality, given to the 14-year-old son of Lorenzo de' Medici, brought Lorenzo's daughter, Maddelena, in marriage to the pope's own son, Franceschetto. Supporters pointed out that at least Innocent was the first pope not to insult his offspring by referring to them as "nephews and nieces."

An odd but interesting conclusion to this area is the tomb of the Stuarts of England. The tall white marble monument, designed by Antonio Canova, shows **James Francis Edward Stuart** (1688–1766), the Old Pretender; **Charles Edward Stuart** (1720–1788), the Young Pretender; and **Henry, cardinal Duke of York** (1725–1807). Two exquisite angels, their torches downturned, steal the show outside the closed door of the tomb.

When James II, the father of the Old Pretender, took a devout Catholic for his second wife, it sparked the Glorious Revolution of 1688. The country was seething with anti-Catholic sentiment; when James Stuart was born, jeopardizing the accession to the throne of the Protestant William and Mary, rumors started that the baby was a changeling. William of Orange and James's daughter Mary were crowned, and James and his new family fled to France, then finally Italy.

From Italy a number of plots and rebellions were hatched to put James III on the throne. An invasion of Scotland failed, and the Old Pretender retreated to Rome. He died in exile.

Next the Jacobites tried to put the Young Pretender in power. Known as Bonnie Prince Charlie, he led his Scottish followers in an uprising but was defeated in 1746 and had to escape to France. He had been a brave and charming young man, unusually precocious, playing the violin beautifully at age four. But without a kingdom, without a purpose, he roamed Europe in an alcoholic stupor. In London he paused long enough to renounce Catholicism and join the Church of England. His wife, Luisa Stolberg, whom he had married when she was 19 and he 52, took up with the poet Vittorio Alfieri. After Charlie burst into her bedroom and tried to strangle her for her infidelity, she took refuge in Rome.

After his brother's death, the cardinal Duke of York proclaimed himself Henry IX of England. He had a medal struck with his claim, "King by the grace of God but not by the will of man," but by then the movement to settle a Stuart on the throne had faded. Instead, as a cardinal bishop, he ruled the See of Frascati and at the end lived on a generous pension from George III.

Across the way is the monument of Queen **Maria Clem-**

entina Sobieski (1701–1735), wife of James Stuart, the Old Pretender. A putti displays her portrait based on a painting by Isaac Sterne. A marble figure holds a flame on her palm.

James was delighted with his pretty bride, whose hair fell almost to her ankles. But he was unable to stop her from the religious fasting that often sent her into unconsciousness. When she was 34, her weakened body gave out completely. Clementina lay in state for three days in a Dominican nun's habit, was dressed briefly in royal attire and a golden crown, then was re-dressed for burial in a nun's black veil. It was promised that when the king regained his throne, she would be moved to Westminster Abbey.

To end your tour, walk back to the center of the basilica to the impressive Baldacchino that houses the tomb of St. Peter. The tomb is a dark, ornate casket held aloft by gilt angels' wings. The metal grillwork above it is a lovely collection of saints' and angels' faces. Seven brass lamps hang in front. The figure kneeling in prayer, created by Canova, is **Pius VI** (1717–1799). He was 82 and in frail health when Napoleon marched into Rome and demanded Pius renounce his temporal power. When he refused, he was exiled to France and died there the following year.

ST. PETER *b. first century, Bethsaida; d. ca.* A.D. *64–68, Rome.* It seems difficult to make the simplest statement about St. Peter without stepping on someone's faith. Roman Catholics believe that he founded the church at Rome and was its first pope. Protestants, unwilling to concede the papacy, assert that he never came near this spot. And Jews and those less religious are frankly skeptical of

miracles such as walking on water and slipping out of locked prisons. Only the jokes about St. Peter monitoring the gates of heaven seem to be agreed on by everyone.

But Peter was an actual personality, born in Bethsaida ("house of fishing") on the Sea of Galilee. Despite a tendency for New Testament writers to portray him as rough-hewn and poor, Peter's family owned their own fishing boat and hired other workers; the area was flourishing owing to the salt industry and fish-pickling centers nearby. It seems likely that Peter was first a follower of John the Baptist, Jesus's cousin. It is further likely that Peter and Jesus met through John, whose mission it was to introduce Jesus as the Messiah. Offered the hope of overthrowing the Roman establishment, Shim'on, renamed Peter by Jesus, quickly joined him.

Peter assumed that Jesus would take over the civilized world and rule from Jerusalem. He did not take it well that, in fact, Jesus believed that he would be killed and was talking about establishing a kingdom in heaven instead. But his response may also have been exaggerated by the writers of the Gospels, who liked to portray the apostles as dullards. By the time the New Testament was written, late in the first century, there was already a movement to downplay the contributions of Jewish Christians and to stress the demands of discipleship by contrasting Jesus's perfection with his followers' failings.

Yet Peter's personality shines through. During the three years of traveling with Jesus, he tries to walk on water, becomes distracted, and sinks. Unable to keep from dozing while Jesus is praying for guidance in Gethsemane, he leaps to the occasion by slicing off the ear of one of the men come to arrest his leader. Who could fail to sympathize with someone who, while warming himself at the enemies' fire, denies their scornful accusations that he is a follower of that madman? But the cock crowed, and Peter awoke to his mission.

Jesus must have known it would take a devout and outspoken personality to continue his message, and appears to have groomed Peter for the task. Peter was equal to it. After the crucifixion he was the first to see Jesus; whatever the real nature of that appearance, he, at least, was convinced that Jesus had triumphed over death as he promised and was indeed the Messiah. Peter rallied the depressed and bedraggled band of believers and began the task of spreading that message.

There followed years of traveling and preaching, attempts to work out how much of Jewish culture Gentile Christians were expected to take on, and theological conflicts with Paul. Peter, who was married, brought his wife on missions; stories about her various martyrdoms abounded. There was also a daughter, Petronilla, perhaps adopted, who legend says was miraculously healed of paralysis.

The evidence suggests that Peter did get to Rome, though probably not in time to establish the church there. After stays in Antioch, Corinth, and Jerusalem, he arrived in the Eternal City sometime between A.D. 54 and 58, though possibly as late as 63. He stayed with wealthy Christian tentmakers, Aquila and Priscilla, whose house is now the site of the Church of Santa Prisca, or, alternatively, with a converted senator, Pudens, and his daughters, Pudenziana and Praxedis. Their home is said to be beneath the Church of Santa Pudenziana.

It is startling to realize that during Peter's lifetime Caligula, Claudius, and finally Nero ruled Rome, and that Peter was caught in the net of Nero's persecutions. He was martyred between 64 and 68, traditionally by crucifixion—upside down, at his own request, so he would not be competing with Jesus. Since 160, belief has been strong that Peter's bones were rescued from the common grave of martyrs and interred on this site, though early Christians, believing that Jesus would be coming back soon, did not consider preserving remains important. But whether or not the bones of this enigmatic man are actually under our feet, his mystique has bloomed over the years into this amazing edifice.

DIRECTIONS AND HOURS: Take Metro Line A to the Ottoviano stop and walk south, or take a no. 64 or 492 bus from Termini. St. Peter's is open daily 7:00 A.M. to 7:00 P.M. (6:00 P.M. in winter).

ROME, NAPLES, and FORMIA
Quick Trips

▲   ▲   ▲

THE CHURCH OF ST. CECILIA IN TRASTEVERE AND SAN PIETRO IN MONTORIO

Trastevere is on the far side of Rome, across the Tiber and almost beyond the reach of the bus line. The Jewish ghetto is located there, along with intimations of anarchy and a string of tiny, fascinating churches. Two churches in particular have legendary characters buried inside. It would make an interesting afternoon to start at St. Cecilia, stop in at Santa Maria in Trastevere for the charming mosaics, and end at dusk at San Pietro in Montorio with its panoramic view of Rome.

St. Cecilia's is entered through a pleasant rosebush-planted courtyard. Once inside the church, the most striking object is the statue of St. Cecilia in a glass case in front of the main altar. She was sculpted by Carlo Maderno exactly as she was found when her tomb was opened in 1599, lying on her side with the three fingers of her right hand extended—the secret sign of early Christians to show a belief in the Trinity.

In 817, when Pope Paschal I was unsuccessfully searching the Catacombs of St. Calixtus for Cecilia's body, he fell asleep and dreamed that she came to him, telling him that he had been close to her tomb that day. Going back, he found the cypress wood coffin with Cecilia inside, her body seemingly untouched by death.

If the crypt is open, you can descend the steps in the front to where **St. Cecilia** is buried behind a grille, along

Opposite: the Appian Way

with her husband, **St. Valerian**, his brother, **St. Tibertius**, and **St. Maximus**. You can also pay a small fee and tour the excavations beneath the church, a fascinating labyrinth of corridors with decorative pavements and sarcophagi. Part of the ruins is believed to be Cecilia and Valerian's home, though no one is exactly sure when they lived or died.

St. Cecilia, daughter of a patrician family, refused to consummate her marriage until her husband, Valerian, became a Christian. Quickly deciding to convert, he and his brother, Tibertius, devoted themselves to their new faith. They were arrested for retrieving and burying the bodies of martyred Christians and sentenced to death themselves. Along with another early Christian, Maximus, they were beheaded outside Rome.

Cecilia buried the three martyrs in the cemetery of Praetextatus and was arrested herself. Given the chance to save her life by sacrificing to the gods, she refused and was sentenced to be suffocated in her bathtub. She survived three days of steam heat without harm, and a soldier was sent to behead her. He sliced at her neck ineffectually—under law only three blows were allowed—and she lingered three days before dying. The patron saint of music and the organ was buried in the Catacombs of St. Calixtus and moved here in 820.

San Pietro in Montorio was built before the ninth century on what was mistakenly believed to be the crucifixion site of St. Peter. Its crowning glory, the *Transfiguration* by Raphael, was moved to the Vatican Museum in 1809, but frescoes by Sebastiano del Piombo (ca. 1518) remain.

If you pull back the carpet on the left side in front of the high altar, you will find the tombs of **Hugh O'Neill** (1540–1616) and **Rory O'Donnell** (1575–1608), tribal chieftains buried far from their native Ireland. The two joined with Spain in a plot against James I and Protestant England. After the conspiracy was discovered in 1607, they fled with a boatload of other Irish noblemen, finally settling in Rome. O'Neill received a pension from Spain and Pope Paul V.

Under the steps of the altar is buried a tragic young woman, **Beatrice Cenci** (1577–1599). The subject of poetry by Percy Bysshe Shelley, a play by Alberto Moravia, a novel by Francesco Guerrazzi, and an opera by Alberto Ginestera, Beatrice was unlucky enough to be the daughter of a wealthy, influential, and sadistic nobleman. After Francesco Cenci was widowed and remarried, he isolated his new bride, Lucrezia, and 18-year-old Beatrice in a remote castle where he could torture them at will.

Beatrice, her brothers, Giacomo and Bernardo, and her lover, Olimpio Calvettie, plotted her father's murder. After he was killed, the body was thrown from a balcony to make the death look accidental. The truth was discovered, and everyone but Beatrice admitted complicity; she was tortured before she finally confessed. Despite pleas to Pope Clement VIII for leniency, everyone but Bernardo, who was too young, was put to death. Cynics believed the pope's primary interest was in Cenci's estate, which he promptly confiscated.

DIRECTIONS: Depending on where you are coming from, take one of the various buses that run across the Pont Garibaldi and down the Viale Trastevere. Get off at the Piazza Mastai and walk two blocks southeast to St. Cecilia's, off the Via Anicia. Then retrace your steps to the piazza and work your way northwest to Santa Maria in Trastevere and San Pietro in Montorio. Consult a local street map for exact locations. The churches are usually open between 8:30 and 12:00, and 2:00 or 3:00 to 5:30.

THE APPIA ANTICA

The Appian Way, whose oldest discovered epitaph goes back to the first century B.C.—"Stranger, I thank you for having stopped by my resting place; may thy business prosper; keep well, sleep peacefully" (Marcus Caecilius)—has some wonderful treasures. It takes time and patience to see them, however, particularly if the no. 118 bus has not yet been returned to service. In that case you will have a long walk (or a short cab ride) from the Colosseum to the Porta San Sebastiano.

You may wish to start at the Catacombs of St. Calixtus, a feisty third-century pope with a prior career as an embezzling banker and rabble-rouser. He is not buried here himself, but seven other popes are. Four of them were murdered under Valerian in the third century. What is believed to be the original burial place of St. Cecilia is in a nearby chamber, marked by a copy of her statue by Carlo Maderno from the church in Trastevere. Along the corridors are fragile frescoes of biblical figures, burial inscriptions, and early Christian symbols, thrilling both because of their age and because they have not been moved elsewhere.

Back outside, the next notable tomb you will see is that of **Cecilia Metella**, an impressive tower now ruined and open to the air. Inside its interior arches are fragments of statuary and pieces of other tombs. Cecilia was the wife of Marcus Licinus Crassus, one of Julius Caesar's generals in Gaul.

Unfortunately, over the ages many of the original tombs along the Appia Antica have been destroyed or stolen. Those that remained have been taken to museums and replaced here by "casts." The most appealing of these are those like window frames with the busts of family members looking out: Hermodorus, Demaris, and Isidis Rabirii, who appear to be father, mother, and son, watch the passing centuries without much pleasure.

DIRECTIONS AND HOURS: If it is running, you can take the no. 118 bus back from Cecilia Metella's tomb. If it is

still not in operation, continue walking to the intersection of the Via Appia Nuova, turn left, and take the no. 664 bus (on the right side of the road) back to the Metro Line A stop. The Catacombs of St. Calixtus are closed Wednesdays and open 8:30 to 12:30 and 3:00 to 6:00.

NAPLES AND FORMIA

Naples is a city of exotic extremes: tenements on a stunning blue bay, *autostrada* bandits in contrast to kindly residents, a volcano that periodically wipes the urban slate clean. Unlike Florence or Rome, Naples has no easily available street maps. Visitors trying to find a street guide at newsstands, hotels, or gas stations will come up empty. It is as if someone decided that there were not enough interested visitors to make such an undertaking worthwhile.

The lack of a street map makes finding a specific grave in a specific cemetery in this city of over a million souls a serious challenge. Enrico Caruso, for instance, is buried in the Cimitero di Santa Maria del Pianto (St. Mary of Tears) on the Nuovo del Campo. We arrived there only after hours of asking directions and only after a generous Neapolitana got into her car and led us to the cemetery gates. The main landmark is an outdoor pottery factory across the way.

Once inside, keep bearing left as you move down the hill into the cemetery. The monument, with Caruso's name and a head of Christ, will loom up suddenly. Inside is his sarcophagus with a bas-relief of two singers, his photo, and a plaque presented on the fiftieth anniversary of his death: "From those who still remember in the United States and Canada."

ENRICO CARUSO *b. February 27, 1873, Naples; d. August 2, 1921, Naples.* Biologists tell us that we procreate to maintain not only family lines but also, by extension, the species. A prime incentive is the pleasure of sex. We can, therefore, only admire the fortitude and persistence, the pleasure and the sorrow of Marcellino and Anna Caruso, for Enrico Caruso was the sixteenth of eighteen children and the first to survive past infancy.

The family's high infant mortality rate was not due to terrible poverty, since the Carusos had an income and a place to live. Rather it was because of epidemics such as the cholera that raged during Enrico's infancy.

Caruso grew up healthy in this teeming city. His fine contralto voice was noticed by teachers early on and his mother sought lessons, although his father, preferring the career of mechanical engineer for his son, offered initial resistance. Caruso survived the pubescent change-of-voice crisis with no loss of quality. More difficult was coping with the death of this mother to whom he was extremely devoted. But within six months his father married Maria Castaldi, a stepmother whose care, love, and interest provided much-needed solace and support for the teenager.

At 18, Caruso took up singing Neapolitan melodies in cafés during the summer months. His sweet tenor attracted the attention of a young baritone, Eduardo Missiano, who introduced Caruso to Guglielmo Vergine, a leading vocal teacher in Naples. The initial audition was not auspicious, but Missiano did not give up and Caruso was back the following week for another try. This time the response elevated to *"so-so"* and Vergine took on Caruso as a student.

Caruso's career had a fitful start; nervous and off-key auditions, a disastrous drunken performance in Sicily. But always there were the spectacular successes when his ravishing tones and dramatic involvement saved his hide and secured his reputation. His performances in *La gioconda* in Palermo won over the chauvinistic hometown crowd who were initially dismayed by the lack of a Sicilian tenor. For his morale and career, these performances were a watershed.

His newfound confidence was further bolstered when he auditioned for the role of Rodolfo in *La bohème* for the composer Puccini. Demanding and not easily impressed, Puccini was greatly moved by the young tenor's rendition and asked Caruso, "Who sent you to me—God?" Success piled upon success. Soon Caruso was earning lavish salaries. His love life sparked into action as well. His liaison with the soprano Ada Giachetti, lasting a little over 10 years, produced two daughters.

In 1903 Caruso's career became centered on the Metropolitan Opera in New York. He quickly became the darling of the management and the public. His fees rose to $2,500 per performance, and had he been greedy he could have earned more. His recordings alone earned him a fortune. No voice of his era was quite so marvelously suited for recording into that horn. He projected where others faded. And there was no arguing that voice. It was lyric, seamless, and mellow. Extending from high C, even D flat in his youth, it reached well down into the baritone range. With age it grew darker and deeper. The high notes were lost and had to be transposed down, but that did not diminish the quality of his appeal. The critics, the public, and his peers all agreed that his was a unique talent that set him apart from all others.

The press followed everywhere, and his liaisons with sopranos Emma Trentini and Geraldine Farrar provided great copy. Trentini announced their marriage. Caruso denied it: "Pah, I don't get married." Trentini declared Caruso a liar and said she was happier without him. Caruso compared the diminutive star to a peanut or a cake of soap. Trentini asked rhetorically, "What does he know about soap?" And so it went until Caruso married the socialite Dorothy Park Benjamin in 1918. If the public was caught by surprise, Dorothy's father, Park Benjamin, was enraged and disowned her.

But Caruso was more than just a good story. He was genuine, playful, and generous. When singing with the distinguished and more experienced Nellie Melba, he stuffed a hot sausage into her hand during his aria "Che gelida manina" in *La bohème.* The soprano shrieked and flung the sausage into the air. On another occasion he squeaked a toy mouse in her ear during a death scene. Because he exuded high spirits and genuine goodwill, Caruso could get away with these antics. To his peers he was complimentary and to stagehands and needy musicians he was generous with money.

On December 11, 1920, during a performance of *L'elisir d'amore* at the Brooklyn Academy of Music, Caruso suffered a hemorrhage which stopped the show. His condition was misdiagnosed as only a ruptured blood vessel in the tongue. Permitted to sing again on the 13th and the 16th, Caruso developed pains in his side. The diagnosis again minimized his condition. Merely neuralgia, declared his doctor.

On Christmas Eve he sang his last performance for the Met. His pain grew intolerable. The experts confirmed pleurisy. Several operations followed, and in May Caruso returned to Italy to recover. For a brief while his spirits rose, but the fever and pain returned as his kidneys failed. The doctors could not relieve the horrible pain, and a little after nine in the morning on August 2, 1921, the world's greatest tenor mercifully passed away. To this day he remains the measure of all tenors.

If you return to the top of the cemetery and start down the hill to the right, you will see a crudely painted sign pointing to "Toto." It will lead you to the mausoleum of **Focas Flavio Comneno de Curtis di Bisanzio e Cle-**

mente, b. November 7, 1898, Naples; d. April 15, 1967, Rome, one of Italy's leading comedians. Inside there are many photos of him.

Just outside the city at the Mergellina Station is the Santa Maria di Piedigrotta Church. Nearby, beneath the railway viaduct, is the Parco Virgiliana, which holds the columbarium traditionally considered Virgil's tomb.

PUBLIUS VERGILIUS MARO (VIRGIL), *b. October 15, 70 b.c., near Mantua; d. October 21, 19 b.c., Brundisium, Calabria.* "Mantua me genuit; Calabri rapuere; tenet nunc Parthenope; cecini pascua, rura, duces" (Mantua gave me birth; Calabria took me away; and now Naples holds me; I sang of pastures, farms, leaders). Virgil's succinct epitaph spells out not only the order of his life but also that of his three great works, the *Eclogues,* the *Georgics,* and the *Aeneid.* These poems have carried Virgil's singing for 2,000 years down to our times. During much of this span his poetry has held enormous sway, for he has been considered the greatest of Roman poets and the most profound poetic interpreter of Roman civilization. When we consider the impact of Roman culture on European history, we can see that Virgil's status was high indeed. It was Virgil, after all, whom Dante chose as the poet's guide through Hell and Purgatory.

Virgil's influence ran through the early Christians, who interpreted Virgil allegorically, especially in the fourth eclogue, which speaks of a child who will bring the peace of a Golden Age. While Virgil was most likely referring to Octavian, his messianic message was easily converted for those who wished to see the Baby Jesus instead. Beyond this, the form that Virgil applied to his poetry was held for centuries to be the correct method of poetic composition. His influence is to be seen in the poetry of his younger contemporary Ovid, down through Dante, Spenser, Milton, Dryden, Tennyson, and Arnold.

Virgil, the quintessential pastoral poet, was raised on a farm on the River Mincio near Mantua. He obtained the best education available and, somewhere between the ages of 10 and 12, was sent to Cremona for further schooling. From there he went to Milan and then to Rome to study rhetoric with Epidius, with an eye toward a career in politics. Finding rhetoric not to his liking, Virgil dropped out and left for Naples to study at the Garden under Siro the Epicurean. He made an obvious impression on his master, for when Siro died it was Virgil who inherited his villa.

There is some question as to whether Virgil fought during the civil war, since his health was habitually fragile. Nor would his spirit have made him an ideal soldier—his gentleness and purity lent him the nickname in Naples of "the Maiden." At the war's conclusion the farm of Virgil's father was confiscated and parceled out to the victorious soldiers as reward for their noble efforts. Such compensation was not unusual, but Virgil fought the action by enlisting the aid of his influential patrons. Whether he was successful is not known.

The *Eclogues* (Selections), Virgil's transformations of Theocritus's pastoral poems, were published in 37 B.C. At first glance they seem to be a romantic escape into the idealized land of Arcadia, where shepherds while away the hours and days in singing and loving. In fact, as in all Virgil's poetry, he developed beneath the surface, through analogy and metaphor, a commentary on the Rome of his day. Here we find not only the fourth eclogue with its messianic prophecy, but also a telling in the first eclogue of the dispossessed Meliboeus searching for new land to farm, and later in the ninth eclogue praise of Caesar, whose soul is the guarantor of ongoing fertility and yield.

The *Eclogues* established Virgil as the foremost poet of his day. He was given a stipend and a house on the Esquiline. His friends, Horace and Varius, and his patrons, Octavian and Maecenas, were important, stimulating, and powerful men. But city life was not congenial to Virgil, and he retreated to Campania where, at the suggestion of Maecenas, he composed the *Georgics* (Tillage of the Land). Published in 29 B.C., these poems bemoan the ruin of the land through ongoing battle, pray for the restoration of traditional agriculture, eulogize the spirit and nobility of farming, and comprise a "practical husbandry" on farming wherein Virgil offers advice to farmers on crops, trees, animals and, most famously, bees, whose characteristics "are those of the Roman ideal: courage, industry, loyalty, and discipline."

The *Aeneid,* a Roman retelling of Homer's *Iliad,* is nothing less than a history of Rome, tracing its origins back to Aeneas of Troy. It is an ideal and romantic history. Its characters rise above the mere human struggles of Homer's cast. The language is rich with exalted metaphor. Virgil demonstrates the futility and cost of human struggle; the destruction, not the ennobling, of what is most valuable in life by the fighting of wars. He paints the enemies of Aeneas with depth and sympathy. They are not straw men present only to exalt the achievements of Aeneas. Rather, their complexity adds a deep layer of ambiguity to the epic, as does Aeneas's love and abandonment of Dido.

In the *Aeneid,* Virgil also celebrates the Roman ideals of *humanitas* (empathy for one's fellows) and *pietas* (fidelity to family and society and to moral guidelines) but in so doing recognizes that the defeated often hold their own views of *humanitas* and *pietas.* Hence the conflict, the depth, and the ambiguity of Virgil's work. It is on the one hand a celebration of Rome, of a Rome that never was, a romantic mythological ancestry fulfilled and made real, and yet it is recognition of the human struggle that underlies and even undermines the myth and the glory.

Virgil came close but never finished the *Aeneid.* Bent on obtaining greater accuracy of detail, he sailed for Greece where he met up with Augustus, who influenced him to return to Italy. On the return trip Virgil became ill and died two days after landing in Brundisium. On his deathbed he urged that the *Aeneid* be burned because it was incomplete. Augustus dissuaded him from this rash course. The poem was published by Varius and Tucca in Rome, and Virgil's fame as the greatest poet of Roman history was ensured.

Up the coast, just outside the seaside town of Formia, is the Tomba di Cicerone. Traditionally considered the burial place of Cicero, it is a towerlike structure with a broken top, surrounded by fir and olive trees. The interior may be seen by appointment, but there is actually very little inside.

MARCUS TULLIUS CICERO, *b. January 3, 106 B.C., Arpinum; d. December 7, 43 B.C., Caieta.* Cicero was the greatest of all Roman orators. Not even Caesar could match his style and power. Cicero could exhort, inflame, and cajole; he could rage or roar with laughter. From the noblest pleas and causes to sycophantic abasement, no style or method was inexpedient. He could reconcile his love of Rome and republican ideals with the necessity for strange alliances and hypocritical stands. Understanding the gap between law and justice, he was able to balance on the wire between their conflicting demands. He was a patriot, an idealist, a pragmatist, a power broker. He knew the system, its rewards and its punishments.

Cicero was born to a family of the equestrian class in the country town of Arpinum. When he was 10, Cicero's family moved to Rome. There his intellect blossomed. As he grew older he studied rhetoric and law and, whenever able, observed the skilled orators of the day. It was his early determination to become nothing less than the greatest orator in Rome. By the year 80 he had entered a legal career and scored his first notable success in his defense of Roscius. But whether because this success offended the dictator, Sulla, or because his health was poor, Cicero left Rome for two years and furthered his study of oratory in Athens and Rhodes.

Cicero returned to Rome after the death of Sulla in 77. The following year he married the wealthy and strong-willed Terentia, by whom he had two children. He was also elected quaestor. In 70, he moved into a position of leadership in the Roman bar with his prosecution of Verres, a notoriously cruel and corrupt governor. His career moved along smartly. In 69 he became curule aedile and in 66 praetor.

More astounding yet, Cicero was elected consul in 63. For a man of his class this was all but unprecedented, for the nobility dominated the government and jealously guarded access to its seats of power. But Cicero won handily, defeating both Catiline and C. Antonius. Cicero's victory was a measure of the power of his oratory, his conspicuous successes, and his obvious political acumen.

Cicero was a staunch republican, and he was conservative. He had no interest in fomenting discontent. His aim was to maintain the republic and to reform it only when necessary. He found it expedient not to offend, and yet when he felt obligated he spoke forcefully. He was a determined foe of Julius Caesar. For the most part he preferred defending the law rather than prosecuting, because the latter was more likely to offend the ruling class. It is ironic, then, that his two greatest successes were obtained as a prosecutor.

Indeed Cicero's greatest hour came in his suppression of the Catilinarian conspiracy. Cicero defeated Catiline in 63 but also ensured his defeat again in 62. Catiline, a man with great ambition, then plotted the overthrow of the government. Cicero, in constant touch with an informant, brought the conspiracy to the attention of the Senate and the public. His adroit handling of the situation protected the republic and ensured Catiline's downfall.

Not all of Cicero's moves were so successful. In 60 he refused to participate in the First Triumvirate. In doing so, he left himself vulnerable to charges by Clodius that he had authorized the execution of certain Catilinarian conspirators without first obtaining the permission of the people. The charge was true but politically motivated. Without the protection of the triumvers, Cicero found himself exiled in 58. Fortunately, his exile was brief; the following year he was recalled to Rome, where he continued with his legal practice and worked on essays.

From now until his death, Cicero's writings would consume much of his time. They cover a wide range of subjects, ranging from the Republic to the orator, to fate, old age, divination, friendship, glory, and moral duty. Cicero was not a philosopher in the sense that he developed his own school of logic or thought. He openly admitted that he borrowed from the Greeks, but he did so in a manner that might be described as popularizations, for his choices demonstrate a clarity and wit often not present in the originals. Further, his choices give us an accurate and revealing picture of the man, his general outlook, his worldview. Cicero's influence extends throughout the ages, through St. Augustine and down to Churchill. His style of oratory has been copied by countless generations. It was a formulaic style spiced with genius and relying most especially on cadence, on the measured delivery of lush language and extended metaphors and elaboration.

When Pompey and Caesar engaged in civil war, Cicero backed Pompey. In a rare display of magnanimity, the victorious Caesar allowed Cicero to return to Rome. His days of official power were over, but still he wielded enormous de facto influence. Although he approved of it, he did not participate in the planning or carrying out of Caesar's assassination. Cicero's love of the republic and distrust of Mark Anthony brought him to preach his virulent speeches against Anthony, known as *philippics.* These ensured Cicero's death when the Second Triumvirate came into power, for Augustus, in a concession to Anthony, allowed Cicero's name to be placed on a list of proscribed citizens.

Anthony's soldiers found Cicero at his estate in Caieta being carried down to the sea on a litter. Cicero, upon seeing the centurion Herennius, ordered his litter to be set down. He then stared at Herennius, stretched his neck out, and was beheaded. The vengeful Anthony nailed his head and hand to a wall in the Forum.

Horrible and inevitable as it was, there was no disgrace in Cicero's death. He had once again spoken for the republic that he loved. And if his critics point to his inconsistencies and political maneuverings, it cannot be forgotten that he died for his words and his actions.

C H A P T E R   7

UMBRIA and TUSCANY

▲   ▲   ▲

ASSISI

If you can be in Assisi in the evening and stand on the street above the lighted basilica, you may experience an incredible peace. Looking down, you will see the large *PAX* formed by hedges in the back lawn; at intervals an unseen sacristan rings the bell in the steeple. The people who pass you smile and nod hello, as if you are there for a common purpose. Even if you have not come to Assisi on a religious pilgrimage, you are invited to share its gentle atmosphere.

You can prolong this sense of peacefulness by touring the Basilica of San Francesco early in the morning. The lower church was completed in 1230 and there is a crypt-like feeling inside, enhanced by the series of low painted arches and polished dark stone floors. The altar to St. Francis in the back is columned and lit by many small green lanterns. Off to the side is a chapel with one of his coarsely woven, much-mended tunics under glass. The frescoes here and in the chapel opposite, no more than fragments in many places, are lovely.

Retrace your path and go down the steps into the crypt, a small, attractive area made of red brick with recessed lighting. Just outside the chapel is a metal chandelier holding several brass birds. Lighting inside is also provided by lamps shaped like birdbaths, which hang from mosaic crosses.

After St. Francis was buried here in 1230, his sarcophagus could be seen for the next 200 years by entering the tomb through a tunnel. Then in 1442 the Perugini sacked Assisi and tried unsuccessfully to carry him away. Next they attempted to convince Pope Eugenius IV that the body would be "safer" in Perugia. Instead, Eugenius ordered the tunnel entrance sealed off completely.

It was not until 1818 that the tomb was successfully excavated. The skeleton inside was examined and certified as that of St. Francis. A new crypt with a suitable entrance was created by Pasquale Belli, but nobody liked its neoclassical design. It was redone in its current form in 1932 by Ugo Tarchi. The bones of St. Francis were disturbed a final time, in 1978, when Pope Paul VI ordered them preserved in a Plexiglas casket, which was then placed in the metal coffin of 1818 inside the original stone tomb of 1230. The tomb rises impressively to the ceiling with grillwork on the sides.

ST. FRANCIS (FRANCESCO BERNARDONE) *b. 1181, Assisi, d. October 3, 1226, Portiuncula. "Paupertatas cum laetitia."* (Poverty with joy.) This was the motto of St. Francis. Citing melancholy as "the Babylonian disease," Francis exhorted others to "take your troubles to God, but when you join your companions, show only joy." Joy was achieved only through great sacrifice and humility. It is, along with charity, the essence of the Franciscans.

Eight hundred years later Francis is still perhaps the most appealing, the most accessible of saints. His humanness keeps shining through. He was a man of voice, an impassioned speaker in the manner of traveling evangelists of our own century, a door-to-door proselytizer in the manner of a Jehovah's Witness. He wrestled with pride and sexual desire. He was scatological. On more than one occasion he preached or walked naked in public. To quell his sexual desire, he would strip and roll in the snow or throw himself into rosebushes. He was inconsistent, arrogant, and stubborn in his rebellion. His struggles are as manifest as his message of love.

The son of a well-to-do clothing merchant, Francis spent his late youth carousing with the wealthy young men of Assisi. Together they drank, danced, sang, and kept company with the demimondaines of the town. Though no beauty, he dressed in a gaudy self-designed patchwork affair made of sackcloth and the finest material available in his father's shop. Francis was in full rebellion against his father, a condition which only worsened with time.

In 1202, in Assisi's war with Perugia, Francis was captured and imprisoned for a year. Upon his release, he experienced his first epiphany, his awakening or conversion. Within a year, another visitation brought him to the step of purgation. He divested himself of his belongings and money, and, at times, those of his parents. As his father's outrage grew, Francis's demonstrations of religious submission became even greater. He was now pausing on the road to kiss lepers on the mouth.

In his wanderings Francis came across a tiny dilapidated chapel honoring St. Damian. Among the ruins there still hung a crucifix in Byzantine style. Falling to pray, Francis watched as, three times, the lips of Jesus moved and told him, "Francis, go and repair my house, which, as you see, is falling all to ruin."

Preferring the literal translation at first, Francis sold some of his father's best cloth and his horse and offered the money as a tribute to St. Damian. Immediately disowned by his father, Francis took refuge in the rude chapel. The church then, like the government now, was the major employer of the time, and most men joined to gain work. But Francis was a devout and a singular one at that. He was now wedded to poverty. Taking his word on the road, Il Poverello (the Little Poor Man) began to gather a small following. In 1210 Pope Innocent III sanctioned Francis and his followers, and Francis became a deacon. It was his sole ecclesiastical rank. The brothers became known as the Frati Minori, or Lesser Brothers.

Rank meant little to Francis. Urging the revival of the Gospel of Simplicity, he showed himself to be both anti-intellectual and antidoctrinal. As such, he was an ancestor of philosophical anarchism. There was no hierarchy within the brotherhood. In 1212 he and St. Clare founded the Poor Clares. Over the years the Little Brothers grew in number and took their message as far as Egypt. Indeed, in 1219 Francis and Illuminato attempted unsuccessfully to convert Sultan Malik al-Kamil.

The Egyptian trip aggravated Francis's chronically poor health. In 1221 he formulated his First Rule, which stressed poverty, chastity, and obedience. But within the brotherhood there was dissent. His severe demands (e.g., open sandals in winter) lacked temperance. For Francis himself, no sacrifice was too great. All must be suffered with patience and humility in order to experience perfect joy.

In 1224 Francis received the stigmata while praying at Mount La Verna in the Apennines. He had now assumed the very likeness of Christ. Moving only with great difficulty, he carried these wounds to his death. Nearing his death, he composed another stanza to his "Canticle of the Creatures." It was a praise of death. On his deathground, lying on sackcloth and sprinkled with ashes and dust, he invoked it as his last frail song. It is said that an exultation of larks took to the heavens singing his praise.

In the wall niches are the remains of four of St. Francis's early companions: Fra Angelo, Fra Masseo, Fra Rufino, and Fra Leone. As with Francis, their activities only emphasize the human appeal of the brothers and their movement. **Fra Angelo** was a noble knight and a special friend of St. Francis. Just weeks before Francis died, he summoned Angelo and Leone to sing his "Canticle of the Creatures" for him. **Fra Leone** was Francis's secretary and confessor. Francis nicknamed him Frate Pecorella or Pecorone because of his large sheeplike head.

Fra Rufino, a first cousin of St. Clare, spent much of his time in the throes of ecstasies and visions. To test his early devotion and sincerity, Francis ordered the shy young man to preach a sermon in church clad only in his shorts. Observing his humiliation and the jeering audience, Francis himself took on the same charge. Stripping naked, he launched an impassioned sermon that first quieted the derision and then converted it to tears of shame and belief.

Tall, handsome, and a trifle dull, **Fra Masseo,** content in his assurance of Christ, took to endlessly cooing like a dove, much to the annoyance of his fellows. Accompanying Francis on many pilgrimages, he proved he had a head for directions. Uncertain at a crossroads which direction to take, Francis spun Masseo until the dizzy brother collapsed on the ground, his tonsure pointing the road to Siena.

The Basilica of Santa Chiara is a 10-minute walk across Assisi, following a well-marked road. The pink and white stone church was completed in 1260 to house St. Clare's body; the basilica's Gothic style is similar to the Upper Church of San Francesco. The church occupies the former site of the Chuch of San Giorgio, the parish church where St. Francis studied as a boy and where he preached his first sermon. It was here that his body was taken after death.

To reach Clare's tomb, you must descend several flights of stairs. When you come into the last chapel, turn left and follow the pictures of the story of her life, from her receiving the palm in 1212 to the rediscovery of her body in 1850. You can go up a spiral staircase and see the propped lid and empty stone sepulchre from which she was resurrected. Her remains are now in an urn, placed behind the re-created figure of Clare in a glass coffin.

ST. CLARE OF ASSISI (CHIARA DI FAVARONE) *b. July 11, 1194, Assisi; d. August 11, 1253, Assisi.* One wonders how St. Clare might feel to learn that, along with embroidery and sore eyes, she was made the patron saint of television. The title was conferred on her by Pope Pius XII in 1958; perhaps he was remembering the Christmas Eve when Clare, too ill to leave her bed for midnight mass, was said to have seen the manger at Bethlehem projected on the wall of her cell.

The oldest daughter of a wealthy Assisi family, Clare was born after her mother, who had had trouble conceiving, petitioned at various holy shrines, even making the arduous trip to Jerusalem. By the age of 12, the tall and pretty Clare had begun turning down marriage proposals, and at 17, she initiated a series of meetings with St. Francis, begging him to take her on as a Franciscan friar.

He refused, unwilling to compromise his order. But on Palm Sunday night 1212 she and her cousin Pacifica went to the friary, the girls dressed as brides to be wed to Christ. St. Francis himself snipped off their long hair and gave them sackcloth robes to wear. Uncertain what to do next with two females, the Franciscans finally escorted them to a convent two miles away.

Despite the pleas of Clare's family to return home, it was not until her sister Caterina, 14, later called Agnes, joined her that their father sent 12 Favaroni relatives to retrieve them. The story is that Clare prayed and the men, who had Caterina by the hair, could no longer budge the tiny girl. It is a more charming story than the one in which a group of peasants, hearing Caterina's screams and Clare's explanation, helped free the girl.

Under the tutelage of Francis, Clare went on to found what is now the Poor Clares, based on strict Franciscan principles. The order neither ate meat nor wore shoes, and slept on the ground. More significantly, they received permission from various popes during Clare's 40-year tenure to practice strict poverty, resisting gifts of land and legacies and living only on alms. As Innocent III pointed out, her request to reject donations was surely the first to come to the court of Rome.

After her father's death, her mother and another sister, Beatrice, joined the Poor Clares. It was a rigorous life of caring for the sick, doing menial tasks, and worshiping God. No time was allowed for reflection or recreation. The visits of Francis, who was playful and often surprising, were high points in the lives of the Clares.

As time passed, Clare was consulted by popes and cardinals and credited with miracles such as saving Assisi from Emperor Frederick II in 1241. She oversaw the spread of Franciscan convents throughout Europe, cautioning an eager founder in Prague not to overdo the privations, "for our bodies are not made of brass." Plagued by poor health herself, she was eventually bedridden, spending her time embroidering altar cloths. But for a religious woman in the Middle Ages, it had been much the happiest of lives.

DIRECTIONS AND HOURS: As you approach Assisi from below, stay to the left side of the city. There is parking around Porta San Pietro and Porta del Sementone; the Basilica of San Francesco, an easy walk, is open daily 7:00 A.M. to 7:00 P.M., except November to March when it closes between 12:00 and 2:00 P.M. The Basilica of Santa Chiara is open daily 6:30 A.M. to noon, and 2:00 P.M. to dusk.

CERTALDO

Certaldo, especially during the siesta hours, has the peaceful feeling of a working village. The Church of Jacopo e Filippo is simple but lovely, with brick walls and high wooden beams. Giovanni Boccaccio's shallow effigy in the floor is life-sized. He is lying with his head on a tasseled pillow, clutching his masterpiece, the *Decameron.* A covering like a nightcap is on his head, and his feet turn up slightly at the end of the frame as if he is in a bed that is too short.

On the left wall is Boccaccio's hooded bust, again holding his book.

GIOVANNI BOCCACCIO *b. 1313, Paris; d. December 23, 1375, Certaldo.* Whether he was exulting over their "bewitching beauty and exquisite grace," or excoriating them as "gluttonous, wayward, and cantankerous," Boccaccio's writings were preoccupied with women. Though he sometimes tried to raise his sexual obsessions to the level of courtly and spiritual love portrayed by Dante and Petrarch, he never succeeded. His sensuality broke through medieval barriers and led a parade that would come to include Chaucer, Shakespeare, Molière, and Keats.

He was born to an unknown French woman and a banker who had gone to Paris to make a quick fortune.

Boccaccio *patri* did not return home with any wealth, but he brought back his three-year-old son. It was never explained whether Giovanni's mother had died or had merely been left behind, but the senior Boccaccio quickly married and gave his son a legal mother.

Their plans were for Giovanni to go into business, and as a teenager he was sent to Naples to learn commerce. When, after six years, this proved unsuccessful, he spent another six unenthusiastically studying canon law. He had already pledged himself to poetry and was enjoying a rapturous life both at the court of King Robert of Anjou and at the resort of Baia. It was rumored that no young woman who arrived a virgin at the Neapolitan playland ever returned home in the same condition, and Boccaccio did his part to make that rumor fact.

In the midst of his dalliances he met a young woman generally believed to be Maria d'Aquino, the natural daughter of King Robert. She was married but began a relationship with the poet. Glorified as his Fiammetta (Little Flame), she inspired several works of prose and poetry, including *Il filocolo* (The Love-Weary, ca. 1340), *Commedia delle ninfe Fiorentine* (The Comedy of the Florentine Nymphs, 1341–1342) and *L'amorosa visione* (The Amorous Vision, 1342–1343). When she tired of him and turned to other relationships, the spurned and furious Boccaccio penned *L'elegia di Madonna Fiammetta* (ca. 1344), recognized as the first psychological novel. Sharpening his revenge, he reversed the situation and made her the jilted, abandoned party.

By then he was back home. Under his father's watchful eye and in no-nonsense Florence, his life seemed restrictive. He was also forced to face the conflict he felt between his unbridled sexuality and the Dantean spirituality he admired. There was sadness as well. Boccaccio's daughter, Violante, born when he was in Naples, died at five or six. He never married or had other children, and for the rest of his life thoughts of his lost daughter would bring tears to his eyes. The warm paternal feeling of his next book, a pastoral romance entitled *Ninfale Fiesolano* (The Nymph of Fiesole, ca. 1345), seems influenced by this experience.

The next experience that affected Boccaccio was the plague that swept Italy in 1348. This Black Death, which started in Constantinople in 1334 and roamed the world for the next 20 years, eventually killed three-quarters of the population of Asia and Europe. The poet was spared but started his masterpiece, the *Decameron* (1348–1353), with a vivid description of plague-ravaged Florence, which lost three-fifths of its population. Seven young women and three young men escape to a villa outside the city and entertain each other with 100 tales.

These stories, told in a luminous and leisurely way but heightened by the backdrop of death, were a collection of medieval tales, the anecdotes of travelers. As one Boccaccio biographer put it, "The learned have amused themselves . . . by tracing origins and parallels for the stories in the *Decameron.* They have surmised India and Persia, smelt out old Greek and Roman authorities, sniffed in old mediaeval histories and chronicles, yelped with joy to discover that Boccaccio even repeated some things from the *Filocolo.*"

In short, the material was already in existence, but he retold it in his own way. Winsome and wily women, clowns, merchants, clergy both holy and depraved, artists, and kings all find their place in the recounting of fortunes lost and found, unexpected adventures, good deeds, and the tricks and treats of love. The *Decameron* has been mined by other writers ever since.

Meanwhile Boccaccio had to support himself. The death of his father and a second stepmother left him with no inheritance and a small half brother, Jacopo. He accepted this responsibility graciously and undertook diplomatic missions for Florence, acting as ambassador to other cities and to Pope Innocent VI. Toward the end of his life he was appointed a lecturer on Dante.

Before he settled into the life of scholarship, he had one more piece of fictional revenge to spew. *Il corbaccio* (The Old Crow, ca. 1355) was written when the tall, round-faced lover with the cleft chin and sparkling eyes was settling into middle age. Gray-haired and frankly fat, he was lonely for the comforts of a home for Jacopo and himself and set his sights on a beautiful widow. She strung him along, encouraging his attentions before finally getting word to him that she already had a more attractive lover. *Il corbaccio* describes a long dream in which the ghost of her dead husband comes to Boccaccio and describes her as she really is: snobbish, bossy, repulsive, and, before makeup, with a face "the colour of bog-mist, goose-fleshy like the birds when they are moulting, wrinkled and scruffy." The poet awakens a free man.

His last crisis came in 1362 when a Carthusian monk came to his door with a deathbed message from another monk. Boccaccio was told that he had only a little while left to live and was to renounce poetry and secular studies and turn to religion and prayer. The shaken poet moved to Certaldo, became more pious, and lived for another 12 years.

On your way out, notice **Beata Giulia** of Certaldo on the right side toward the back. She was born here in 1319 and is designated a *romita agostiniana* (Augustinian hermit). If you look through the grille, you can see her skeleton in a glass coffin, dressed in an embroidered robe and hood with artificial flowers around her skull.

On the main street, the Via Boccaccio, is the poet's supposed family homestead. Restored in the last century on the basis of rumor and hope, it does not appear to be open to visitors.

DIRECTIONS AND HOURS: It is easiest to park in (or take the train to) the lower section of Certaldo and climb up to the walled city. The Church of Jacopo e Filippo is open between 8:00 A.M. and noon and between 3:00 and 6:00 P.M.

TORRE DEL LAGO

You would expect Giacomo Puccini to have waterfront property, and you will not be disappointed. A charming statue of the composer stands among the palm trees in front of his house; he is shown with his hands in his coat

pockets, a cigarette held between his lips. The town itself has been Puccini-ized, with street names like Via Bohème and Viale Butterfly. The composer's home is on Viale Giacomo Puccini.

Because the house is private property, the procedure for tours is restrictive, but it is the only way you can get inside. Guided tours are given on the half hour between 10:00 A.M. and noon and 3:00 and 5:00 P.M. There must be at least 10 people to trigger a tour, but no more than 25. The narration is in Italian—but with an expressive guide and your own exclamations of *"Molto bello!"* a lot can be communicated.

The house is worth exclaiming over. In Puccini's studio you can see the piano on which he wrote many of his operas, and a table with an inkstand and blotter, this furniture set perpendicular so he could easily swing back and forth between them. There are many photos of the composer, alone and with other people, and in the back corner of the studio is his white plaster death mask.

Puccini's shooting room displays rifles and boots. His waterproof cloak and leather bag still hang on a peg, as if he might be coming for them shortly. But such a fantasy fades when you see the adjoining private chapel where he and his family are buried. It is a solemn place with an arched stained-glass window behind an altar, showing a faceless modern Christ. The arch is echoed by a white marble bas-relief of a woman hiding her face in her arm. A larger copper arch surrounds her, with the names and dates of Puccini's wife, Elvira; daughter, Rita; and son, Antonio. Puccini himself is in the black marble sarcophagus on the floor beneath.

GIACOMO ANTONIO DOMENICO MICHELE SECONDO MARIA PUCCINI *b. December 22, 1858, Lucca; d. November 29, 1924, Brussels.* For all that Giacomo Puccini was influenced by other composers, it seems as if he might have risen fully formed out of the mists of Torre del Lago. Giuseppe Verdi dominated Italian opera, yet only *Gianni Schicchi* shows his influence, and only *Il tabarro* delves into the verismo style of Leoncavallo and Mascagni. The vast portion of his output derived from no obvious source. For Puccini, Wagner might never have written. It is an oddity because Puccini did not have the autodidact's freedom from history, nor was he a revolutionary breaking the rules and exploring new forms. If anything, he drew from the long Italian legacy of lyrical, passionate melodies.

Of course, there was his family's history as well. Starting in 1739, four generations of Puccinis had served Lucca as musicians and organists. (Puccini's name, starting with Giacomo, bears their first names in chronological order.) Although Puccini's father died when he was five, his mother made do with thrift and the help of a generous pension. At school Puccini's laziness prompted one teacher to comment that he came just "to wear out the seat of his trousers." Eventually he would attend the music conservatory in Lucca. This better held his concentration. His progress was noted locally, and he received high praise for a *Mass* written for his graduation in 1880.

Later that year Puccini attended the Milan Conservatory as a scholarship student, and here he studied composition with Amilcare Ponchielli. Puccini's opera *Le villi* (1884) was a success and drew the interest of Ricordi, the famous publishing house. An alliance was formed, to the mutual benefit of everyone concerned. Ricordi published all of Puccini's operas, sticking by the young and relatively unknown composer even after the failure of *Edgar* in 1889. *La bohème* (1896) solved all issues of doubt and debt. Thereafter, the profits rolled in for Ricordi and Puccini, though the publisher, first the father and then the son, maintained correspondence with Puccini, cajoling and admonishing him to finish his work. Ducks, as they well knew, were a greater inspiration.

Even with success, Puccini was not the most dedicated of men. Given his druthers he would opt for hunting, smoking, and dalliances before composition. For years Puccini lived with Elvira Gemignani, a married woman who ran off to Milan with him. It was quite the scandal, but their love was impassioned and public judgment took a backseat. Upon the death of Elvira's husband, the couple married in 1904. But by then Puccini had begun to carry on discreet sexual liaisons. Elvira's innate jealousy was piqued to vengeance. Suspecting Doria Manfredi, a servant on the estate, of being involved with her husband, Elvira gave her no rest from accusations. In despair, Doria killed herself. The autopsy showed Doria to be a virgin, and Elvira served five months in jail. Puccini fled to Milan. The couple later reunited, but there was little affection left.

Puccini's life was otherwise quiet. He avoided intimate contact even with friends. He was not unsociable, just not emotionally forthcoming. He did maintain a volatile relationship with Arturo Toscanini, who conducted three of his premieres. They were friends and then enemies. At times they could not remember which. One Christmas Puccini sent the then-hated Toscanini some panettone. Upon realizing they were still feuding, he wired Toscanini: "Panettone sent by mistake. Puccini." The swift reply confirmed the worst: "Panettone eaten by mistake. Toscanini."

On the stage his successes poured forth. *Madama but-*

terfly (1904) had to be rewritten but quickly joined *Tosca* (1900) and later *Gianni Schicchi* (1918) and posthumously *Turandot* (1926) as his greatest works. His style changed little over the years, although he did borrow new ideas when they appealed to him, as with the use of a whole-tone scale from Debussy in *La fanciulla del West.* He also closely studied the music of the locales of his stories. He was after authenticity and desired his Americans to be American and his Japanese to be Japanese, as much as it was possible to do that musically. While intellectuals still insist that he relied on manipulated emotions and facile melodies with which to seduce his audiences, the public has never doubted his success. *Turandot* is in fact the last opera written that is a mainstay of the operatic repertoire. The public responds because the characters are real. They are human. When Mimi dies or Cio-Cio-San commits suicide, there is no doubting the loss and the tragedy.

Puccini maintained two nervous habits throughout his life. One was a jerking of his knee every time he heard a wrong note sung. This harkened back to his early training when his Uncle Magi kicked him in the shin every time he sang off pitch. The other habit was smoking several packs of cigarettes a day. By early 1924 he was complaining of a chronic sore throat and cough. He attempted a rest cure and blamed the condition for distracting him from finishing *Turandot.* Diagnosis by several specialists in Florence confirmed that the condition was cancer of the throat. X-ray treatment in Brussels was sought. On November 22 an operation was performed, and seven platinum needles were stuck in his throat in an attempt to destroy the tumor. Puccini wrote, "I seem to have bayonets in my throat; they have massacred me." Yet the doctors were optimistic. By the 28th he was lunching with his family at a nearby hotel, but that night he relapsed badly and the next morning his heart succumbed to the stress.

At *Turandot*'s premiere at La Scala, Toscanini ceased conducting in the third act. Turning to the audience, he explained that this was where Puccini had stopped composing. From the balcony came the cry "Viva Puccini," and the audience erupted into a prolonged and emotional ovation.

DIRECTIONS, HOURS, AND ADMISSION: Coming from Florence, take A11, exiting at Route 1. Follow the signs for Torre del Lago Puccini. Once in town, turn right onto Viale Giacomo Puccini and follow it to the end. Puccini's house is open daily. Hours are 9:00 A.M. to noon and 3:00 to 7:00 P.M., except in winter, when they are 2:00 to 5:00 P.M. Tours cost L 5,000.

FLORENCE
San Lorenzo, the Capelle Medicee, and the Duomo

▲ ▲ ▲

SAN LORENZO AND THE CAPELLE MEDICEE

The Medici family was known for its balls. These appeared in varying numbers and designs on their coat of arms, though the origin of the symbolism has been lost. The preferred legend was that an ancestor, Averado, had slain a giant who was terrorizing the peasantry, and suffered damage to his shield from the giant's club; as a reward, Charlemagne allowed him to commemorate his victory by showing the dents as red balls on a gold background. It was also suggested that the red balls represented pills (as the name Medici hints) or even coins, bringing the family down to the level of pawnbrokers.

Another ancestor, Giovanni di Bicci de' Medici, advised the family, "Always keep out of the public eye." But like a giant wave, the family fortune and influence crested in the 15th century, and its descendants rode it out until the death of the last Medici in 1743. By all accounts, it was a spectacular run.

Before the Capelle Medicee were created, the family was involved with the adjoining church, San Lorenzo. Consecrated in A.D. 393, it was a neighborhood church, red-roofed and modest, until 1418 when Giovanni di Bicci de'

Opposite: San Lorenzo (Photo by Gayle Simon)

Medici retained Filippo Brunelleschi to build a new sacristy which would serve as the family tomb. The exterior of San Lorenzo is like an actor without makeup. Furrowed rows of brown brick form the foundation, but the final face has yet to be applied.

As you enter the arched and columned interior, designed by Michelangelo, walk all the way to the front altar. In the pavement in front of the altar is the memorial slab of **Cosimo di Giovanni de' Medici** (1389–1464), known as Cosimo the Elder. Attributed to Verrocchio, the slab is made of red, white, and dark green marble. The design swirls and shapes itself into circles and squares; in each corner is a gold shield, this time with six red balls. Cosimo is designated by his title *Pater Patriae.*

Cosimo was a narrow, sallow-faced man whose nose hooked down to his upper lip. He did everything he could to keep his family out of the public eye. Married to Contessina de' Bardi, a plump, cheerful daughter of one of Florence's oldest families, Cosimo spent much of his time away on business, accompanied by a Venetian slave girl, Maddalena.

The Medici bank flourished; despite Cosimo's attempts at keeping a low profile, the rival Albizzi family was not fooled and carried out a plot in which Cosimo was thrown in prison for "treason." He would have been beheaded and his assets seized had there not been an immediate outcry from the other Italian cities and some of the local populace. (It is fair to say that much of the local protest was fueled by Medici ducats.)

Cosimo was exiled to Padua for 10 years, but after only a year the Albizzis could not hold Florence and the Medici banishment was revoked. Cosimo, in turn, banished 70 of the other leading families that he felt might pose a threat, so many that there were complaints he was emptying Florence. His response was, "Seven or eight yards of scarlet will make a new citizen."

He returned to his attempts to escape notice, riding a mule instead of a horse, disguising his enormous wealth, and making any initiatives in government appear to come from someone else. He was hardly successful. According to Aeneas Silvius de' Piccolomini, the future Pope Pius II, Cosimo ruled in everything but name.

But Cosimo was no warload. Attracted to learning, he established the Platonic Institute and the immense Medici Library, the first of its kind in Europe. He liberally supported artists and architects, including Donatello, Fra Lippi, Fra Angelico, Brunelleschi, and Luca della Robbia.

In later years Cosimo's disposition darkened from the pain of arthritis and gout. A little while before he died from kidney failure, his wife asked him why he sat with his eyes shut. "To get them used to it," he snapped. By then, having lost both his sons and a beloved grandson, he was resigned to leaving.

To your left in the far corner is the Old Sacristy. **Giovanni di Bicci de' Medici** (1360–1429) and his wife, **Piccarda Bueri** (1368–1433), are interred here. Their white marble sarcophagus is decorated with garlands of fruit, the family coat of arms, and putti holding scrolls with their inscriptions.

Giovanni was the Medici who advised his descendants to keep a low profile. A shrewd, humane man with a large, determined chin and hooded eyes, he well understood his fellow citizens' propensity to turn on anyone who seemed too powerful. Quietly he tended his wool workshops and very quietly handled the immense papal finances.

Set into the wall between the Old Sacristy and the Chapel of the Relics is the monument of two of Giovanni di Bicci's grandsons, **Piero "the Gouty"** (1414–1469) and **Giovanni de' Medici** (1421–1463). When the tomb was built, it was considered a wonder. The red and green sarcophagus has ornate metal sides, pawlike feet, and two tilted cornucopias on top from which fruits and nuts spill. The arch is filled with bronze grillwork. Intriguingly, Verrocchio supported the whole monument on the backs of two small turtles.

Despite his unappealing nickname and constant pain from arthritis, Piero the Gouty was calm and pleasant. He survived two attempted coups and attacks on his life and had a long and well-regarded marriage with poetess Lucrezia Tornabuoni. Fond of beautiful and expensive curios, Piero also supported the artists of his day and invited Botticelli to live at the Medici Palace.

Giovanni de' Medici was less handsome than his brother, Piero. He had the large family nose and the curse of eczema, and his dedication to eating made him immense. He was likewise dedicated to music, art, and wit, even when it was directed against the family. A capable banker and prudent businessman, Giovanni was fond of his wife and son but also of the beautiful Venetian slave girl he had purchased. Unwilling to relinquish any of his great weight, he died from a heart attack at 42.

In the second chapel on the left is one of the more interesting monuments in San Lorenzo, that of Countess **Berta Moltke Witfeldt** (1831–1857) completed in 1864 by

Photo by Gayle Simon

Jules Dupré. In the romantic style of the times the sculpture shows the young woman, hair flying, being carried off by a kindly angel.

Inside the last small chapel on your right before reaching the altar again is a monument to Donatello, who is buried in the crypt of the church. This uninspired memorial, created over 400 years after the artist's death, shows him lying in dark bronze, hands clasped, under a marble cameo of a Madonna and Child. Marble designs, accented by gold paint, decorate the wall above. It is better to remember Donatello by his bronze pulpits and other works of art in San Lorenzo, including the interesting sarcophagus of the Martellis nearby which is textured like a wicker basket.

DONATELLO (DONATO DI NICCOLO BETTI BARDI) *b. ca. 1386–1390, Florence; d. December 13, 1466, Florence.* Because no one could predict Donatello's future fame, no one paid much attention to his birth. The artist himself could never remember how old he was and listed his mother's age as 84 on tax declarations in both 1431 and 1433. Plainspoken and rough-hewn, Donatello was impatient with statistics or financial accounts.

Before attempting sculpture, he began his training as a goldsmith, working with Ghiberti and Brunelleschi. A marble *David* and *St. John the Baptist* are considered his earliest extant work; while they have the static look of cathedral art, the realism of the fabric and the emotion in their faces mark a departure, an indication of the drama and emotion of his mature work. In his statues of the prophets *Zuccone* (ca. 1423–1425) and *Jeremiah* (1427–1435), the psychological tension is more apparent, a bitterness bordering on an almost insane intensity. The artist's polychromed *Penitent Magdalena* (ca. late 1430s to 1450s) is truly horrifying, showing the beautiful prostitute as a hermit saint. He makes her an emaciated crone, baggy-eyed and gap-toothed, her lovely hair a tangled ruin; sentimentality has given way to immense power.

By contrast, Donatello's bronze *David* (ca. 1446–1460) is rich in sensuous feminine curves and smoldering emotion. David's partial nakedness—he wears a floppy hat and knee-high boots—makes him more sexual than the classical Greek nudes, an impression enhanced by the position of one jaunty hand on his hip. From the back, with his long hair, he looks girlish. It was the first bronze freestanding statue since antiquity, but some of Donatello's contemporaries saw it only as an unabashed admission of the sculptor's homosexuality and reacted with outrage. At that time, after five offenses a homosexual could be sentenced to death by fire.

It was widely known, of course, that Donatello liked to hire his apprentices for their beauty. After one such youth left him precipitously, the artist got permission from Cosimo de' Medici to track him down and kill him. Instead, when found, the boy began laughing and Donatello joined in, prompting a relieved Cosimo to claim that he had known all along that would happen.

Although Donatello spent periods living and working in Siena, Pisa, and Padua—his reliefs of the *Entombment of Christ* and the *Miracle of the Irascible Son* are particularly compelling—he always returned to Florence, claiming that the adulation he received elsewhere made him nervous. In Florence, where he could expect nothing but carping criticism, he was spurred on to greater achievement.

In Florence, his patron and friend, Cosimo de' Medici, also kept him under his financial wing. Never lacking in commissions, the sculptor hung a basket of money in his studio so that anyone who needed cash could help himself; not surprisingly, he was chronically behind in the rent. But indigence seemed part of his self-image. When Cosimo gave him a new red cloak with a cowl, he wore it a few times then put it aside, claiming it was "too fine."

Another Medici gift, a small farm on which Donatello was supposed to retire, was as poor a fit as the cloak. Unable to keep financial records, the sculptor grew testy when his cattle were confiscated for unpaid taxes and bad weather ruined his fruit. He prevailed upon Piero de' Medici to give him a small pension instead and moved happily back to the city. His wish to be buried near Cosimo was likewise granted.

As you go around to the side and enter the Capelle Medicee, you will find yourself in the Crypt, an area of low lighting, two-tone gray and white plaster, and squat arches. Prior to 1858 the coffins had been simply placed on the floor. But in September 1857, at the instigation of Leopold II, the bodies were exhumed and identified, then placed in the ground behind brass railings. **Leopold II** (1797–1870), a member of the House of Lorraine, was not a Medici himself but made himself at home; his large marble slab is behind the altar at the back, flanked by two mourning figures.

Only two years after the exhumation, Leopold II found himself forced to abdicate. He and his family had to flee so quickly that they left behind a whole fleet of monogrammed carriages, which form the basis of the Museo delle Berline (Museum of Coaches). Unfortunately, it has been closed for some time.

There is a strong sense of women and children in the Crypt, their remains divided between two tombs. Unlike other noble families, the wives have been separated in death from their husbands, with the men in the chapels upstairs or in San Lorenzo.

Eleonora da Toledo (1522–1562) was the mirror image of her husband, Cosimo I, as perfectionistic and critical in her own sphere as he was in his. Oddly, the pair tolerated each other's faults well. Cosimo was not troubled by her love of gambling and capricious changes of mind, and she allowed him his secretiveness and ill-tempered silence. Toward the end of her life she had trouble keeping food down and died, heartbroken, two weeks after her favorite son, Garzia.

Eleonora's daughter, **Isabella di Cosimo de' Medici**, made the mistake of marrying the wrong man. Paolo Orsini, faithless and violent, engineered her death so he could wed his mistress, Vittoria Accoramboni. After dinner one evening he signaled to accomplices to let down a rope through the ceiling, then, pretending to kiss Isabella, garroted her with the rope.

He announced to the world that she had died of an apoplectic seizure, but the truth was found out and Orsini fled to Venice. (Coming full circle, after he died and left Vittoria his fortune, his brother, who had expected to be his heir, stabbed Vittoria to death.)

Archduchess **Joanna of Austria** (1548–1578) would

have considered it supremely unfair that she is buried in the city she hated. The Florentines, mistaking her homesickness for hauteur, did nothing to make Francesco's pallid wife feel at home, though her father-in-law had the courtyard of the Palazzo Vecchio decorated with murals of Austria. When she died at 30, gossips accused her husband's mistress, Bianca Capello, of poisoning the unhappy duchess.

Anna Maria Ludovica (1667–1743), the last Medici survivor, was an awkward, masculine young woman who, when proffered as marriageable, was turned down by Spain, Portugal, and France. She was finally accepted by Johann Wilhelm, the elector palatine, but his wedding gift to her was syphilis, which caused miscarriages, sterility, and finally widowhood. Deeply religious, Anna Maria was proud of her position as the last Medici and greeted visitors soberly beneath a black canopy in a room of silver furniture. She bequeathed the family property and art to the new regime with the proviso that the collection had to stay in Florence and remain available for the enjoyment of the world.

From the Crypt, go up two flights of stairs and enter the Chapel of the Princes. The huge richness, the sheer detail, stuns the senses; visitors do not even reach the bottom of the immense sarcophagi. The room's colors are the rich shades of burnt sienna, dark red, and gold. Only two of the six niches—those of Ferdinando and Cosimo II—contain statues.

When **Cosimo I** (1519–1574) was a baby, his father, Giovanni, spied him at a window with his nurse and ordered her to toss him down. After trying unsuccessfully to change her master's mind, she finally closed her eyes and let the child drop, unable to watch whether or not Giovanni caught him. He did, and approved of his son's stoic attitude.

Perhaps after the first terror there is no other, for Cosimo grew into a cold, unemotional warlord, creating a powerful Florentine navy to beat back Spanish encroachment. Darkly handsome, he appeared to take little pleasure in anything but hunting boar, deer, and pheasant. Even when hunting he was secretive and he confused his retinue by moving from bonhomie and intimacy to suddenly rebuffing attempts at familiarity.

Next come two of Cosimo's sons. **Francesco I** (1541–1587), grand duke of Tuscany and husband of the unhappy Joanna of Austria down in the Crypt, was neither the warrior nor the captain of industry his father had been.

Taciturn, indifferent to appearance and dress, he had two life goals: first to obtain Bianca Capello and then to pursue scientific experiments.

When they first met, the beautiful and ambitious Bianca was living in a tenement with a bank clerk with whom she had eloped from Venice. She was ready for a change. Once the relationship was under way, her husband was set upon and stabbed to death "by persons unknown."

Francesco moved into seclusion with Bianca in the Villa Pratolino, an estate that boasted Swedish reindeer, rare shrubs from India, clockwork figures in fountains, and topiary fantasies. He succeeded in inventing new methods of cutting crystal and making porcelain, and developed ingenious ways of making fireworks. Bianca, obsessed with trying to get pregnant, surrounded herself with doctors and fortune-tellers.

When the couple died on the same day of malarial fever, the rumor was that they had been poisoned by one of his scientific experiments.

Ferdinando (1549–1609) was far more congenial to the Florentines than his brother had been, and more interested in the welfare of the city. Quickly resigning his posi-

tion as cardinal, he assumed the throne and stabilized finances, built hospitals, and made his father's navy even more powerful. He established Leghorn as a city of religious tolerance, a haven for persecuted Protestants and Jews. He also charmed the populace by providing dowries to poor girls to aid them in attracting husbands.

When Ferdinando married Christine of Lorraine in 1589 (he had never actually taken his clerical vows), thousands were put to work creating triumphal arches, banquets, and concerts; the celebrations climaxed in a musicale at the Pitti Palace, which included fire-breathing dragons, exploding volcanoes, and a courtyard flooded to reenact the storming of a Turkish fort by Florentine galleys.

Ferdinando's son, **Cosimo II** (1590–1620), upheld the family's reputation for staging fantastic entertainments. Sociable but uninterested in finance or science, he did one act of significance before dying at 30: he offered Galileo sanctuary and the protection of the Medicis against religious persecution.

Ferdinando II (1610–1670), Cosimo II's son, bulbous-nosed with a handlebar mustache, was exceedingly good-natured; he lost his temper only when he was not allowed to win at games. Interested in collecting scientific instruments, which he displayed in the Pitti Palace, Ferdinando was also fascinated by the art of *pietre dure,* mosaics created of gold, crystal, and semiprecious stones, and commissioned many of these works.

The cross he had to bear was his wife, the icy and triple-chinned Vittoria della Rovere. A few weeks after Cosimo III's birth, Vittoria had discovered Ferdinando fondling a handsome young count. Their quarrel about it went on for 20 years. Nor was Ferdinando lucky in his death. Suffering from dropsy and apoplexy, he was bled by his doctors, who then cauterized his skull and placed four live eviscerated pigeons on his forehead. It did not help.

Cosimo III (1642–1723) was the sad sack of the family, plump, melancholy, and religious. When as an adolescent the boy preferred going to church to attending plays and frequenting brothels, his anxious father, Ferdinando, decided he needed a wife. Unfortunately, he chose Marguerite-Louise, a niece of the Sun King, and Cosimo's opposite: high-spirited, hysterical, and avaricious, she pretended that the Medici were trying to poison her. Her hope was to be sent back to France. After 12 years the pair were allowed to separate. Marguerite-Louise returned home, donned a blond wig, and became a gambler; after turning religious, she died at 76 as the mother superior of the convent at Saint-Mandé.

Cosimo, on his own, first imitated her extravagance and turned obese, refusing to allow on his table a capon that weighed less than 20 pounds. As his waistline increased, his tolerance dwindled. Fines were imposed on Christians who sought employment under Jews; if they could not pay, they were stretched on the rack. Florentines found guilty of sodomy were beheaded, and even the May Day festival was banned because of its "pagan roots."

As he grew older, Cosimo reverted to type, eating alone and drinking only water, and attending several masses a day. Obsessed by religion, he collected and venerated relics, including a piece of St. Francis Xavier's intestine. He lost interest in tormenting the citizens of Florence; when he died at 81, few mourned but no one cheered.

Some of the most appealing features of the chapel are the panels of the altar, which seem to glow with an incredible brightness. They are made of *pietre dure,* which shows pictures of fruit, flowers, and religious objects.

The New Sacristy, undertaken by Michelangelo, was not completed by him, but he worked on its architectural design and statuary from 1520 until 1534 when he left for

Rome. Despite its high cupola and arches, the room feels small. The statuary here is on a more human scale.

As you enter, on your left is the tomb of Lorenzo, duke of Urbino. The luxuriant marble figure of a young woman, Dawn, appears to be waking slowly and perhaps unwillingly. Dusk, on the other side of the sarcophagus, is an older man who looks weary. Above them Lorenzo sits, dressed as a Roman general. He is looking away as if lost in thought, his finger crooked to hide his mouth, and appears very young.

Lorenzo di Piero de' Medici (1492–1519), the nephew of Pope Leo X, went from being a nice young man, energetic and ambitious, to a tyrant who enjoyed ordering people around. In 1516 he captured Urbino and was proclaimed duke, but was badly wounded by gunfire. He never recovered from the injury, wasting away and dying at 27.

The companion piece, across the room, is the tomb of Giuliano, duke of Nemours. Day is a muscular male nude whose face is rough and unfinished. Unlike the other three, he is staring out into the room. The highly polished Night is far more interesting. She is sleeping, but not easily; her body is contorted, her mouth pursed. On her head she is wearing a star and crescent moon, and around her are grouped objects denoting wakefulness and sleep: the heads of poppies, a barn owl, and a grotesque mask like a nightmare.

Giuliano is shown as a young, curly-haired man, dressed as what is called a "captain of the church" and holding a commander's baton. His head is turned to the left in a pose that suggests arrogance. When people pointed out that the figure did not much resemble the dead duke, Michelangelo replied that in a few centuries "no one would remember what Giuliano looked like anyway."

Giuliano di Lorenzo de' Medici (1478–1516), the younger brother of Pope Leo X, was the opposite in temperament of his nephew, Lorenzo. Raised in exile, when the Medicis were returned to power in 1512 he walked modestly into Florence and went to stay with a friend. He was charming and kind, accepting both his arranged marriage to Philiberte of France and the title duke of Nemours. But by then he was dying of consumption, a flickering candle, and left no legitimate heirs.

Because of the unified design of the first two monuments, the third suffers by comparison. It shows an unfinished Madonna and Child, flanked by two statues done by Michelangelo's assistants. St. Cosmas, on the left, was sculpted by Giovanngelo da Montorsoli; St. Damian, on the right, by Raffaello da Montelupo. In the plain marble tomb beneath are Giuliano and his brother Lorenzo the Magnificent.

Giuliano di Piero de' Medici (1453–1478), as painted by Botticelli, is a young man with a nose as long and thin as a taper and an impressive chin. Popular and athletic, he delighted in tournaments and festivals. Perhaps he never would have emerged from the shadow of his older brother, Lorenzo, but he was robbed of the chance to try by his assassination in the cathedral during the Pazzi Conspiracy.

LORENZO DI PIERO DE' MEDICI *b. 1449, Florence; d. April 8, 1492, Florence.* Known as Lorenzo the Magnificent, the elder son of Piero the Gouty was precocious and athletic, though without his brother Giuliano's good looks. Sallow and crooked-featured, Lorenzo had an ugliness that was more arresting than displeasing. He was infectiously joyous, inexhaustibly energetic, and would compose and sing songs or tell jokes for hours. He had a gift for friendship and engaged in such diverse activities as breeding racehorses, making architectural drawings, and studying Plato.

By the age of 15, Lorenzo was being sent on diplomatic missions, and five years later, amid incredible festivity, he married Clarice Orsini of Rome. By all accounts they tolerated each other, though she remained convinced of her superior lineage and had little interest in literature, philosophy, and art. Nor could she understand his witty circle of friends or his championing such artists as Michelangelo, Botticelli, Ghirlandaio, and Verrocchio. But neither was she bothered by his philandering, attached as she was to their seven children (three others died in infancy).

Before Lorenzo could settle into this comfortable life, however, he had had to deal with complications from his brother's assassination. Furious that the Pazzi Conspiracy had failed, Pope Sixtus IV excommunicated "that son of iniquity and foster-child of perdition, Lorenzo dei Medici, and those other citizens of Florence, his accomplices and abettors." The Florentines warned Sixtus about the dangers of abusing his office and a few months later excommunicated *him.*

But other armies had joined Sixtus against Florence, and it was only through good fortune and Lorenzo's clever, in-person negotiations with Naples that peace was restored. Once the Neapolitan alliance had been made, other provinces backed off, and Sixtus was left to stew in his venomous hatred. He soon died, and his successor,

Pope Innocent VIII, was more agreeable. Lorenzo sealed their friendship by marrying his daughter, Maddalena, to the pope's son.

Remarkable poet and master statesman that he was, Lorenzo had no talent or interest in finance. The Medici bank was tottering near failure, and to keep up his lifestyle he had to borrow from a trust fund for two young cousins. He also helped himself to the public treasury. During this time he was plagued by attacks of gout and what may have been intestinal cancer. The disease was described as eating him away from inside, "limbs, intestines, nerves, bones, and marrow." His charm turned to irritability with the pain. He was only 43 and did not want to die. Unable to walk or hold a pen, he went into a coma and finally let go.

A sad coda is the fate of his doctor, Piero Leoni, who did not believe that Lorenzo's illness was fatal. Up to the end, he was assuring the family that all would be well if Lorenzo stayed warm and dry and out of the night air, and ate no pears or grape seeds. Falsely accused of poisoning and witchcraft after the death, Leoni threw himself down a well.

DIRECTIONS, HOURS, AND ADMISSION: The church and chapels are on the Piazza San Lorenzo and can easily be located on a city map. The Capelle Medicee are open every day but Monday 9:00 A.M. to 1:00 P.M. Admission is L 8,000.

SANTA MARIA DEL FIORE (DUOMO)

The Duomo is the most famous sight in Florence, its red dome the landmark in every photograph of the city. Consecrated though not completed in 1436, it has a history and architecture that are bound up with one of the few persons of note buried inside, Filippo Brunelleschi.

Although the exact burial place of Giotto is no longer known, he is commemorated by a bust in the rear right-hand side of the cathedral. A more dramatic monument is his bell tower just outside.

GIOTTO DI BONDONE *b. ca. 1267, Colle di Vespignano; d. January 8, 1337, Florence.* "Once Cimabue thought to hold the field as painter; Giotto now is all the rage, dimming the lustre of the other's fame." So wrote Dante while discoursing on fame in *Purgatorio*. There is a legend that Dante and Giotto were friends and this is the cause of Giotto's mention. More likely the men met but were not compatible, and the verse served as an admoni-

tion to Giotto that he too would suffer eclipse. Dante's warning fell well wide of its mark. Almost seven centuries later, Giotto is still very much with us.

Giotto revolutionized art, bringing to it an element of physical realism and visceral emotion not seen in the stylized representations of his predecessors. In Boccaccio's *Decameron* Pamfilo relates that Giotto could "recreate with pencil, pen or brush so faithfully, that it hardly seemed a copy, but rather the thing itself." Realism is of course relative. Looking at Giotto's art today, we would scarcely label it realistic. Giotto lacked a firm knowledge of anatomy and, because perspective had not yet been developed, his scenes have a certain flatness.

Despite these "failings," these limitations, Giotto's art still carries a potent impact. It was he who moved away from the stylized, formulaic methods of his Byzantine predecessors and indeed from his putative teacher, Giovanni Cimabue. Giorgio Vasari puts forth a fabulous story of Cimabue discovering Giotto's talent when, touring the countryside, he spotted the young boy elegantly scratching the outline of a sheep on a large stone. So impressed was the master that he made immediate arrangements for the boy to be taken to his studio as an apprentice.

The truth is that we know little of Giotto's life. He did come to Florence, probably in his early teens, and may have studied under Cimabue. Certainly he was influenced by him. He is reported to have been down-to-earth and to have possessed a sharp wit. We know that he married, had sons and at least three daughters, and that he was a shrewd investor in real estate. The first verification we have of Giotto's presence in Florence is dated 1301. By then he was well past apprenticeship, had completed his extraordinary *Crucifix* (ca. 1290) in Santa Maria Novella, and was about to embark on the famous frescoes found at the Arena (or Scrovegni) Chapel in Padua. His revolutionary work was already under way.

It is the *Crucifix* that first shows Giotto's new style. His Christ is not an icon; he is convincingly human. He is not God on the cross; he is a man suffering a torturous death. The formulaic features of the past are displaced by the reality of arms stretched to bear the weight of the body. His head sags, and his lips are parted in wearisome pain.

Giotto's crowning achievement is his frescoes for the Arena Chapel. There are other noteworthy frescoes: the Bardi and Peruzzi Chapels in Santa Croce, those in the Upper Church of San Francisco in Assisi, and yet others now lost to reconstruction or overpainting. The Arena Chapel is a simple barrel-vaulted, rectangular space with no intrusive architectural features. On the walls are 39 scenes depicting the story of Mary, Christ, and the Final Judgment. The soft colors are lit by five windows. The effect is cumulative. It is a seduction into a world of great drama and emotion. It is at once ancient and new. His forms and his use of combined narrative (multiple events in one scene) are to be found in the art of our century. Like all great artists, Giotto offers something for every age.

Three years before his death Giotto was placed in charge of the works of the cathedral in Florence. Though not an architect, he designed the famous Campanile and supervised the first phases of its construction. This splendid colored tower of pink, green, white, and black stone, "horrible" to Ruskin, is never obvious. Like all Giotto's work, it must be studied. For Sean O'Faolain it is a "brilliant, strange, tropical bamboo" that has survived for us to admire.

Down the stairs and to your left, behind bars, is the tomb of Brunelleschi. A dried pinecone wreath, as tall as a 10-year-old, stands to one side. The tomb itself is just a brass-bound slab in the ground.

FILIPPO BRUNELLESCHI *b. 1377, Florence; d. April 15, 1446, Florence.* As with Giotto, little is known of Brunelleschi's early life. We can rely only on what is grandly termed the Biography by, of course, the Biographer. This anonymous (some attribute it to Antonio Manetti) source was unfinished but appears to be highly accurate. In it Brunelleschi appears as a diminutive, energetic, generous,

individualistic man who exhibited a tenacious, at times self-destructive, stubbornness and a weakness for practical jokes.

At 15 Brunelleschi was an apprentice goldsmith, and by 21 (1398) he was sworn as a master goldsmith. Fleeing the plague in Florence in 1400, he received his first commission for the Silver Altar at Pistoia for which he executed several of the figures, though his true accomplishments are shrouded in history and debated by scholars.

The following year saw Brunelleschi entering the competition in Florence for the doors of the Baptistery of San Giovanni. The theme was Abraham's aborted sacrifice of his son Isaac. The choice of theme was an interesting one, for Florence was hoping for similar divine intervention to stay the threatening armies of Giangaleazzo Visconti. As the contestants worked on their samples, Florence learned of its salvation when Giangaleazzo and his forces were fatally defeated by the plague. The original seven entries were whittled down to a fight between Brunelleschi and Ghiberti. As the world well knows, Ghiberti was the winner, and his panels are still one of the major attractions of Florence. Brunelleschi never forgave him.

Brunelleschi's entry panel exists and shows why it was such a strong contender. His figures are bolder, exhibit greater drama, and push outside the boundaries of the panel. Abraham's hand holds Isaac's head, his thumb pushing his chin up, revealing and stretching the neck for the sacrificial slice. The rescuing angel arrives at the last second, grasping Abraham's arm and staying the slaughter. Ghiberti's action, meanwhile, is wholly contained in the quatrefoil panel. The figures are more finely sculpted in a shallower relief, and there is a greater flow and unity. More practically, Ghiberti's techniques involved less metal and would have been considerably less expensive.

The defeat, however, was a victory for the arts, because Brunelleschi turned from goldsmithing and took up architecture. In 1404, he first became actively involved with the design of the Florence cathedral. This work would last throughout his lifetime. Many of his duties were shared, nominally at least, with Ghiberti, whom, some have said, Brunelleschi did his best to embarrass by setting up situations that would show off his greater knowledge of engineering. Ultimately Brunelleschi designed the dome and solved the problem of how to build it without the need for wooden centering, which would have required a small forest to construct.

He erected a double dome that relied on massive timbers and intricate brickwork, the whole being reinforced with iron chains. A graceful lantern of Brunelleschi's design tops the dome. Its eight buttresses form a continuation of the eight great ribs and cap them as if to keep them from springing up and apart. The dome, and particularly the lantern, display the classical influence and the use of mathematical ratios which Brunelleschi so favored.

In 1412 Brunelleschi adopted Andrea Cavalcanti, who later became known as Il Buggiano (after the town where he was born) and served as Brunelleschi's assistant in many of his projects. These included the Ospedale degli Innocenti, San Lorenzo, Santo Spirito, and perhaps most impressively, the Pazzi Chapel. All these buildings were completed after Brunelleschi's death, and the detailing, both exterior and interior, is certainly not all to his design. What is most obvious is the marvelous sense of space, geometry, and proportion. It is mathematical elegance made visual. It is classicism adapted and molded to a current use and style.

Brunelleschi's talents did not stop here. He developed and systematized the use of one-point perspective, a technique quickly adopted by painters of the age. He was also busily engaged with military projects and fortifications, developing new machines, designing a more efficient air pump for the cathedral's organ, and, in his spare time, writing poetry and studying Dante. Not surprisingly, he remained fully engaged until his death in 1446.

DIRECTIONS: The Duomo can be located by looking for the famous orange dome that dominates Florence. It is located on the Piazza del Duomo and is open between the hours of 8:00 A.M. and 6:00 P.M.

CHAPTER 9

FLORENCE
Santa Croce

▲   ▲   ▲

Santa Croce at first seems too wild to be tamed. Besides its size, there are too many monuments and too many floor slabs. Half of them are memorials for people who are actually buried elsewhere, so unless you know that da Vinci and Cherubini are in France and Dante in Ravenna, for instance, it is easy to be fooled.

The huge, high-raftered church was begun in 1294 but delayed by financial crises and natural disasters such as flooding and the plague. It was finally consecrated in 1433. There followed another kind of disaster in 1565 when Cosimo di Giovanni de' Medici assigned Giorgio Vasari to redo the interior. Vasari, known for his biographical volumes, *Lives of the Artists*, would have done better in this instance to confine himself to writing; he had the famous frescoes on the walls of Santa Croce whitewashed out and erected altars with contemporary paintings instead.

The monument of Michelangelo was also designed by Vasari, but it has a certain charm. Painting, Sculpture, and Architecture lounge listlessly around Michelangelo's bust, women on a sweltering August afternoon with nothing much to do. The scrollwork on the sarcophagus seems to mimic that on the Medici tombs that Michelangelo designed, but the upper painted area of canopy and cherubs is all Vasari. It has the intriguingly flat look of stage scenery.

Michelangelo is actually buried in the floor in front of the second altar.

MICHELANGELO DI LODOVICO BUONARROTI SIMONI *b. March 6, 1475, Caprese, Italy; d. February 18, 1564, Rome.* The story of Michelangelo is a tricky one. Known as Il Divino to his contemporaries, he has been mythicized and apotheosized by every succeeding generation. His image needs, as his Sistine Chapel ceiling received, a thorough cleaning. A genius he was, but divine he was not.

Not only was Michelangelo short and squat, but his face was led about by a badly disfigured nose, the product of a punch from Torrigiano, a fellow apprentice of his youth who had grown tired of his boasting. As he left home, his father adjured him not to bathe. In old age he certainly followed this advice, living in squalor and wearing his leather boots for so long that they could not be removed without taking a layer of skin with them. Family loyalty, however, was paramount, and throughout adulthood he helped support his father and his younger brothers, gradually enlarging and enriching the family holdings. But he was a martyr who could trowel on guilt as easily as he did plaster. "I have borne every kind of humiliation . . . risked my very life in a thousand dangers, solely to help my family."

Born in the tiny Tuscan town of Caprese, of which his father had been mayor, Michelangelo moved with his family to Florence when he was but one month old. There he was let out to a wet nurse whose father and husband were stonemasons. He later joked that he got the hammer and chisel through her milk. At 13, he left his ill-tempered and abusive father and apprenticed himself to Francesco Ghirlandaio, from whom he learned painting and fresco technique. His early influences were Masaccio and Giotto as well as antique statues, which he studied firsthand in the house and gardens of Lorenzo de' Medici.

His talents developed quickly—fast enough in fact for him to pass off forgeries (a drawing aged brown by candle flame and a "recovered" bust smeared with soil) while he was still a teenager. His first major surviving work is a statue of a youthful, swaying, drunken *Bacchus* (1496–1498). In sharp juxtaposition, his next work was the famous *Pietà* (1499), showing the grieving Mary holding the body of the dead Christ in her capacious lap. The virtuosity is extraordinary. Stone becomes voluptuous folds of cloth and tactile flesh. Absent, however, is a true sense of sorrow on the Virgin's face. She is idealized youthful beauty, as young as Christ. Perhaps she represents Michelangelo's own mother, who died when he was only six.

In 1501 Michelangelo started working on a giant marble block that had been lying about the cathedral in Florence for 35 years. With the first blow he removed a knot on what was to be the chest of David. Almost two and a half years later it was completed and set to stand outdoors in the Palazzo della Signoria. The torso is Greek, but the head and hands are outsized and heroic, emphasizing the immediate anticipation of encountering Goliath.

After run-ins with the pope on the uncompleted tomb of Julius II, Michelangelo was, surprisingly, recalled to Rome in 1508 to start work on the Sistine Chapel ceiling. For the next five years it would monopolize his life. The restoration reveals the vibrant colors he and his assistants applied on the wet plaster as they stood, not lay, on a scaffolding suspended from the ceiling cornices.

In 1532 he met and became obviously enamored of a handsome young nobleman, Tommaso de' Cavalieri. His letters and poems bear out his strong attraction. Indeed his whole career points to his obsessive attraction to the male figure. His female nudes are masculine figures with clumsily attached breasts. But was he homosexual? There is no record of active homosexuality, and he may even have died a virgin. An attraction there was, but its sexual significance lies buried under the vagaries of sensibilities, styles, and Neoplatonic ideals now 450 years old.

Michelangelo continued to sculpt, producing the Slaves, the Prisoners, and Moses, all for the much-delayed papal tomb. He then moved on to the statues of Day and Night, and Dusk and Dawn for the Medici tombs. In later years he turned to architecture, most notably seen in the Laurentian Library, the public squares, and his design for St. Peter's, which still dominates Rome.

His work, which revitalized Rome, continues by its visibility to vitalize it today just as his paintings and sculptings have held centuries of admirers in awe and reverence.

Broken nose and skinned feet. Flesh and blood. And genius.

As you move deeper into the church, you will pass the memorial cenotaph to Dante Alighieri, who is buried in Ravenna. The official church guidebook sternly characterizes this monument as "unpleasant."

The next chapel holds the remains of the poet **Vittorio Alfieri** (1749–1803). His monument, executed by Antonio Canova in 1810, is wedding-cake white, an impression enhanced by its rounded base and draped floral trim. The figure weeping over his cameo is Italy, but she appears more like a visitor who has stopped by to pay her respects rather than an integral part of the work. Notice the interesting details such as the towers on her head, the tragic masks at the corners, and the lyre that has eyes. When Alfieri's mistress, the countess of Albany, was told that the amount she wanted to spend would only bring a bas-relief, she upped Canova's commission and got a full statue.

In the next alcove is the tomb of Niccolò Machiavelli. Diplomacy sits on his claw-footed sarcophagus. In one hand she holds his cameo, in the other what appears to be a tassel she has just cut from a roll of material. His inscription reads, *"Tanto nomini nullum par elogium"* (For such a great man, no eulogy is sufficient).

NICCOLÒ MACHIAVELLI *b. May 3, 1469, Florence; d. June 22, 1527, Florence.* Conflict has swirled around Machiavelli far more after his death than it did during his lifetime. In its adjectival form, his name has become a commonplace. His philosophy as espoused in *The Prince* is known to high school students, scholars, and world leaders. "The ends justify the means." Pragmatism is the defining Machiavellian idea. Ruthlessness is no evil if used toward the defined end. But the question that has been kept alive is what did Machiavelli really intend in his writing? The answer is far from simple and has been reinterpreted over and over, each interpretation expressing the concerns of its own times. The inevitable struggle and dialectic of historiography. And still Machiavelli continues to talk to us over the centuries.

Machiavelli was born to Bernardo di Niccolò and Bartolomea Nelli. He was a lawyer, while she was likely a religious poet. The family's ancestors had served the city of Florence well and had held numerous posts of importance. But his parents lived without the money and prestige of their forebears. Like faded families of any era, they wore ancestral achievement with pride and petitioned for

SANTA CROCE

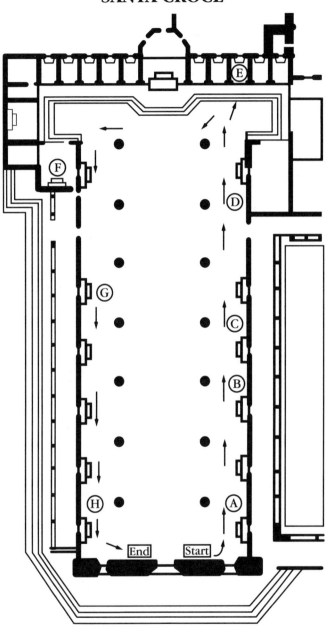

A Michelangelo
B Vittorio Alfieri
C Niccolò Machiavelli
D Gioacchino Rossini

E Bonaparte Family
F Sofia Zamoyska
G Lorenzo Ghiberti
H Galileo

its restoration. It was not forthcoming. Nevertheless, Machiavelli received an adequate education grounded in politics, religion, and the classics. His admiration for the Greeks and Romans would stay with him throughout his life.

The time of Machiavelli's emergence was one of turmoil for Italy in general and for Florence in particular. The year 1494 saw the invasion of Italy by French armies under Charles VIII. In Florence the Medicis were overthrown, and Savonarola ruled for the next four years. Machiavelli was employed in the new republican government. After the death of that despotic priest, Machiavelli came to the attention of the *signoria* for his bureaucratic talents, and he attained the post of chancellor of the Second Chancery, which merged with the Magistracy of the Ten. From there he advanced to diplomatic duties and direct service to Pietro Soderini, the prince of Florence from 1502 to 1512.

Through his travels, his contact with people of influence, and the direct tutelage of the infamous Cesare Borgia, Machiavelli greatly broadened and refined his outlook on political ends and means. Yet even given the influence of Cesare, there is nothing to indicate that he was about

TANTO NOMINI NVLLVM PAR ELOGIVM
NICOLAVS MACHIAVELLI
OBIT AN A.P.V. CDDXXVII

to emerge with the cold practicalities that guide the philosophy of *The Prince*. Perhaps the turning point was the ascension of the Medicis in 1512. Not merely deposed from power, Machiavelli was made to pay for his loyalties. He was imprisoned, six times tortured on the rack, and then exiled to his small estate in San Casciano. Through his ordeal he did not confess, for it is likely that he had nothing to reveal. He was a dedicated civil servant, and his practicality was guided by the ideals of republicanism. He did not profit from his position or his connections. There is no evidence that his methods were ever Machiavellian. As an outcast, he entered into poverty.

His second and far more influential career was about to begin, and, ironically, it was a career forced on him by his exile. Machiavelli desperately sought to ingratiate himself with the Medicis, but forgiveness was not quickly forthcoming. In the interim he had to make do, and he turned to writing. The subject would of course be political, for in this regard Machiavelli was monomaniacal. *The Prince* was written within months of his release from jail. It was circulated among friends and even the Medici, but it caused little comment. Publication did not come until 1532, five years after Machiavelli's death.

What did stir public notice and comment were *The Art of War* and his comedic and satirical play *Mandragola*. He wrote other plays, satires, and political commentaries. His crowning work, started in 1520, was the unfinished *History of Florence*. Rarely read, this book sets forth his political thought, and it is in sharp contrast to *The Prince*. The latter is the exception to Machiavelli's consistent devotion to republican ideals. It is perhaps the most widely read political book in all history. This slim volume, with its pithy and epigrammatic style, is easily and even entertainingly read. It may, however, not represent Machiavelli's true thought. There exists the possibility that it is satire. Certainly, it grew out of the bitterness of his deposal, torture, and exile. But was his bitterness so great that it overrode all sense? Would he have laid in the hands of his enemies a guide to success? Or was this satire without laughter? And what of the writings that follow and give no hint of a similar outlook?

The answer is unknown. Over the centuries Machiavelli has been viewed as the despot's advocate, a secular apologist, a realist, a nationalist (i.e., Italian) unifier and patriot, a mirror of his times (and therefore one whose guidelines are specific rather than universal), a political scientist, a satirist. Finally eligible for political office in 1525, he became secretary of a commission for the defense of Florence. Witnessing the successful uprising of the republicans against the Medici, he yearned for restoration to his old position at the Magistracy of the Ten. Before the bitter news that he was denied his wish could reach his ears, an acute abdominal infection quickly ended his life. What remains is the certainty that Machiavelli, lit with different colors, will star in a new production on the historical stage.

By the fifth chapel, you may begin to sense a certain sameness in monument design. The tomb of Gioacchino Rossini, like that of Machiavelli, has a footed sarcophagus, a mourning woman, and a cameo of the deceased. Rossini, who died in Paris, was initially buried in Père Lachaise Cemetery but was brought back home in 1887 after protracted negotiations with his French wife, Olympe, whose understandable wish to be buried with her husband met with the severe disapproval of Verdi, among others. She finally relented, saying, "I shall remain there alone: I make this sacrifice in all humility; I have been glorified enough by the name that I bear."

GIOACCHINO ROSSINI *b. February 29, 1792, Pesaro; d. November 13, 1868, Paris.* What a wonderful thing a Rossini overture is! It has vivacious wit, whistleable melodies, imaginative orchestrations, all leading up to the famous quick-tempoed crescendo of a Rossini finale. It is as bracing and invigorating as a morning shower and is ideal for lighting a fire under the day's slow starter. Only the most churlish of tone-deaf curmudgeons could possibly resist its charm.

Like most famous composers, Rossini demonstrated precocity in both performing and composing. As a child, he sang in the opera and played piano, violin, and viola. By the age of 12, he had composed his Sonate a Quattro, the third of which bears the earmarks of his future efforts. By 18, his first performed opera, *La cambiale di matrimonio,* had been well received in Venice, and the next Venetian season featured *L'inganno felice,* a smash hit.

None of this, however, gained Rossini wealth or even very wide renown. Following the pattern of his childhood when he traveled about with his parents, talented but second-rank musicians, Rossini scampered from city to city promoting his music and composing two or three new operas each year. His earnings barely exceeded his expenses.

The composition of the quintessential comic opera, *Il*

barbiere di Siviglia (The Barber of Seville), in 1816 changed all this. It was written in 13 days, fast even for Rossini, who, if he took his time might need another week, for Rossini had no compunctions about liberally lifting from prior works. The soon-to-be famous overture had already served duty for three other operas. Why not a fourth? Also lifted were arias and ensembles that were interpolated into the newly written score. The result was seamless and breezy, and fame and fortune belonged to Rossini.

When Rossini was 15 and studying in Bologna, he heard and met the beautiful and talented Spanish soprano Isabella Colbran, then 22. It took them 15 years to get married. When they did so in 1822, their age difference and her large dowry caused tongues to wag, with more than one accusing Rossini of opportunism. While there is no evidence to support this, it is true that the relationship was no hotbed of passionate love. Affectionate and cordial, they drifted to separate domiciles after eight years. In 1832 Rossini took up with Olympe Pelissier, who became his mistress and, after Isabella died in 1845, his wife.

Even before he met Olympe, Rossini had all but stopped composing. After a string of brilliant successes including *La cenerentola* (1817), *Semiramide* (1823), and *Le siège de Corinthe* (1826), Rossini finished his operatic output at the age of 37 with the production of *Guillaume Tell* in 1829. The reason for the abrupt cessation is unknown. Certainly he needed no further wealth or fame to inspire his muse. And undoubtedly he saw public taste shifting to the romantics, a group of composers for whose "excesses" he had no patience. From here on he composed only his *Stabat Mater,* the *Petite messe solennelle,* and a curious group of short songs and piano pieces that he called "Sins of My Old Age." Presaging Satie, these bear witty titles like "Les hors d'oeuvres," "Mon prelude hygenique du mati," and "Gymnastique d'ecatrement."

Rossini's life turned to lionized leisure. He expanded his reputation as a gourmand (witness tournedos Rossini), met with Wagner, offered pithy and acidic commentary on new music, and held musical soirees at his home. There the lucky elite would crowd together to hear opera stars perform, with the master accompanying in the old style (no pedal) from the keyboard. He complained of many ailments, some real, others hypochondriac, saying that he had "all of women's ills. All I lack is the uterus."

The real ills took hold. He developed rectal cancer and suffered terribly at the last. "Open the window and throw me into the garden; I'll do well there; I won't suffer any more." His suffering ended, but his music has survived opposing fashions and is enjoying a renaissance.

On the floor are numerous slab tombs; the one near Ugo Foscolo is particularly interesting. It depicts two well-worn soldiers of fortune who fought as mercenaries for Florence in the 15th century.

Ten small chapels, containing interesting artwork, flank the altar. The names of those interred in them will probably be unfamiliar except for the Bonaparte Chapel, third from the right, which holds Napoleon's niece, **Charlotte Bonaparte** (1802–1839), and her mother, **Julie Bonaparte Clary** (1774–1845). Charlotte's pretty bust is by Lorenzo Bartolini.

Joseph Bonaparte was made king of Naples and Spain in 1808 by his brother but was forced to abdicate five years later. He retreated to Bordentown, New Jersey, where he enjoyed life for many years as a gentleman farmer. Although Julie Clary, small, slender, and dark-eyed, was considered charming, Joseph found her company suffocating and could not bear to have her near. He was more attached to his daughters, especially Charlotte, who spent several years with him in New Jersey. In 1824 she returned to Europe to marry her first cousin, Napoleon Louis. The marriage was brief and strained; Napoleon Louis died mysteriously in 1831. Charlotte survived him for eight years, succumbing to a brain hemorrhage at 37.

Another notable tomb is in the Salviati Chapel, which is directly across the church from Ugo Foscolo and up three steps. **Sofia Zamoyska** (1780–1837), a Polish noblewoman, is propped up on a chaise and has obviously already left this life. The marble folds of the blanket and gathers on her nightgown are extremely realistic, a trademark of Lorenzo Bartolini. Also buried in this chapel under the pavement is **Giovanni Gentile** (1875–1944), known as the philosopher of fascism owing to his early and enthusiastic support of Mussolini.

Come back inside, turn right, and walk to the next altar. In the floor is the simple slab of **Lorenzo Ghiberti** (1378–1455). A perfectionist in his art, after winning the competition to design one of the bronze baptistery doors, Ghiberti spent 21 years working on the north portal and 23 years on the east door—dubbed the Gates of Paradise by ecstatic Florentines. His one failure came when he was appointed along with Brunelleschi to construct the cupola of the Duomo. The incensed Brunelleschi, uninterested in sharing the glory, successfully set traps to show that Ghiberti was not worthy of the honor.

Near the back doors is the last monument of interest, that of Galileo. His bust, which shows him as a skinny old man with one hand holding a telescope, is refreshingly individualized. The sculptor and tomb designer, Giovanni Battista Foggini, has placed the scientist under a scallop shell. Geometry looks heavenward, while Astronomy holds a scroll showing a brass sun.

GALILEO GALILEI, *b. February 15, 1564, Pisa; d. January 1642, Arcerti, Italy. "Eppur si muove."* (And yet it does move.) This was Galileo's legendary murmur as he rose before the Inquisition after recanting the Copernican theory of the universe. Before his interrogators he at last appeared abject and submissive, but his vaunted pride had not been totally subdued. Then 70, Galileo was encumbered with a troublesome hernia and searing attacks of arthritis, his ills magnified by hypochondria. He was tired and emotionally spent by long inquisitional delays, and he was terrified by blatant threats of torture. His arrogance

had netted him enemies over the years, the demeaned detritus of his scientific castings, and it was for arrogance more than scientific theory that he was tried.

The eldest child of six, the redheaded Galileo was born into a contentious household. His father, a strong-minded music teacher, struggled to support the family, while his mother, who could boast noble though distant relations, pressed for fulfillment of loftier status. At the age of 11, Galileo was sent to a monastery in Vallombrosa. By 15, he had declared his intent to become a novitiate, but his father whisked him away, talking to him of a future in the wool trade.

But his father recognized his talent, and wool gave way to medicine and that in turn to mathematics. At the University of Pisa he became known as "the Wrangler" for insolently questioning the petrified teachings of dusty professors. There he had determined, by using his pulse to time a swinging lamp in the cathedral, that pendulums were isochronal. Turning it around, he developed a pendulum device to measure pulse rates. As a professor at the university, he dropped objects of different size and weight from the famous leaning tower, thus demonstrating the principle of equivalence, which states that the rate of fall is a function only of distance (i.e., time) and not of mass or weight.

In 1592 Galileo shifted his teaching duties to Padua, then part of the Serene Republic of Venice. He assumed paternal duties as well, fathering three children with Marina Gamba, a young, lusty, illiterate woman of easy virtue. The couple never married. Marina and the children lived in cramped lodgings near Galileo's mansion.

While in Venice, Galileo learned of the invention of the telescope by a Dutchman, Hans Lippershey. The military use of such an instrument and the monies that would accrue to its maker leaped to Galileo's mind. He entered into feverish activity and in a short time had built a far superior telescope. The market was his. He demonstrated its ability to spot distant fleets at sea, but he also aimed it at the skies, where he showed that the moon's surface was not smooth. He charted four moons of Jupiter (obsequiously named after four Medicis), the phases of Venus, and sunspots. Later he would similarly refine the microscope.

Financial concerns badgered Galileo. He had to support not only his own family but frequently his brother's family, and he was held responsible for his sisters' dowries. Striking a profitable arrangement, he moved to Florence in 1610. His astronomical observations strengthened his belief in the Copernican model, but here he ran into trouble with Rome. The stocky Galileo was a feared speaker, both forceful and entertaining. His writings, spiced with an unhealthy dose of measured acerbic wit, followed suit. In 1616 Cardinal Bellarmine instructed Galileo that Copernican thought was erroneous and that he was not, in any way, to teach or defend it.

But Galileo could not refrain. In 1632 he published *Dialogue on Two Chief Systems of the World,* which contrasted the views of Ptolemy and Copernicus. His detractors, many of them Jesuits, and many harboring past insults, leaped at their chance, convincing Urban VIII that the doltish Ptolemaic advocate in Galileo's book was none other than the pope himself. Thus the Inquisition convened, and, since it was stacked with men of ignorance, superstition, and bile, only the penalty lay in doubt.

That penalty was the banning of his book, the forbidding of further teaching, and house arrest. He moved to Siena and then settled in Arcerti, outside Florence. There he completed *The Discourses on the Two New Sciences,* his lasting contribution to physics. He continued to observe the skies with his telescope until blindness overtook him. But he received visitors. Hobbes and, ironically, Milton paid their respects. His last year was enlivened by an epistolary love affair, a passionate end to a passionate life.

DIRECTIONS AND HOURS: Santa Croce is located on the Piazza Santa Croce, two blocks north of the Arno, and can easily be located on a city map. It is open daily but closed between 12:30 and 3:00 P.M.

FLORENCE
English Cemetery

▲   ▲   ▲

If Columbus discovered America in 1492, Americans discovered Italy less than three centuries later. In the 1700s, long before Horace Greeley advised heading west, explorers such as John Singleton Copley, Benjamin West, and Thomas Jefferson came east to investigate. The next century brought a flurry of visitors who published their findings under titles such as *Italian Sights Seen Through American Spectacles* and *A Boston Portrait-Painter Visits Italy*. By then the English had already established permanent colonies.

Mary McCarthy blames Robert and Elizabeth Browning for creating "a tooled-leather idea of Florence as a dear bit of the old world," an idea which attracted "old maids of both sexes . . . studying Tuscan wild flowers, collecting ghost stories, collecting triptyches and diptyches, burying their dogs in the churchyard of the Protestant Episcopal church, knowing (for the most part) no Florentines but their servants."

But that is not the impression one gets of the expatriates buried in the English Cemetery. To judge from their epitaphs and their lives, they were hopeful and brave, pioneers in an unfamiliar land. What makes it more poignant is the way the cemetery has been abandoned. No one has been buried here for over 100 years, and there are no caretakers on the premises, no one to give information about the Americans, British, Germans, and French who died so far from home.

The cemetery is compact and walled in, the size of a city block, and can easily be explored in an hour or two. You will need to press the bell so that one of the other businesses in the building can let you in. As you enter, go to your right. The woman kneeling in shocked sorrow is mourning **Arnold Savage Landor** (1818–1871), the oldest son of poet Walter Savage Landor. The poet himself is buried in the interior of the cemetery. Notice the immense detail in the marble, including the carefully sculpted fringe balls on the woman's shawl.

Turn right at the first path. About four rows up, facing into the cemetery, is a monument with a cameo of **Theodore Parker**, "The Great American Preacher born at Lexington, Massachusetts, United States of America, August 24, 1810, Died at Florence, Italy, May 10, 1860. His name is engraved in marble, his virtues in the hearts of those he helped to free from slavery and superstition."

Parker, the youngest of 10 children, began his ministerial career by attending Harvard Divinity School and in 1837 became a Unitarian minister. But he shocked Boston in 1841 when he preached a sermon, "The Transient and Permanent in Christianity," that questioned whether its doctrines were a unique revelation from God.

His lectures on slavery and other social issues took him around the country, often into stressful situations. He risked imprisonment trying to free a slave by force. Constantly under attack from his colleagues and in a bloodless marriage the warmhearted and whimsical Parker suffered spells of depression. When he contracted tuberculosis in his forties, he traveled around Europe in an attempt to stabilize his health. He died at 49 in Florence.

At the top in the back and to the left of the center path are **Beatrice Shakespeare** and **Claude Shakespeare Clench**, described as the last descendants of William Shakespeare.

To your left is the **Delisser** monument with a frieze of the Parthenon showing three unconnected pillars—perhaps signifying D. Delisser, who died in 1844 at 48; Ellis William Delisser, who died in 1845 at 19; and Adelaide Delisser, 13, who perished a week after her brother.

A few rows down the hill is the unusual design of a serpent making a circle by biting its tail, set against a sunburst. It is the monument of **John Fombelle**, who "filled the highest judicial appointment in the presidency of Bengal."

Up toward the front on the terrace is the skeletal Grim Reaper on the monument of **Andrea di Mariano Casentini** (1855–1870) and just in front, under a plain stone, is the author Frances Trollope.

Fanny Trollope (1780–1863) is best remembered for two things: her highly critical book, *Domestic Manners of the Americans*, and her son, Anthony. It hardly matters that she wrote 100 more books and had six other children.

Domestic Manners of the Americans (1832) brought fame and desperately needed cash. None of her subsequent books, with titles like *The Young Countess or Love and Jealousy* (1848), were as financially successful, but she published two or three romances a year and made a decent living. Mr. Trollope, who had undertaken to write an *Encyclopedia ecclesiastica*, an alphabetical history of Christianity, was not as fortunate. He died in 1836 when he was still on *D*.

Fanny's relationship with Anthony had always been problematic. Enterprising and sharp-tongued herself, she found him clumsy and slow, lacking in charm. When Anthony handed her a manuscript of a novel in 1845 and asked if she would give it to a publisher, Fanny and other family members were dumbfounded. She did so, without reading it, and the rest is literary history. Fanny published her last book in 1856, the year that Anthony completed *Barchester Towers.*

In the center section rests a conflux of poets. The monument to **Walter Savage Landor** (1775–1864) has a quote from a poem written by Algernon Swinburne in his memory: "And thou, his Florence, to thy trust Receive and keep / Keep safe his dedicated dust, His sacred sleep. / So shall thy lovers come from far, Mix with thy name / As morning star with evening star His faultless fame."

Although brilliant, Landor was expelled from Rugby for a witty rebelliousness and from Oxford for shooting at a rival's shuttered window after a row. He next attempted to create a castle in Wales, only to have to flee lawsuits and other complications in 1814. He and his pretty wife, Julia, eventually settled in Florence, where four children were born amid great rancor. At 60, he turned over the villa to his wife and family and moved to England.

Landor spent 21 years in Bath, writing and visiting friends in London. But at 82, convicted of libel, he escaped to Florence, to a family that refused to take him back. Landor wandered Lear-like through the stifling Italian streets until William Wetmore Story and Robert Browning compassionately made arrangements for him.

Landor, though critically acclaimed, was widely unread. Between 1824 and 1853 he published *Imaginary Conversations*, nearly 150 dialogues between such figures as Diogenes and Plato, Galileo and Milton, and Henry VIII and Anne Boleyn on the eve of her beheading. His poetry was published periodically throughout his life and ranged from the lyrical to the epic.

Elizabeth Barrett Browning, who liked Landor but characterized him as a "poor headstrong old man," has a sarcophagus with a cameo in profile of a woman with braided hair and the initials EBB.

ELIZABETH BARRETT BROWNING *b. March 6, 1806, Durham, England; d. June 29, 1861, Florence.* When Elizabeth Barrett Browning was born, her father was already searching for a home that would keep his family isolated. His need to control the lives of his wife, Mary, his baby daughter, Elizabeth, and the 11 more children still in the wings was absolute. This domination was to provide the main drama of Elizabeth's life.

Elizabeth, nicknamed Ba (for baby), was not old enough to protest when, at the birth of a son 15 months later, her jubilant father ordered a holiday for the family slaves down on his Jamaica sugar plantation. But she was furious at 14 when Edward was sent away for a formal education and she was not. She knew Greek and Latin, read the classics voraciously, and had already produced a privately printed epic poem, *The Battle of Marathon*. Burning at the inequity, she developed undiagnosable ailments (such as feeling her spine was "swollen") and spent her adolescence in bed. As an invalid, she was the center of family attention and excused from mundane household tasks.

Yet it was a mixed blessing. The prescribed cures for "female maladies" at that time were to undergo complete (and debilitating) bedrest and take opium in the form of laudanum—a habit Elizabeth was to continue nightly for the rest of her life. Her health improved in her twenties, but most of her energy went into animated correspondence. Years earlier, she had decided that people were disappointed when they met her in person, and she became reluctant to give them that opportunity. Only her cocker spaniel, Flush, whom she tried to teach to read, was allowed to love her unconditionally.

Elizabeth's first collection, *The Seraphim and Other Poems*, had been published in 1838 to good reviews, though Elizabeth's use of near rhymes (i.e., ways/grace and faith/breath) irritated some critics. That book was followed by two volumes in 1844, called *Poems*. Oddly for a writer, she was more eager to receive criticism than praise, writing gleefully to a friend about a review that was said "to cut me into gashes." The fact that her work was being criticized presumably meant that it was being taken seriously.

In 1845 she began corresponding with Robert Browning, though both lived in London. When they finally met, instead of its ending the relationship as she always feared, the two poets fell in love. But now Elizabeth had to worry about her father's reaction. Edward Barrett had long proclaimed that none of his children were going to marry, expecting them to stay in his household forever.

To be fair, Elizabeth had fostered a particular closeness with her father, weeping when he went away on business and dissolving in tears of joy at his return. He worried about her health, and they still participated in nightly prayer sessions in her room. Too, the prospective bridegroom was six years younger than Elizabeth, and an unemployed poet still living at home.

Nevertheless, in September 1846, the pair were secretly married in a local church and embarked for Italy. Mr. Barrett, notified by mail, was astonished, then enraged. For the rest of his life he returned his daughter's letters unread. Henrietta and Alfred, two of Elizabeth's siblings who also married, received the same treatment.

Elizabeth and Robert were happy in Florence. Their son, Pen, was born when Elizabeth was 43, after a series of miscarriages. She doted on the boy as she had on Flush, but she did not neglect Robert or her work. In 1851 she published *Casa Guidi Windows*, followed by *Aurora Leigh* in 1857 and the political treatise *Poems Before Congress* in 1860. Her 1850 collection of *Poems* included "Sonnets from the Portuguese," the 43 poems she had written for Robert during their courtship. A persistent theme in her work was what she feared: the betrayal of a woman by a man.

In the end it was Elizabeth's body that betrayed her. Over the years her respiratory weakness had come and gone, hiding, then unexpectedly reappearing. But this time an abscess on her lung burst, and there was no reprieve.

Next to EBB is the wife of painter Holman Hunt, **Fanny Waugh Hunt** (1833–1866), who died in childbirth. Holman Hunt,* a Pre-Raphaelite painter whose most famous work is *The Light of the World* (1853), used Fanny as his model in *Isabella and the Pot of Basil* (1866).

DIRECTIONS AND HOURS: From the Duomo walk east on Via dell' Oriuolo, then northeast on Via Borgo Pinti to Donatello Piazzale. The English Cemetery is open daily 9:00 A.M. to noon and 3:00 to 6:00 P.M. You will need to ring the bell to be admitted.

---

*Buried in St. Paul's Cathedral; see *Permanent Londoners.*

CHAPTER 11

FLORENCE
Artists' Churches

▲ ▲ ▲

CHURCH OF THE OGNISSANTI

The Church of the Ognissanti (All Saints' Day) would be your typical neighborhood church—if it did not contain paintings by Botticelli, Ghirlandaio, and Taddeo Gaddi. But this is Florence. The church was founded in 1256 by an order of Benedictine monks skilled in making wool and was rebuilt in the 1600s.

As you enter Ognissanti, in the floor to your right is a geometric black and brown design, the family crypt of the explorer Amerigo Vespucci. Although Amerigo is not buried here, he is said to be the young boy to the right of the Madonna in the Ghirlandaio painting of the *Madonna della Misericordia Protecting the Vespucci Family*. A relation by marriage, the beautiful Simonetta Cattaneo Vespucci, who was believed to have been Botticelli's model for Venus in *Birth of Venus* (ca. 1485) and Flora in *Primavera* (ca. 1478), may be in the crypt. Sadly, she died very young of consumption.

In the right front of the church is the chapel where Botticelli is interred. The chapel itself is ornate, but the artist is buried in the floor under a monument the size of a dinner plate. It has a gold heraldic lion on a shield of dark blue.

SANDRO BOTTICELLI (ALESSANDRO DI MARIANO FILIPEPI) *b. 1445, Florence; d. 1510, Florence.* The name Botticelli, when properly accented, has a romantic cadence that fits perfectly with the enchantment of the *Birth of Venus* and *Primavera*. Do we really have to know that *botticelli* means "little tub" or that the artist, at least in his self-portrait in *Adoration of the Magi* (ca. 1475), was stocky, heavy-lidded, and broken-nosed, looking out with impatient scorn toward his audience?

Probably we do, if only because so little else about him is known. We know that he rarely strayed far from the neighborhood around Ognissanti where he was born, a restless and indifferent student whose older brother tried to get him interested in goldsmithing. But Botticelli moved on to painting as an assistant to Fra Lippi until 1467. He next joined the workshop of Verrocchio, in the company of Leonardo da Vinci, seven years younger. The two debated about landscape and perspective, and Leonardo later wrote that Botticelli claimed it was possible to throw a paint-soaked sponge at a panel and create a background from whatever resulted. Leonardo declared that Botticelli "painted bad landscapes," but it is hard to believe that the older artist was not teasing him. Backgrounds were not primary—he mixed ancient, medieval, and Florentine architecture at will—yet in *Primavera* over 190 flowering plants have been identified.

In the 1470s Botticelli was filling commissions for tondo (round paintings) and did many *Adoration of the Magi*, following conventions such as including a peacock as a symbol of the Resurrection since its flesh was believed never to decay. Botticelli was invited to Rome in 1481 to help decorate the walls of the Sistine Chapel. The subjects, the *Youth of Moses* and the *Punishment of Korah, Dathan, and Abiram* (who rebelled against Moses in the wilderness), were probably dictated by Pope Sixtus.

Afterward Botticelli packed up quickly and went home, though not before having to formally bill the notoriously slow-paying Pope. Back in Florence he was part of the Medici court with Lorenzo's love of the mythic—a combination that produced the wonderful *Primavera*, celebrating the coming of spring, and the *Birth of Venus* from the sea, in which she is being blown by the Winds to land where she can be decently clothed. To enter the room of the Uffizi where both paintings reside, along with his *Adoration of the Magi* (ca. 1475), *Pallas and the Centaur* (ca. 1482–1483), and others, is a heady experience indeed.

Botticelli's women follow the German convention of the thrust-out belly, though less exaggerated, a posture Florentines considered beautiful and becoming to a woman. The chaste beauty of Simonetta Vespucci may reflect the distance at which Botticelli wanted to keep women in his own life. He allegedly had a nightmare one time that he was married, and got up and walked the streets of Florence to keep the dream from coming back.

How different would Botticelli's subsequent paintings have been had Girolamo Savonarola not swept the north with his denunciations of sinful Renaissance Florence? The artist did not abandon his Medici friends and patrons as many did, but his paintings were now of religious subjects and darker in mood. His *Pietà* (late 1490s) and *Calumny of Apelles* (ca. 1797–1798) have been suggested as his protest against the excommunication and martyrdom of Savonarola in 1498. But the gracious and intellectual world of the Medici, driven out of Florence in 1494, had also been destroyed.

Botticelli painted little after 1500. He was a man who saw life simply. Earlier on, when his next-door neighbor, a weaver, disturbed his concentration with the clatter of his looms, the artist threatened him with violence and was brought into court. Now at 55 he refused to adapt and change to meet High Renaissance demands. Vasari condemned Botticelli for letting himself sink into poverty and obscurity. Indeed, his art lay dormant until Rossetti and the Pre-Raphaelites (who also loved red-haired models) woke it into its own spring. And it has been spring ever since.

On your way out, across from Botticelli's painting of St. Augustine, notice a charming bas-relief memorial for a child. His mother holds him as he stands lightly on the palm of her hand, reaching toward the sun.

DIRECTIONS AND HOURS: Ognissanti is located on the north side of the Piazza Ognissanti on the Arno. It is open between 9:00 A.M. and noon.

SANTISSIMA ANNUNZIATA

Santissima Annunziata, built in the 13th century, is a favorite of Florentine society and the church of choice for weddings. The entrance is an impressive cloister with some wonderful frescoes high on the walls. A bust commemorates the painter of several of the frescoes, **Andrea del Sarto** (1486–1530), who is buried in the floor near the high altar. The interior of the church is dark and dramatic, richly clotted with paintings and gilt shrines.

It seems difficult to find a church or museum in Florence that does *not* contain a religious painting by del Sarto. Unlike some of his contemporaries, he finished all commissions promptly—a necessity, perhaps, given the modest amounts he was paid. His finances improved briefly when the king of France, who admired his work,

sent for him and paid him generously in gold. But del Sarto's wife begged him to come home, and he went back to working at a subsistence level. Lucrezia del Sarto, a widow several years his senior, was considered a shrew. But he was in love, and all the women he painted had his wife's features.

Del Sarto survived the siege of Florence, only to die of plague in the aftermath. The biographer Vasari admired his colors and the sense of the bodies beneath the clothing but believed that del Sarto's "timidity of mind" and lack of ambition kept him from being a genius. Still, his paintings are everywhere.

In the chapel right of the altar is a sculpture by **Baccio Bandinelli** (ca. 1493–1560) of the *Fallen Christ*, with skulls and crossbones at the corners. The artist and his wife are buried here. Had he not had such a discordant personality, Bandinelli might have accomplished more. He was constantly embroiled in litigation, which he greatly enjoyed, but his quarrels took away from his work time and a number of sculptures were left unfinished. He is perhaps best known for his *Hercules and Caius* (1534) and his *Laoccoön* (ca. 1523–1525), now in the Uffizi. He also worked on the tombs of Leo X and Clement VII in Santa Maria sopra Minerva in Rome (ca. 1534–1536); the observer fingering his beard in the bas-relief on Clement's tomb is said to be a portrait of Bandinelli himself.

Left of the altar down a corridor at the end is the chapel where **Giambologna**, or **Giovanni da Bologna** (1529–1608), is interred. His work here includes the crucifix and bronze reliefs with *Scenes of the Passion*. Giambologna is said to be the first sculptor in Western history to abandon the theory that works of art have only one correct point of view, forcing his viewers to look at a sculpture from various angles.

Supported by the Medici, he maintained a large studio. The Bargello contains his masterpiece, *Flying Mercury* (1564). The *Rape of the Sabine* (ca. 1583) shows both the vitality of his human flesh and his use of spiraling forms.

Most of the other artists here are buried under an in-ground vault in the Capella di San Luca. It is kept locked, but you can ask the sacristan to show it to you. He will take you through an outdoor courtyard, the Cloister of the Dead, and into a small chapel decorated with marble sculptures of major biblical figures. Jacopo da Pontormo, Benvenuto Cellini, and many others are under the trap-door decorated with skulls and the phrase "Semper velim vita morte floreat" (Let him always flourish whether in life or death).

By the time he was 18, **Jacopo da Pontormo** (1494–1557) had lost his parents, his grandparents, and even the

younger sister for whom he was responsible. The tailor who commissioned his first work died before it was finished. In the face of so much death, the teenager apprenticed himself to Andrea del Sarto and was given a commission by the Servite friars; when it was done, Michelangelo commented, "This youth, if he lives and continues to pursue art, will attain to heaven."

Pontormo did live and continued to pursue art, creating paintings that are now in the Uffizi, the Pitti Palace, and the National Gallery in London. In 1522 he came across an engraving by Albert Dürer and began painting in a German mannerist style. Not everyone was pleased. A frustrated Vasari commented that Pontormo took "pains to learn what others avoid, abandoning a good style which pleased everyone."

Pontormo's portraits continued to be masterful, however. A solitary soul who never went to festivals for fear of being crushed, he refused to let death be discussed in his presence. He kept mortality at bay until the age of 63, when he succumbed to edema.

BENVENUTO CELLINI *b. November 3, 1500, Florence; d. February 13, 1571, Florence.* Benvenuto Cellini opens his famous autobiography by advising all men who have achieved anything of excellence to write their own life history but not to do so until they are at least 40 years old. This age, he reasons, lends a contentment and freedom not found in younger minds. He then immediately begins his story by lying about his "ancient" lineage.

But this was all part of Cellini's character. He bragged, swaggered, murdered, and fought his way through life. He was the premier goldsmith of his time and one of the great sculptors of the century. His autobiography, though flawed by rodomontade, is still the best-read contemporary account of those times. With wonderful color and presence the range of society is covered, starting with his patrons (kings, popes, cardinals, and Medicis) and running on through artists, workmen, apprentices, prostitutes, and criminals. Dictated over a five-year period (1558–1562) to a young assistant, the book was not published until 1728. It is now considered a classic.

By 13 Cellini had begun to learn goldsmithing. His skills developed rapidly. What also sprang into prominence was the family temper. When he was 16, both he and his 14-year-old brother were exiled for six months for brawling. It is interesting that Cellini describes this brother as having an "extreme boldness and fierce temper," for it serves as an equally apt portrayal of himself.

Cellini's studies continued in Siena, Bologna, and Pisa before he settled in Rome in 1519. After he found work in a master's shop, word of his talent spread and he soon began receiving commissions of his own. He moved back to Florence, where his success caused much envy among his former employers. The situation deteriorated into a fight in which Cellini killed a cousin of his first employer. With the aid of a friar, Cellini was able to escape Florence disguised as a monk, and once again he headed for Siena. Ultimately he settled in Rome until 1540.

Of his Roman period, not a great deal remains. He worked primarily on making seals, coins, and medals for popes, cardinals, and the wealthy families of the time. No doubt much of what he accomplished was later melted down by thieves or by his patrons so that jewels could be retrieved and the gold resold. When not creating work requiring the finest detail, he was busy creating enmity among his fellow artists with his abusive and outspoken ways. He committed yet another murder and in 1538 was imprisoned in Castel Sant'Angelo by Pope Paul III for the theft of certain jewels with which Clement VII had entrusted him. Even here adventure awaited, for he was able to escape this gloomy, impregnable fortress, if only for a few weeks. Recaptured, he was released toward the end of 1539.

In 1540 Cellini moved to France for a stay of five years under the patronage of Francis I. Here he designed the famous saltcellar, one of the greatest creations ever done in gold. The main figures, Neptune, god of the sea (salt), and Tellus, goddess of the earth (pepper), are reclining nudes executed in gold. The aesthetic inspiration springs from Michelangelo's figures in the Medici Chapels, although his female figure is far more delicate than any done by Michelangelo. To the side of Neptune is a hollow ship that holds the salt; to the side of Tellus is a temple in Ionic style that contains the pepper. Other creatures adorn the top, and sea and earth are enameled green and blue. The base contains more figures yet and more brilliant enameling. While the saltcellar seems gaudy at first, close observation reveals marvelous and inventive detailing and design.

A return to Florence for a short visit turned into a lifetime stay when in 1545 Cellini was offered a commission by Cosimo de' Medici. This was for a large bronze statue of Perseus that would adorn the Piazza della Signoria. The project took nine years, and in doing it he broke new artistic ground. With bronze he could make the figure slimmer and decorate it with finer and more detailed decoration than one could do with marble, as Michelangelo's *David*. The casting of the statue, which is over 10 feet high, is described with great drama in the *Autobiography*, for in the process Cellini nearly burned down his studio.

Cellini did not stick with metals, however; around 1550 he had started working in marble. His most famous work was his *Crucifix,* completed in 1561. In the meantime his stock was falling. The Medicis were temperamental and paid slowly, fellow artists resented his success, and prison intervened in 1556 and 1557 for assault and then for sodomy. Perhaps confinement gave him time for thought, for his *Autobiography* emerged over the next four years. He wrote some treatises and then married in 1565, after already having fathered numerous children with several women. Marriage was not a palliative. Continuing his contentious behavior, he took up litigation as a method of petty revenge and entertainment and did not stop until he died three months after his 70th cantankerous birthday.

Members of some of the city's noble families are buried outside in the cloister. You can see a large, long-haired bust of a Medici cousin, **Ferdinando** (d. 1736). He was the son of Maria Strozzi, another prominent name in Florentine history. The attractive knight of a horse in bas-relief belongs to the **Amerighi** family.

DIRECTIONS AND HOURS: Santa Annunziata can be reached by walking north from the Duomo for several blocks on Via de Servi to Piazza Annunziata. The church is open daily between 8:00 A.M. and noon and between 3:00 and 6:00 P.M.

C H A P T E R   1 2

EMILIA-ROMAGNA
Bologna, Ferrara, Ravenna, Predappio, and Rimini

▲   ▲   ▲

BOLOGNA

The primary reason to go to Bologna is to eat, to enjoy its unparalleled pasta and cream. Oddly, for a city with its history, there are few famous people buried here. But the Certosa, the public cemetery of Bologna founded in 1334 and consecrated in 1801, is well worth a visit.

Enter at the gate nearest the stadium and move left. In the second section you will see the two large soldiers commemorating those *caduti in guerra* (fallen in war). Turn left at the levitating angel of the Veronesi family, and walk back to the simple monument of Nobel Prize–winning poet **Giosue Carducci** (1835–1907).

From his first collection of poetry, *Rhymes* (1857), to *The Barbarian Odes* (1887) and *New Rhymes* (1889), he rarely wrote on personal themes, retaining his early dislike of romanticism. Politics, both ancient and current, were his obsession and fueled his work. The same Carducci who defied priests as a young man continued to attack Catholicism and Christianity in such poetry as "Hymn to Satan," often alienating even his friends.

He was awarded the Nobel Prize in 1906. A year later he died from influenza complicated by pneumonia. Plans to bury him in Santa Croce in Florence were never completed.

Near Carducci's monument, in a marble tomb deco-

Opposite: Child's monument in Bologna

rated with laurel, rests the composer **Ottorino Respighi** (1879–1936). Respighi was a traditionalist who joined with nine other Italian composers to issue a manifesto against "modern" music, decrying it to be without "human content." Born in Bologna, he studied with Rimsky-Korsakov and Max Bruch. He is best known for his brilliantly orchestrated, though some say meretricious, tone poems *The Fountains of Rome* (1914–1916), *The Pines of Rome* (1923–1924), and *Rome Festivals* (1929). His suite *The Birds* (1927) and his popular *Ancient Airs and Dances* (1917, 1923, 1931) carry a direct and sincere charm.

There is an abundance of wonderful statuary in the Certosa. Of particular note, in the right front section (Chiostro Maggiore), is the unusual monument to **Giuseppe Capi**, which shows a bas-relief of several family members cheerfully involved in the running of a printing press. Also in this section are some very old monuments. One of the most beautiful is the white marble bust of **Maria Barberini**, the niece of Urban VIII, who died in 1621 at age 20.

The small chapel at the center front of the Certosa has stones dating back to the 16th century. Its walls are decorated by marquetry showing musical instruments, street scenes, a skeleton standing in an archway, and the head of St. Peter lying on a tombstone.

Finally, on the far side in the columbarium area is the marble drawer of **Ernesto Maserati** (1898–1975), "Pioniere dell' Automobile." His cameo smiles out from behind the wheel of a car. Maserati began by building race cars with three of his brothers. In 1927 he drove and won the Tripoli Grand Prix for racers in the 1.5-liter class. By 1930 the Maserati 16-cylinder was winning most international races. The Maserati was the only European-made car to win the Indianapolis 500.

DIRECTIONS AND HOURS: If you are driving, the easiest way to reach the Certosa is to follow signs for the stadio *(stadium). The cemetery is on the other side of the Via Corso and is open daily 8:00 A.M. to 5:00 or 6:00 P.M.*

FERRARA

Ferrara is a cheerful and lively city, but if you go there in the near future you may find most of it closed for *restaurazione*. To visit one of the most enigmatic women of her generation, Lucrezia Borgia, you are instructed to go to the Church of Corpus Domini and ring the bell of the closed order of nuns. But instead of being admitted to see the family's tomb slabs in the choir, you may be told that the church is still undergoing restoration, completion time unknown, and is not open to visitors.

LUCREZIA BORGIA *b. April 1480, Rome; d. June 23, 1519, Ferrara.* Given the reputation Lucrezia Borgia has had to carry through the centuries, an albatross of incest and poisonings around her delicate neck, it seems incongruous to find her buried in a convent. But 20th-century research has found that she was more sinned against than sinning.

Certainly the golden-haired child was always the pawn of her father, whether as a political asset or, as was rumored, in his bed. When Cardinal Rodrigo Borgia was ready to make a play for the papacy, he encouraged his widowed mistress, Vannozza Cattanei, to marry again for appearance' sake. By doing so, however, she was required by law to give up guardianship of her children. Three-year-old Lucrezia and eight-year-old Cesare were taken from their mother and placed with a cousin of Rodrigo.

The next decision that Lucrezia's father, now Pope Alexander VII, made for her was marriage, at 13, to a sullen and melancholy widower, Giovanni Sforza of Milan. Four years later, not having realized the diplomatic and political gains he had hoped for from the union, the pope decided that they should divorce. A shocked Lucrezia sought refuge in the convent of San Sisto and Sforza fought the suggestion, but when promised that he could keep her entire dowry, he signed a paper stating that the marriage had never been consummated. The union annulled, Lucrezia was restored to a *virgo intacta.*

The populace knew better. When a handsome young chamberlain of the pope was fished out of the Tiber shortly after the divorce, it was rumored that he was the father of a child born to Lucrezia in March 1498. Others said that the baby's father was Cesare or Pope Alexander. Little Giovanni Borgia was "legitimized" by two papal bulls, first as the son of Cesare and "an unmarried woman of Rome," then as the offspring of the pope himself.

Both father and son Borgia were lusty and compulsive womanizers, fully capable of incest. By then Cesare was suffering so badly from "the French disease," syphilis, that he wore a mask to hide the pustules on his face—a face that had once been known as the most handsome in Rome. Lucrezia, affectionate, extravagant, and addicted to fashion, was deeply attached to both men.

Her next husband, Alfonso di Bisceglie, was chosen by Alexander to strengthen ties between Naples and the Vatican. This bridegroom was gentle and affectionate, and the couple were very much in love. Their son, Rodrigo, was born in 1499. Within the year, however, Alfonso was murdered. The "assassins" were never found, but the death was blamed on Cesare, who had a reputation of doing away with rivals of any kind. It was from Cesare that the family got its reputation for poisoning; he employed his own strangler and chemist, and studied the ways in which cups, flowers, and saddles could convey lethal doses.

Alfonso di Bisceglie's death ended Lucrezia's happiness, particularly since consenting to her father's plans for a third marriage meant having to give up baby Rodrigo. But after much negotiation, in late 1501 she was wed to Alfonso d'Este, and Rodrigo was left behind in Rome.

Lucrezia spent the last 17 years of her life in Ferrara with an uninspiring husband. She tried to recapture the ecstasy of love through flirtations with the poet Pietro Bembo and with Francesco Gonzaga, her husband's brother-in-law, until, abandoning the search for romance, she turned to religion. Joining a lay order of St. Francis, Lucrezia became active in caring for the sick and dying.

By that time she had suffered through the deaths of Pope Alexander in 1503 (either by malaria or by the poison he had intended for a cardinal he was dining with), Cesare in battle in 1507, and, most bitterly, her son Rodrigo, who succumbed to malaria at 12. Her own health was compromised by constant pregnancies. Lucrezia used sojourns at the cloister as birth control but found herself expecting for the eleventh time at 39. After a difficult birth she contracted puerperal fever and died a week later.

At her death Lucrezia's reputation as a good-hearted, if sometimes misled, woman seemed secure. It took Victor Hugo 300 years later to popularize her as a moral monster, claiming that "the people's fables often make up the poet's truth."

DIRECTIONS AND HOURS: If you are driving, park outside the Porta Romana and walk into the interior of the old town. Corpus Domini is located on the tiny Via Pergolato, but all through this area are street maps of the main points of interest. When the church is open, the hours are Monday to Friday 9:30 A.M. to noon and 4:00 to 5:30 P.M.

RAVENNA

Ravenna is an ancient city, deservedly famous for its mosaics, Theodoric's Mausoleum, and Dante's tomb. But you must slice through a lot of industrial-modern fat to locate

these treasures. Although there is no historic *centro* to Ravenna, the suburban secretions do hide a pearl or two.

Dante's Chapel is downtown and the logical place to start. It stands next to a churchyard and contains one room with variegated marble walls. Above Dante's sarcophagus is a relief done by Pietro Lombardo, showing the poet in profile, standing lost in thought at his desk. One elbow leans on an open book on a lectern. His epitaph, written by Bernard Canaccio, translates as follows:

> I sang the rights of monarchy, the heavens, and the infernal lakes which I had visited as long as fate decreed. And then my soul was translated to a better place and even more happily rejoined its Maker in Heaven. Here I, Dante, lie buried, in exile from my birthplace; a son of that loveless mother, Florence.

In fact, Florence tried many times after Dante's death to reclaim her son's body. In 1519 a group of Florentines appealed to the Medici pope, Leo X, for its return; Michelangelo, one of the signers of the petition, promised to build Dante an impressive tomb in Florence. Their request was granted, but when the delegation arrived and opened the sarcophagus, it was empty. It was learned centuries later that Franciscan monks had bored a hole through the wall and slithered out the bones to keep them in Ravenna. The bones stayed hidden in a walled-up door, forgotten about until 1865 when they were discovered and verified, then returned to the sarcophagus.

Surrendering with apparent good grace, the Dante Society of Florence donated the perpetually burning lamp inside the chapel in 1908.

DANTE ALIGHIERI *b. June 5, 1265, Florence; d. September 14, 1321, Ravenna.* To demystify Dante, it may help to realize that his name was a shortened version of Durante. Images of pianos, bananas, and "snozzolas" leap to mind; although Dante's nose was less spectacular, it was aquiline and prominently placed. His eyes were large and brown, his jaw pronounced, and he had an air of hope, not unlike Jimmy Durante's response to the world.

Born to a Florentine family of noble lineage but modest circumstances, Dante was well-educated, specializing in poetry and classical literature. Politically, his family was Guelf as opposed to the Ghibelline party of feudal nobility. A year after his father's death in 1283, he married a Ghibelline, Gemma di Manetto Donati. Such political differences were not uncommon, but in 1301, when Dante was serving as a member of a protest delegation to Pope Boniface VIII, the "Black" faction of the Guelfs seized power in Florence and exiled the "Whites," Dante among them. Separated from his children and his wife, who declined to follow him, Dante never saw Florence again.

At the time of his exile in 1302, he had already produced *La vita nuova* (The New Life, 1292), a collection of sonnets innovatively written in Italian instead of Latin. The 31 poems chronicle his beginnings as a poet and his explorations into courtly love. Such explorations dwelled at least as heavily on the varieties and colorations of the feelings experienced as on the object herself, though it was here that Dante introduced Beatrice, a young woman he had known and been close to in childhood. She is generally assumed to be Beatrice Portinari, later married to a banker, Simone Bardi. Her tragic early death in 1290 transformed her in Dante's eyes into a figure of saintliness and innocence who would reappear as his spiritual guide in the *Commedia* (Divine Comedy, 1321).

With his property confiscated and under threat of death by fire if he returned to Florence, Dante wandered from city to city for several years, supported by sympathizers. He also supported himself by lecturing on philosophy in university cities and by writing. *De vulgari eloquentia* (ca. 1304) is an exposition on spoken Italian, chronicling its various dialects and its suitability to poetic expression. Dante was instrumental in establishing his native Tuscan dialect as the literary language of Italy. *Il convivio* (The Banquet, ca. 1307) contains 14 of his poems with philosophical interpretations.

The *Commedia* begins in the "dark wood" of middle age in which nothing satisfies, no direction is clear. Seeing a mountain illuminated by sunlight, Dante tries to climb it, only to be beaten back by sin. Virgil, representing human reason, appears and guides him through the *Inferno*'s nine circles of the damned. Then they begin the arduous climb up the mountain of *Purgatorio*, striving toward the light of God. For the final phase, when human reason is deemed insufficient, Beatrice appears and takes over.

If Dante had not been cheated out of so much—his home, his financial holdings, and his family—by the capricious wind of politics, would he have had enough rage to fuel the *Commedia*? From the beginning, with its now-famous inscription, "Abandon hope, all you who enter here," the *Inferno* is shocking. Among the lost souls are Francesca and Paolo, unhappy lovers who were murdered by her hunchbacked husband, and Count Ugolino, who constantly betrayed others, forever gnawing on the skull of Archbishop Ruggieri, who betrayed him. But here are also Ulysses and Brunetto Latini, Dante's beloved teacher and mentor, placed among the Sodomites.

Yet by the time the *Commedia* was completed, Dante had gotten through the wasteland of his own *Purgatorio* and was on his way toward Paradise. He had been invited to the court of Guido da Polenta in Ravenna and settled there permanently; his children, Pietro and Antonia, a nun, were already living in the city. In 1321 da Polenta sent him to Venice as an ambassador to help avert war. Developing a "fever" on his way home, he died in his adopted city at 57.

Galla Placidia is no longer in the mausoleum that bears her name. In truth, she probably never was. But it is a good excuse to see the beautiful Byzantine mosaics for which Ravenna is famous. *Somebody*, after all, spent time in the three stone sarcophagi, and Ravennians still maintain that it was Galla, flanked by her husband, Constantius, and their son, Valentinian. The story goes that until the 16th century a mummified figure in queenly attire could be seen through a crack in the sarcophagus. The body was destroyed when children left a lighted candle in the opening.

When you enter the mausoleum, you cannot help but be dazzled by the deep blues, golds, and whites, the colors still vivid after more than 1,500 years. On the arched walls there are the early Christian symbols of doves, stags drinking at the everlasting waters, and Christ as the Good Shepherd. There are also apostles and the martyr St. Lawrence.

Galla Placidia, daughter of Emperor Theodosius, was a good woman, disappointed by her children. The spoiled Valentinian was fonder of horses and astrologers than of work when he took over the throne at 18. Placidia shuddered, but turned her attention to filling churches with beautiful Byzantine mosaics and aiding the poor. Next she had to live through a mother's worst nightmare: her daughter, Honoria, spiteful because she was forbidden to marry the man she loved, sent a gold ring to Attila the Hun, offering herself to him. Fortunately for Ravenna, he did not accept.

Theodoric's Mausoleum is just outside the city in a grassy park. It rises about 52.5 feet, and its dense Istrian limestone is estimated to weigh 300 tons. Seen from the outside, the structure is imposing, but it requires an act of imagination to picture the way it must have been originally when it was carved and bedecked with statues. The worn stone gives just a hint of the "tong-like" decoration.

At the top, beneath a dome, is the huge marble bathtub that doubled as his sarcophagus. There is evidence that **Theodoric** (454–526) had the mausoleum built around

520. One legend was that the Goth conqueror had heard predictions that he would be struck by lightning for his crimes and had this shelter built to protect him during storms. It did not help. The fissure in the dome was made by a divine thunderbolt striking Theodoric as he huddled inside.

As a young child, Theodoric was sent to Constantinople as a hostage to make sure that his Ostrogoth father kept his treaty with the emperor of the East. In 473, the 19-year-old Theodoric was released to rule the wandering tribe of barbarians from whom he had been separated, and in 488 the eastern emperor agreed that if Theodoric could conquer Italy he could keep it. Four years later his opponent, Odoacer, surrendered. Theodoric sliced him in two and established himself as "king of the Goths and Romans in Italy" at Ravenna.

Although he could not read or write, Theodoric was profoundly respectful of Roman civilization. He dressed in a toga, addressed the Senate in stilted Latin, and formed a brigade to protect the hundreds of statues that stood around the city. (Roman thieves had a penchant for hacking off bronze body parts and melting them down.)

Theodoric's goal was to unite the best in Roman culture and law with the new Christian faith. He ruled well, showing no favoritism to either group, and kept himself carefully subordinate to the emperor of the East. It could have worked, but it didn't. The emperor became jealous of his greater power, and the Italians resented being ruled by a barbarian. A minor theological question—Was Jesus made of the same or of only similar material to God?—became the rallying point.

Suspecting conspiracies, Theodoric reverted to his Gothic roots and had any suspects tortured and killed. One of these, the Roman statesman Boethius, was one of Theodoric's ministers. He wrote *The Consolation of Philosophy* while in prison and was executed in 524 without a trial.

Whether the story of lightning striking him is true or not, Theodoric died a disappointed man.

DIRECTIONS, HOURS, AND ADMISSION: If you are driving to Dante's Chapel, locate the main street in Ravenna, Via di Roma, and turn west on Via Mariani; park in the Piazza Garibaldi and walk one block south to Via Guido da Polenta. The Chapel is open daily 9:00 A.M. to noon and 2:00 to 5:00 P.M. The Mausoleum of Galla Placidia is north about eight blocks on Via Pietro and is open daily 8:30 A.M. to dusk; admission is L 5,000. To reach Theodoric's

Mausoleum, drive east to Via Darsena, which runs by the train station, and go north until you reach Via Cimitero. The mausoleum is open 8:30 A.M. to dusk; admission is L 4,000. If you come by train, walk along Via Carducci, which becomes Via Mariani, and follow preceding directions.

On the way to Predappio is an unexpected treasure. The beautifully maintained Indian Army War Cemetery across from the Forli municipal cemetery is "a gift of the Italian people for the perpetual resting place of the sailors, soldiers, and airmen who are honored here." There are 495 burials, and 768 names are recorded on the Cremation Memorial. Fifteen of the dead have never been identified.

What makes this cemetery particularly moving is that most of the men were in their twenties and thirties and died so far away from home. The stones are identically shaped but have individual insignias: elephants, eagles, and old-fashioned oared ships representing regiments with names like the Punjab or Sikh.

PREDAPPIO

There is only one reason to go to Predappio; whether you do so or not depends in part on your sensibility and your sense of history. Benito Mussolini is buried in the Cemetery of San Cassiano just south of town. You will know you are in the right place when you are approached by smiling older men handing out brochures of "war souvenirs"—black shirts, brass eagles, and key chains with Il Duce's profile. Their obvious sympathies cast an ominous chill: the thought that what should have been eradicated fifty years ago is still being glorified.

After you enter the cemetery, walk straight back to the chapel. The family crypt is to the right of it and downstairs. In the room are the dictator's wife, **Rachele Mussolini** (1893–1979), her bust looking tired and sad; the busts of **Alessandro Mussolini** (1854–1910) and **Rosa Maltoni Mussolini** (1858–1905), Il Duce's parents; and his son, Captain **Bruno Mussolini** (1923–1941), a handsome young man in a flight jacket who died in 1941 when the warplane he was piloting crashed. Bruno's widow, **Gina Ruperti Mussolini**, has an appealing expression. She survived the war but drowned in Lake Como when she was trapped under a motorboat on the way to a friend's wedding.

Mussolini's daughter, **Anna Maria Mussolini Negri** (1929–1968), who died at 38, is shown in a smiling photo-

graph above her granite sarcophagus. Plagued with health problems including polio as a child, she was rushed to the hospital after contracting chicken pox from one of her daughters. She died two weeks later from complications.

Benito Mussolini is set apart from the family, his sarcophagus in an alcove, blocked by iron fencing with his trademark *M.* In glass cases flanking his oversized, seemingly sightless, bust are boots, a black shirt, a helmet, and a miniature of his sarcophagus. He is remembered by a number of floral tributes.

BENITO MUSSOLINI *b. July 29, 1883, Varano di Costa; d. April 28, 1945, Mezzegra (Lake Como).* From the beginning, Benito Mussolini was a behavior problem. When forced by his pious mother to attend church, he would sit on the aisle and pinch people viciously as they walked by, or climb into a tree afterward, and pelt departing parishioners with acorns and rocks. In school, he threw an inkwell at a priest who tried to correct him and stabbed another student for making him smear what he was writing. His ruling passion was vengeance tinged with sadism.

As a teenager, he was a skilled orator; though his classmates avoided him personally, they came to respect his gifts.

After graduation Mussolini taught school for a year. When his contract was not renewed, he left for Switzerland just before he was drafted into the military. There he worked hard to survive, hauling bricks, living in a packing case, and stealing picnic lunches from old ladies. The experience crystallized his lifelong hatred of the rich. In 1904 he returned to Italy to serve in the army, then wrote for various Socialist newspapers such as *La lotta di classa* (The Class Struggle). When he was 26, experienced in seducing young women, he turned his attention to his stepsister, 17-year-old Rachele Guidi. In the face of his parents' opposition to their marriage, Benito brandished his pistol, announcing that it held one bullet for Rachele and five more for himself. The parents gave in.

In 1914 he broke with the Socialists by advocating Italy's entrance into World War I. His newspaper, *Il popolo d'Italia* (The People of Italy), soon had a circulation of 100,000. Setting an example, he reenlisted, eventually enduring a cannon explosion that left over 40 pieces of shrapnel in his body. After the war it seemed natural for him to organize other veterans into a new party. The Fascists, adopting the black shirts and the fez caps of the Arditi, proclaimed Mussolini *Il Duce* (the leader). He scored his first substantial triumph in 1922 when the Fascists took over the trains and prepared to march on Rome. King Victor Emmanuel III, who had heard the Blackshirts chanting "Long live the king!" prudently decided to make Mussolini prime minister.

The Fascists restored order and prosperity to postwar Italy, stabilizing the lire, increasing the wheat crop, and making the trains adhere to schedule. New roads, bridges, and hospitals were built. "Be proud to live in Mussolini's time," the posters proclaimed, and millions were. Each little boy was given his own black shirt and toy machine gun and initiated into the glories of the state. Mussolini, after a few blunders such as ordering a green plaid suit with red trim and dunking his bread in his wine at state banquets, learned to comport himself with dignity. His early belligerence seemed replaced by a new thoughtfulness. Yet his energy was already shifting to the paranoia of hanging on to power. Free elections disappeared, along with opposition newspapers—and any opposition at all.

He had an admirer in Germany. Adolf Hitler, six years younger, began to be known as the Führer (leader) and patterned his Nazi Brownshirts after the Fascist militia. He came to Italy in 1934 to meet with Mussolini and invited him back to Berlin. Yet it was Mussolini who became the follower. He taught the Italian army to goose-step, allowed Hitler to invade Italy's ally, Austria, and, most tragically— for Mussolini had never held with racial or religious prejudice—fell under the spell of Hitler's anti-Semitism. He began talking about a "pure Italian race" and made it illegal for Jews fleeing Nazi persecution to settle in Italy. He also made it illegal for Italian Jews to join the armed services, teach school, or own a large business.

In May 1939 Mussolini formally signed "the Pact of Steel" with Hitler, a prescription for war that his son-in-law, Gaetano Ciano, begged him to tear up. But Il Duce, with dreams of military glory, would not listen, though he maintained Italy's neutrality. He wanted the spoils of war without the bloodshed and watched on the sidelines as Poland, Norway, Denmark, Holland, and Belgium fell; he finally dragged his troops into France at the tail end of Germany's invasion. By then Hitler had realized how little help Italy would be, and he canceled Mussolini's plan to invade Yugoslavia. Afraid Hitler would also veto attacks on Greece and Albania, Il Duce went ahead on his own.

In 1942 when Allied planes bombed Italian cities, Fascist party popularity sagged. Mussolini, bedridden with an acute gastric ulcer, could do nothing. Finally, the almost-forgotten king stepped forward. With the help of the grand council, Victor Emmanuel III forced Mussolini's resignation as dictator in July 1943.

As he left his meeting with the king, Il Duce was spirited away in an ambulance, told that, as the most hated man in Italy, there were fears for his safety. He actually seemed relieved by his confinement; when Hitler rescued him in September, he was reluctant to go. Now 60, he looked shrunken and powerless, a hairless doll losing his stuffing. Hitler propped him up and set up a new Fascist regime, placing Mussolini in the northern village of Lake Garda. The puppet government went after the "traitors" who had helped depose Il Duce, including his daughter Edda's husband, Gaetano Ciano; Mussolini split the family by consenting to his execution.

But Mussolini knew his power was illusory. As he told a journalist, "My star has set." A few weeks later, attempting to leave Italy, he and his young mistress, Clara Petacci, were executed along with 15 others by the Italian resistance and their bodies taken to Milan's Piazzale Loreto. Il Duce and Clara were hung inside down from the girders of a gas station, but not before his corpse was urinated and spat upon and shot five times by a woman who had lost five sons in the war. Ironically, it was the Allies who rescued him and took his body to a local morgue.

DIRECTIONS AND HOURS: Coming from Forli, take Route 9 and turn south at the exit for Predappio. The cemetery is just south of Predappio on your right and is open daily from 8:00 A.M. to 5:00 P.M.

RIMINI

Just as Federico Fellini is very different from Benito Mussolini, so the resort town of Rimini is a more light-hearted place to visit. The film director is buried in the large Civico Cimitero. After you walk through the main gates, turn right at the third path (Section D), and at the corner of Section O you will see a dark brown mausoleum. It is made of bricklike stone with a small bell on the top and has the name Urbano Fellini e Suoi (Son). The metal-grilled door is bedecked with flowers and notes to Federico Fellini and Giulietta (Giulia) Masina. Two small brass birds on a limb decorate their tombstone.

FEDERICO FELLINI *b. January 20, 1920, Rimini; d. October 30, 1993, Rome.* As an evening coastal storm darkened and lashed the town of Rimini, a violent clap of thunder caused the Fellini house to shudder as Ida Fellini gave birth to her son Federico. A theatrical, even cinemagraphic, debut. Rimini was the seaside town that was to form such a strong impression on Fellini, and which he was, in one form or another, to revisit throughout his directorial career. The people who marked his youth, his guides, initiators, and companions, are seen in various reincarnations, their presences enlarged through the mythology of memory.

For his critics, these resurrected souls of the screen were seen once, twice, thrice too often, much like being forced to watch an ever-circling small-town Fourth of July parade. Fellini's supporters, however, were enamored with the way characters were reclothed and with his manner of exploring another facet of the same theme. Through the exploration came a development and deepening of characters and themes: his obsessive relationship to women, love versus sex, and guilt and alienation.

There was little in his childhood to suggest his artistic bent. Much of his early history was self-reported and was either gloriously enriched or purely invented. At best it is highly unreliable. We do know that his father was a middle-class salesman whose airs of sophistication exceeded his experience. His mother was handsome, mischievous, and devoutly religious. Parochial school provided memories of Sisters, some affectionate, some mean, and the beach provided voyeuristic thrills: blond women from the north bronzing in the sun and Saraghina, (the sardine girl) who, for a fee, lifted her skirts and displayed her charms for the awestruck boys of town. His interest in priestly ambitions was fleeting and later turned to stern opposition. His interest in women never faltered.

By the age of 18, Fellini had headed out for Rome. His start came in journalism, writing humorous pieces and drawing illustrations and caricatures for the satirical magazine *Marc' Aurelio* and for a film periodical, *Cinemagazzino.* He soon got part-time work at Cinecitta studios, and as the war swung into full gear, avoided the draft with much help from his friends.

In 1943 he met and within five months married Giulietta Masina. By then he was already involved in writing scripts for film, but it was his collaboration with Roberto Rossellini on *Rome, Open City* (1945) and *Paisan* (1946) that marked his first substantial work. Equally important was his work with Rossellini as an assistant. His observance of

Rossellini was an inspiration that let him see that movies could be made with "the same direct complicity and rapport with which a writer writes or a painter paints." In 1946 he began cowriting with Tullio Pinelli, and the two provided the screenplay for Fellini's directorial debut, *Variety Lights* (1950) followed by *The White Sheik* (1952), both starring Giulietta Masina. Neither film fared well with the critics, although historical reconsideration has been more favorable. *The White Sheik* was notable also for Nino Rota's score, the first of a long and happy collaboration that provided some of the finest film music ever written.

With *La strada* (1954) there could be no argument from the critics. It is arguably Fellini's masterpiece and may well have a staying power that will overshadow the more controversial *La dolce vita* (1960) and *8½* (1963). The movie's tragic and moving story is simply filmed. For Fellini, it was "the story of a man who discovers himself." And while Gelsomina was his favorite of all his characters, it was Zampano with whom he most clearly identified.

This closeness is doubly interesting because Masina achieved her greatest fame for her remarkable portrayal of Gelsomina. It may well be that Fellini's fear of losing himself by losing her is what kept him allied to her in their marriage. A friend once stated that Fellini's courage was expressed on the screen. In his personal life he took few risks. It was an attraction to and perhaps romantic sentimentality toward bourgeois life that anchored Fellini. Through movies he explored his bohemian yearnings and wanderings, his fantasies and confusions. It is true that he had affairs and that Masina could not provide the excitement and glamor he craved. But he feared that if he lost her he would lose his center, and so he remained in the marriage.

By the time of *La dolce vita* and *8½*, Fellini had moved into a surrealist mode. Shot within theatrical sets, they portrayed the reality of life within a circuslike atmosphere. Many were scandalized by *La dolce vita* for its portrayal of the empty promiscuity of café society. At its opening one outraged well-to-do viewer spat in Fellini's face. (The name of Paparazzo, the photographer portrayed in the movie, would become part of a world vocabulary for a detestable group.) *8½* focused on a filmmaker's block in creating a new movie. In it is the marvelous scene where the director acts as ringmaster trying to bring sense and order to the circling characters of his life. In *Amarcord* (1973) Fellini revisits his youth and some of these same characters with great affection and humor. Life is a circus, portrayed and accepted for its vast comic and cosmic absurdity.

Fellini was a large man who ruled the movie set by force of his outgoing personality. Wearing a wide-brimmed black hat, he waved his hands and arms about as he joked, cajoled, and clowned in an effort to get the performances he wanted. He had little use for interpretation, scoffed at references to books and movies he had not read or seen, and declared interpretation to be a crutch of the intellectual. He was the ringmaster, affectionate and demanding, taking the characters of his life and imagination and transporting them onto the screen for our pleasure, inspiration, and bemusement.

Fellini died in his beloved Rome after a stroke and a heart attack.

GIULIETTA MASINA *b. February 22, 1921, San Giorgio di Piano; d. March 23, 1994, Rome.* Fellini's wife of fifty years died of cancer less than five months after her husband passed away. Starring in Fellini's first two films, she reached the pinnacle of her success as Gelsomina in *La strada.* The role fit her waiflike appearance. Indeed, Fellini referred to her as Lo Sippolo (Lovable Little Waif).

Masina also starred in Fellini's *Nights of Cabiria* (1957) and *Juliet of the Spirits* (1965). The latter movie focused on a woman's hallucinatory reactions to the pending dissolution of her marriage after she discovers her husband's infidelities. For some, the movie was based on Fellini and Masina's own marriage. But whatever their difficulties, they remained together. She often acted as a buffer against a public intruding on Fellini's private life. And she was available to play muse and critic for his various ideas and inspirations. Masina retired from the screen for twenty years, returning for her last Fellini role in *Ginger and Fred* (1986).

As you are leaving, notice the interesting old Egyptian structure across the way, and, on the main path, the modern mausoleum of Zelio Zanni with its elongated Christ. He is remembered as the "Inventor and installer of the votive lamps of this cemetery."

DIRECTIONS AND HOURS: The Civic Cemetery is located outside Rimini on the road from Ravenna. Look for the Bar Romani on Via Popilia and park on that street. The cemetery is open daily 8:00 A.M. to 1:00 P.M. and 3:00 to 5:00 P.M.

NORTHERNERS
Milan, Arqua Petrarca, and Padua

▲   ▲   ▲

Walking up the wide steps of Milan's Cimitero Monumentale, you could shout for joy at the beauty of the sculpture around you. To your left is a life-sized mason, *constructore* **Enrico Pogliani** (d. 1857), reclining uncomfortably on the bricks of his trade. Nearby are the **Redaellis**, first shown as young and gloriously nude, then in the modesty of old age, Elvira's thick braid now a scanty bun. Their inscription puts them "in the hands of God." Outside on the right is the monument of Dr. **Pietro Lazzati** (d. 1871), which shows him delivering a baby and binding up a soldier's leg as if planning to amputate it.

The Famedio, the sheltered hall at the top of the steps, honors some of Italy's famous sons. **Alessandro Manzoni's** (1785–1873) stone sarcophagus stands in the center of the room under a domed ceiling of gold stars sprinkled against deep blue. On two sides of his tomb angels in dark bas-relief bless his cameo or a cross; on the ends one angel writes in a book while the other strums a lute.

Giuseppe Verdi loved Manzoni, and wrote a *Requiem Mass* in his honor. The Scapigliatura (Disheveled Artists) hated him, deriding him as "a statue that is still standing . . . without any value in the new literary or poetic climate." Even Edgar Allan Poe had an opinion, praising *I promessi sposi* as "a work which promises to be a new style in novel-writing," though he doubted that it was completely original. Still, on the basis of that one novel, rewritten three times, Manzoni was called the Charles Dickens, the Leo Tolstoy, the Sir Walter Scott of Italy.

The first version of *I promessi sposi* (The Betrothed) was published in 1827. Its 600 pages tell the story of two villagers, Renzo and Lucia, who are engaged but prevented from marrying by the powerful Don Rodrigo. Lucia takes asylum in a convent but is abducted by the don and must be rescued by Cardinal Borromeo. Renzo goes to Milan and becomes involved in 17th-century famine, war, and the plague. Despite such obstacles, the pair at last marry. Manzoni's underlying theme is God's hidden hand in human life.

In the corner of the Famedio is a larger-than-life **Carlo Cattaneo** (1801–1869), looking very serious. Exiled to Switzerland for leading the 1848 revolt in Milan against Austria, Cattaneo believed that it was the philosopher's duty to take a hands-on role in solving society's problems.

Back in the opposite corner is the head and collar of another exile, **Giuseppe Mazzini** (1805–1872). A true hero of Italy, it was as a student in Genoa that Mazzini first embraced the idea of a united Italian republic. He joined a secret revolutionary group, the Carbonari, but was betrayed in 1830, jailed, then exiled to Marseilles. He continued to plot and in 1834 was condemned to death in absentia. Working tirelessly for Italian reunification from outside the country, he returned for a brief triumph as one of the ruling triumvirate of the Roman republic; unfortunately the republic only lasted from February to July of 1849. Escaping to London, he continued his agitation and wrote extensively on philosophy, politics, and literature. Shortly before his death Mazzini retired to Pisa.

Next to the entrance gates is a very human-looking Verdi. His bemused expression and the rumpled scarf wrapped around what appears to be a brass-buttoned pea jacket give him the look of an old sea captain trying to get a fix on tomorrow's weather. Unlike the others, Verdi's remains are no longer here. After a month-long stay, he was buried at the Casa di Riposa per Musicisti in Milan, a home for elderly indigent musicians he had endowed.

GIUSEPPE VERDI *b. October 11, 1813, Roncole; d. January 27, 1901, Milan.* A photograph of Giuseppe Verdi's 10-person household staff is oddly revealing. The five men and five women look sullenly away from the camera, as grim as characters in *La traviata*. It is not what one might expect. Surely, working for a national celebrity could not have been *that* bad.

But life seemed to conspire to keep Verdi himself off-balance. His beloved only sister, Giuseppa, died at 17. His patron, Antonio Barezzi, paid for Verdi to go off to the

Milan Conservatory, but when the small, pockmarked teenager arrived, scores in hand, he was not admitted. His piano playing was judged inferior, and he was considered "too old." Instead, he signed on with a series of private teachers with the expectation that he would take over the position of music director in his hometown. It was a modest enough hope, but the Busetto Philharmonic and the conservative clerical faction began dueling, and Verdi was caught in the crossfire. He was finally appointed in 1836, after a delay that had to be considered insulting.

Quickly he married his patron's daughter, Margherita, and wrote his first produced opera, *Oberto* (1838). Then, between August 1838 and June 1840, his baby daughter, his son, and finally Margherita herself were carried away by illness, his family reduced to a few mementos in a small copper box. Grief-stricken, Verdi finished the opera for which he was under contract, a weak farce called *Un giorno di regno* (King for a Day, 1841). It was greeted by jeers and catcalls at its premiere.

That final blow made him give up music forever. But forever, in this case, lasted less than a year. The director

CIMITERO MONUMENTALE

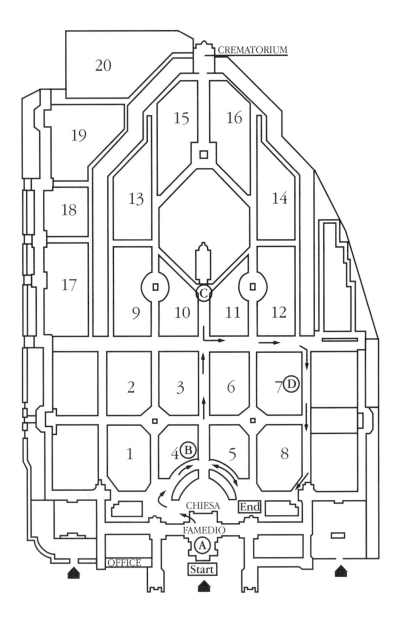

A Alessandro Manzoni
   Giuseppe Mazzini
   Giuseppe Verdi
   Salvatore Quasimodo

B Pasquale Crespi
C Dina Galli
D Arturo Toscanini
   Vladimir Horowitz

of La Scala pressed the libretto of *Nabucco* (Nebuchadnezzar) on him, and the opera premiered in March 1842. The plight of the captured Israelites in Babylon mirrored that of Italians straining under Austrian rule, and the chorus, "Va, pensiero," became a national anthem, bringing Verdi instant fame.

For the next 10 years he fought bouts of malaise with work, writing 16 operas, including *Rigoletto, Il trovatore*, and *La traviata*. He insisted that he wrote because he found the word *millionaire* to have a "full, lovely meaning," compared to "empty" words like *talent, glory*, and *fame*. During this time he formed a relationship with soprano Giuseppina Strepponi, a young woman who had strained her voice through overuse and damaged her health by constant pregnancies. At least four times she had left behind infants at the local charity hospital or given them to other people to raise. She and Verdi did not marry until 1859, well past her childbearing years.

Long before that, angered by his parents' rejection of his paramour, Verdi "divorced" them. Separation papers were drawn up; he would provide them with a horse, a house, and an allowance, but they would otherwise go their separate ways. He remained close to his former father-in-law and patron, Antonio Barezzi, instead.

Strepponi bore the worst of Verdi's moods, delighted when he appeared happy, cast down when he was brusque. She often came to the defense of the servants who were the victims of his tirades over offenses as small as forgetting to close a window. When he traveled, he threatened to fire them if they so much as left the premises of the estate. Small wonder that they would not smile for the camera.

If Verdi's moods were often grim, a full range of emotion infused his music. Its blackness was absolute, but its ecstasy cascaded in explosions of beauty. Reviewers reproved him for the melodrama of the librettos he chose, but his audiences loved every hair-raising moment. After *Aïda*, written in 1871 for the opening of the Suez Canal, and the *Requiem Mass* (1874), written in Alessandro Manzoni's honor, Verdi capped his career with *Otello* (1887) and *Falstaff* (1893).

A stroke in 1901 ended his love-hate relationship with the world; one of his final salvos was to refuse the Milan Conservatory's request to name itself after him.

Finally, on the wall near the entrance is a coffin-sized marble plaque giving only the dates for poet **Salvatore Quasimodo** (1901–1968). The modesty of the memorial seems to verify the assessment of his young mistress, Annamaria Angioletti, that "his own country until the time of his death, and even on that occasion, showed him hostility, envy or malice."

When Quasimodo was awarded the Nobel Prize in 1959, the sentiment at home was that the prize should have gone to one of Italy's two older poets, Eugenio Montale or Giuseppe Ungaretti. But Quasimodo had moved from the evocative language of the French symbolists to the more committed stance of social awareness; it appears that this involvement was what was being rewarded by the Nobel Committee. In the award they praised his poetry "which with classical fire expresses the tragic experience of life in our time."

When you are done in the Famedio, stop for a moment on the back porch before going down into the cemetery, so you can appreciate how large the monuments actually are. A cemetery employee riding on a bicycle seems dwarfed by the marble scenes frozen above his head. For over a century this has been the final resting place for Milan's elite.

As you come down the stairs and move to the left of the semicircle, you will see that what looked like an abstract bird at a distance is actually dark angels, rising and falling in contemplation of the deceased members of the **Bonelli** family. Across the way, and more modest, is a chillingly beautiful young World War I soldier, **Luigi Fossati**, his cleated boots and cloth-wrapped legs sprawling as if he has just fallen in battle a moment before.

There are also surprises. The huge stone woman in mourning on the **Pasquale Crespi** monument appears suitably conventional, but walk around to the back and you will find a grinning baby Bacchus impishly lifting one leg. Below him the door leading into the crypt is dominated by the twisted metal shape of a bat.

Stop for a look at the monuments on the second half of the semicircle—there is a wonderful boy angel in elongated style—then go back and walk down the center path. It is the lifelike details that make many of these monuments so compelling.

On the right, behind a touching couple of World War II vintage, is a striking, almost shocking tableau of one man tugging at a pair of recalcitrant oxen while another equally frail figure guides a plow behind them. Over the scene broods the huge brownstone face of a woman. It is depressing, yet the nose of the nearer ox shines a bright,

unexpected brass, since passersby cannot resist patting the naughty beast.

Across the way, on your left, is a bearded Grim Reaper with the largest scythe imaginable. But it does not help; eyes downcast, he does not appear to be enjoying his work. Farther up there is the dark metal statue of a charming, laughing boy who looks as if he was caught mid-anecdote. It is a face, an expression, that packs an emotional charge, which many sorrowing maidens do not.

Almost to the Ossario Centrale there are three figures half-crouched, almost running. The configuration bears a resemblance to the photograph "Raising the Flag at Iwo Jima," but instead they are carrying tools, a hammer and a shovel.

At the foot of the Ossario is the unforgettable green-bronze statue of **Dina Galli** (d. 1951) holding up a Puck's face and covering her own. Born in Milan, Galli formed theatrical companies here and in Venice. Although she announced her retirement from the stage in 1926, she continued to act for several more years.

Cross the road and turn right at the amazing woman flying upward against the glass of the **Polli** monument. Soon you will come to the small elegant mausoleum of Arturo Toscanini on your right. Women in deliberately shallow granite relief decorate its four sides; the most interesting is holding a toy soldier on a horse with wheels.

ARTURO TOSCANINI *b. March 25, 1867, Parma; d. January 16, 1957, New York.* For a good part of his adult life

Arturo Toscanini was idolized, cajoled, and pampered. His friends often displayed great obsequiousness so that the world's most celebrated conductor would continue to honor them with his presence. The old man thrived on it and controlled those social occasions as he controlled his orchestras. One came to listen, to receive, but not always to enter into dialogue. On one famous occasion he even bullied his host into coercing the host's young son to give him his toy magnets. For his own children he was gruff, controlling, and unavailable. And for Carla, his wife, although they achieved compatibility in later years, there were the adoring women and the many ill-concealed affairs.

But oddly, behind the autocratic facade there appeared to be genuine humility and a true lack of pretense. He did not indulge in self-promotion, and he abhorred theatricality. His podium gestures ranged from a biting slash of the baton to the most tender caress of his hand, but he was unaware of these gestures. They were simply an outgrowth of the music.

Toscanini's dedication and immersion in music were

total. He *was* one of this century's greatest conductors. Unlike fellow conductors such as Bruno Walter or Wilhelm Furtwängler, who had wide-ranging interests, Toscanini was far more limited in scope—he knew and studied poetry but music was his world. He believed in the sacredness of the printed score. Tempi and dynamics were meant to be followed, not contorted to the whims of the maestro. As to the first movement of Beethoven's *Eroica*, he asserted, "To some it is Napoleon, to some it is Alexander the Great, to some it is philosophical struggle; to me it is Allegro con brio."

Toscanini's father was a tailor of vaporous ambition who preferred living in the glory of his fighting days with Garibaldi. His mother was an unsmiling martinet by whom Toscanini had no memory of ever being kissed. The family was respectable but poor. Recognizing Toscanini's talent, his second-grade teacher, Signora Vernoni, pled with his parents to send him to the Parma Conservatory. The money was somehow found, and Toscanini spent nine years studying cello, earning the nickname "the Little Genius," and, at 16, passing his final exams with the highest possible marks.

Three years later, playing in an orchestra in Rio de Janeiro, his fabled memory quickly helped him make the transition from the pit to the podium. During a crisis wherein the conductor resigned and the assistants proved to be inept, Toscanini was urged by his fellow orchestra members to step up and save the performance. It was *Aïda*, and he did it from memory. Returning to Italy, he conducted second- and third-rate orchestras, concentrating on opera. His rise was meteoric. Before he was 30 he had led the world premieres of *Pagliacci* and *La bohème*, had taken over at La Scala, and was earning international notice for his conducting of Wagner's operas. In 1901 it was he who conducted at Verdi's funeral.

By 1908 he was with the Metropolitan Opera in New York. Arriving with much fanfare, he quickly obtained the adoration of the critics and the public. Stories of his memory grew, like Pinocchio's nose, to prodigious lengths. He knew by heart 60 operas, then 100, and finally 160. Of no exaggeration was his insistence on total control and his volcanic tantrums. He demanded his players and soloists subserve totally to one vision, to one personality: his. No one slid by. Performers now practiced, memorized, and thought. New levels of excellence were required, and no one wanted to be subjected to that temper. Many performers were grateful for being pushed. Some resented it. Excellence and fidelity. But not inflexibility. Turning off an aggravating metronome, he exploded, "Bah! One is not a machine. Music must breathe."

He was a staunch antifascist whose populist, democratic beliefs further ingratiated him to the public. On the podium, though, he was an autocrat. He cut through the heavy, lugubrious Wagnerian veil that choked so many interpretations of his day.

Toscanini's fame crested with the formulation of the NBC Symphony Orchestra in 1937. The orchestra was handpicked for him. The recordings and broadcasts from studio 8H became legendary. And here Toscanini was used. He was made an icon of advertising, apotheosized for the profit line of NBC.

There exist wonderful photographs of Toscanini conducting, intense and scowling, his face lined with fierce concentration. How sad the end, then, when in 1954 during his last performance, conducting the Bacchanale from *Tannhäuser*, his fabled memory failed him. His beat wavered on the brink of dissolution, and the orchestra followed. The radio engineers panicked and switched to the maestro's recording of Brahms's *First Symphony*. Toscanini recovered, and *Tannhäuser* returned to the auditorium and the airwaves. At the end the Old Man walked offstage, not returning for bows or encores. His career was over and, three years later, his life as well.

This cemetery is the resting place of not only Toscanini but his son-in-law, Vladimir Horowitz, as well.

VLADIMIR HOROWITZ *b. October 1, 1904, Kiev; d. November 11, 1989, New York.* Called "the Tornado from the Steppes," Vladimir Horowitz was, in terms of technique and presence, the most electrifying pianist of the 20th century. For sheer virtuosity, he has been likened to Franz Liszt, whose fabled temperament and abilities towered above the history of 19th-century keyboard performers. Horowitz played Scarlatti with the evenness of strung pearls, Schumann with flowing simplicity, and Rachmaninoff with thunderous power. His tone, aided by slightly sharp tuning, was brilliant, bronze, and orchestral.

He was also a showman. His ability to wow the public was not lost on him. The showstoppers came at the end of recitals, guaranteed to ignite an impassioned audience of adoring fans, fans who waited on line up to two days for tickets for his return to the stage in 1965.

Horowitz's mother, uncle, and sister all displayed musical talent. Obviously gifted but not a prodigy, Horowitz graduated from the Kiev Conservatory at 16. He played recitals with a fellow conservatory graduate, Nathan Milstein, the soon-to-be great violinist, but fame eluded him until he performed as a last-minute fill-in with the Hamburg Philharmonic in 1926. Playing the Tchaikovsky B Flat Minor Concerto, he stunned and then roused the audience to a fevered ovation which erupted before the performance's end. The piano "lay on the platform like a slain dragon" while, according to a German reviewer, Horowitz modestly smiled and bowed.

That reception did not go unnoticed. He was soon in demand the world over. With fame came contacts and with contacts came an introduction to Rachmaninoff, who became the young man's friend and mentor. A fabulous pianist himself, Rachmaninoff, playing a piano reduction of the orchestration, led Horowitz through the intricacies of his Third Piano Concerto, later a signature piece for Horowitz. Contacts also brought Wanda Toscanini before his eye, and they married in 1933. Horowitz's relationship with the Old Man was scarcely one of equals, for Toscanini intimidated and even, it is rumored, bullied him.

His constitution could not stand up to such public and private pressure. Ill, nervous, neurotic, and hypochondriac, Horowitz entered the first of three retirements, this one from 1936 to 1938. His abilities upon his return were undiminished. His fees and percentages (up to 80 percent) were enormous, but spending was no burden as he accumulated fancy clothes, elegant cars, and an art collection boasting fine examples of paintings by Picasso, Roualt, Modigliani, and Renoir.

By 1953 Horowitz was again retired. He and Wanda had been separated for four years, the marriage strained by Horowitz's homosexual flings, his fragile temperament when concertizing, and the emotional problems of their daughter, Sonia, a child to whom he was largely a chilly, nonapproving father. Her death in 1975 at age 40 was rumored to have been a suicide. Wanda grieved, but Horowitz seemed to experience the death more as relief from an emotional burden.

His Carnegie Hall recital in 1965 marked his triumphant return to the stage, but 1969 to 1974 measured yet another period of seclusion from the concert hall. With age came a diminished repertoire, increasing mannerisms that pulled and distorted the pieces he played, and, most fearful of all, memory lapses.

Although Horowitz was never known as an intellect or even as a great musician as opposed to a great performer, even his adoring public had to admit that their hero was slipping. But his legacy exists in his recordings and in several generations of younger pianists who tried to imitate his flash, his virtuosity, his tone. They failed of course, for they could not imitate his fire—the coiled energy that propelled his performances to levels far above mere technical display.

As you continue down the path, the amazing statuary continues. Just when you think you have had your fill of angels, you come across one in black granite who has butterfly wings growing out of her shoulder blades. The quote, from Dante's *Purgatorio*, translates as "We are worms, each one born to form the angelic butterfly, that flies defenseless to the Final Judge."

Nearer to the Famedio is a horrifying, skeletal pair of ghouls, heads shrouded, mouths gaping, cached in a beautiful group of plantings.

Unlike in many cemeteries where the most monuments are segregated in the older section, in the Monumentale you can wander anywhere and strike gold. On the way to the Crematorio, at the back of the cemetery, you will come across two heartrending monuments to the prevalence of early mortality. On the **Biraghi** tomb, against a backdrop of curling waves, tiny Jeanne in a ruffled dress is being led away from her mother by an angel. On the **Rozzi** monument the child is stretching out her arms to her mother, who, eyes shut, is in the cleft of a tree as if already becoming part of it.

Near the Crematorio you can find **Piera Rabitti** wistfully wearing her bridal gown, and the jaunty bust of **Edoardo Ciceri**, whose flat pancake cap and handlebar mustache echo the photograph of him on the front of his stone. There is also the fixture of every large cemetery, a pyramid complete with Sphinx and Egyptian maidens.

On your way out, detour to your right to see the statuary in the niches on the sheltered side of the building. The figures are almost too large and too heroic to be emotionally moving, but this is a sight you won't see in other cemeteries.

DIRECTIONS AND HOURS: The Cimitero Monumentale is located just off Via Carlo Farini, adjacent to Garibaldi Station. Nos. 29 and 30 buses stop directly in front of the cemetery. It is open 8:30 A.M. to 6:00 P.M. from April 1 to September 30, from 8:30 A.M. to 5:00 P.M. during the rest of the year, and is closed Mondays.

ARQUA PETRARCA

Arqua Petrarca is a delightful town in the hills outside Padua. It affords you the added pleasure of being able to visit Petrarch's home as well as his gravesite. Situated on the top of the mountain, the house has unbroken views of the countryside and is surrounded by a lush walled garden. Inside, the floors are tile, and the walls have fading frescoes of Grecian nudes, sailing ships, and bucolic country scenes. Petrarch's studio, on the upper floor, is furnished with only a rustic leather chair, a slatted wardrobe, and two built-in niches holding books.

The rest of the house is given over to various artists' interpretations of Petrarch and Laura, displays of his books in glass cases, and visitors' registers under glass. Lord Byron paid his respects on September 12, 1819, and the poet Giosue Carducci visited on July 18, 1874.

FRANCESCO PETRARCA *b. July 20, 1304, Arezzo, Tuscany; d. July 18, 1374, Arqua.* The most appealing thing about Petrarch is his natural lightheartedness. Living a no-

madic life after his father was exiled from Florence, the infant poet was almost drowned in the Arno; at seven he was shipwrecked outside Marseilles. His law studies ended in 1326 when his father's death and the dishonesty of the executors left Petrarch and his brother, Gheraldo, penniless. But instead of becoming bitter they concentrated on curling and perfuming their hair and stepping out in society. Petrarch had a gift for friendship, and closeness with other people brought out the best in him.

By 1332 he was writing poetry and had a patron, Cardinal Giovanni Colonna, from the wealthy Roman family. Thus sponsored, he toured France, Germany, and Switzerland, searching the libraries of monasteries for "lost" manuscripts in classical Latin and marveling at all he encountered. At 33, he retreated to a rustic farmhouse in Vaucluse, where he was to spend the next 15 years writing, studying Latin, and cultivating two small gardens. Yet he was not without ambition. He let influential friends know that he would like to be Rome's poet laureate. On Easter 1341 he was given Roman citizenry and a laurel wreath which he placed on the tomb of St. Peter.

It is difficult to date Petrarch's writing since he revised so extensively throughout his life, but two of his earliest works were an epic poem, *Africa*, about the Second Punic War, and *De viris illustribus*, which began as biographies of Roman heroes and later expanded to include illustrious religious figures back to Adam. He also began writing poems in Italian, a lifelong collection of *Rime,* many of them inspired by his love of "Laura."

Who Laura actually was remains a mystery. Some scholars have tentatively identified her as Laura de Noves, whom Petrarch met on Good Friday in 1327 at the Church of St. Clare in Avignon, but nothing else is known about her other than that she was married (to someone else) and died of the Black Death in 1348. Perhaps keeping Laura's identity a mystery was a deliberate decision on Petrarch's part. He was thus able to write about her universally and also have his way with her—at least in verse.

Even before Laura died, Petrarch, under the influence of the writings of St. Augustine decided that his attachment to her, albeit from a distance, was taking away from his spiritual development. This insight inspired two more works, *Secretum meum* (1342–1343), consisting of three dialogues between Augustine and himself with Truth as the moderator, and *De vita solitaria* (1346), which developed the joys of the solitary life with its triple consolations of study, nature, and prayer.

The religious life was always a concern. As a young man Petrarch had taken minor ecclesiastical orders and was supported by a stipend from the church. It kept him from marrying, though not from fathering a son and a daughter by an unknown mother. Giovanni (1337–1361) was a disappointment; Petrarch was closer to Francesca (b. 1343), who brought him special pleasure by bringing her husband and young family to live with him.

Before finally settling in Arqua in 1370, the poet moved around Milan, Padua, and Venice, often on the run from outbreaks of the plague. Venice gave him a house and a role in the life of that republic; in return, he promised to leave Venice all his books. An insult by four young men in 1367, however, caused him to pack up and move to Padua. Here he completed the *Trionfi*, a kind of Scissors, Paper, Rock game in structure. Carnal love triumphs over the human heart but falls before Chastity (Laura). Laura dies, but her Fame triumphs over Death; Fame is trumped by Time. In the last triumph, Eternity conquers Time, with Laura reappearing in heaven. Moving beyond medieval conventions, his poetry defined true emotion; by incorporating classic Greek and Platonic thought, he opened the door to let the Renaissance rush in.

Petrarch's death was as he might have wished. He died at work in his library, sitting at his desk, his head resting on a manuscript by Virgil.

After visiting Petrarch's house, retreat back down the hill to the landing with the village church. His plain monument stands in the courtyard with an epitaph he composed himself: "Frigida Francisci lapis hic tegit ossa Petrarca. Suscipe Virgo parens animam sate Virgine parce. Fessa & iam terris celi requiescat in arce." (This stone covers the cold bones of Francesco Petrarch. Virgin mother, lift up his spirit, son of a Virgin. And weary now of earth, let it rest in the peace of heaven.) Although initially buried in the parish church, his body was moved six years later to this sarcophagus by his son-in-law, Francesco da Brossano.

DIRECTIONS, HOURS, AND ADMISSION: Turn off Route 10 at the sign for Arqua Petrarca and climb the road to the village. You may want to park in the churchyard and walk the rest of the way, following the signs for his house. The hours are 9:30 A.M. to 12:30 P.M. and 3:00 to 6:00 P.M., but there is the sense that, unlike everything else here, they are not carved in stone. Admission is L 6,000.

PADUA

The cobbled streets of Padua are alive with pilgrims buying statuettes of St. Anthony, drinking cappuccino in cafés, and being photographed with pigeons on their heads. Yet there is a sense of reverence on entering the Basilica of Sant'Antonio, a feeling that many of the visitors have come on a spiritual mission. Since its completion in 1263, the basilica has attracted pilgrims, but over time the building has evolved from a simple church to a complex with eight domes, two bell towers, and two minarets.

As you enter the basilica, turn and look at the wall behind you. There is a monument to Father **Antonio Trambetta** (1436–1517), who taught philosophy and theology at the University of Padua. During his long lifetime he also held posts as the bishop of Urbino and archbishop of Athens. Trambetta's bust is surrounded by designs made from books, an hourglass, and a globe.

Nearby on the left is a monument to a Venetian admiral, **Alessandro Contarini** (1486–1533), which has a bas-relief of sailing ships—perhaps representing his victory over the Turks at the Battle of Corfu.

Move down the right aisle to the first large chapel, which contains the bodies of **Erasmus da Narni** (d. 1443), better known by his battle name, Gattamelata (Calico Cat), and his son, **Giannantonio da Narni** (d. 1455). Two worshipers holding candelabra kneel on the steps of this elaborate memorial. The marble angels standing high on the altar are elevating a Monstrance (a metal case showing the Host). Captain Gattamelata, the son of a baker, was an energetic and brilliant military strategist who beat back the Milanese and captured Verona for the Venetians in 1440.

The same year he suffered an apoplectic stroke and re-tired to Padua.

Gattamelata can also be seen on horseback outside in the courtyard, in a statue by Donatello—the same statue whose head Donatello bashed in out of annoyance when the Venetians were pressuring him to finish the work.

The next major chapel, that of St. James, has frescoes by Altichiero da Zevio, dominated by a scene of the Cruci-fixion with eight dancing angels. The body of St. Felix is buried under the altar, but which of the 67 St. Felixes he might be is not exactly clear.

It is now time to move across the way and approach the Tomb of St. Anthony. Walk up the two marble steps and around to the back where you can actually touch the green marble of the sarcophagus. Attached to the tomb are many ex-votos, some in Sacred Heart shapes but oth-ers simply small framed photographs with dates and nota-tions. A number of them are of children, perhaps because St. Anthony is invoked to help cure infertility.

Although the chapel is ornate, the most interesting works of art are the nine marble high reliefs with scenes from St. Anthony's life, done by different artists. In the dome over the tomb is the inscription "Gaude felix Padua, quae thesaurum possides" (Rejoice, fortunate Padua, pos-sessor of this treasure).

ANTHONY OF PADUA (FERDINAND DE BULHOES) *b. 1195, Lisbon; d. June 13, 1231, Arcella.* For a saint who lived only 36 years, Anthony did not get an early start. As an Augustinian monk he still kept one foot in the world, until 1219 when he joined the Franciscans and was sent as a missionary to Morocco. He was willing to be martyred by Moors but fell ill instead and was sent home. When his ship was blown off course and landed in Sicily, he met with Francis of Assisi and was assigned to a hermitage near Forli.

It was quickly discovered that Anthony had a gift for preaching; his sermons were eloquent and passionate, grounded in scholarship as well as rhetoric. On one occa-sion in Rimini when the populace refused to listen to his message, he is said to have gone to the water and preached to the fish until they stood up on their tails to listen. Known as "the Hammer of Heretics," Anthony was particularly hard on false doctrines and worldly clergy.

The reliefs around the tomb illustrate some of his more famous miracles. In the *Miracle of the Believing Donkey*, by Donatello, a visitor to Rimini from Provence would not believe that Christ was present in the sacramental bread and wine, asserting that he would believe it only if his donkey knelt and worshiped them. The obliging animal did so immediately. In the *Miracle of the Irascible Son*, also by Donatello, Anthony replaced the limb of a young delinquent who had kicked his mother, then cut off his foot in remorse.

After 1226 Anthony settled in Padua, attacking corruption and wrongdoing in the city. As a Franciscan he advocated for the poor, working to abolish debtors' prisons and performing miracles. A novice who borrowed his prayer book without permission claimed he saw a "fearful apparition" and quickly returned the breviary, leading to the association of St. Anthony with the recovery of lost objects.

By 1231 he was suffering from dropsy, his zeal filmed over by weariness. He was sent to Camposanpietro to rest but died on the way back while staying at a Poor Clare convent. His body was returned to Padua. The following year Anthony was canonized, and in 1946 he was declared a doctor of the church. When his remains were uncovered and examined years after his death, the tongue that had preached such eloquent sermons was found by his exhumers to be "fresh and red."

Against the wall to the far right of St. Anthony is the startling tomb of **Pietro** (d. 1673) and **Domenico Marchetti** (d. 1688), done in 1690 by Giovanni Comini. At the top is a skeleton with angel's wings that is blowing a long, thin trumpet. Below are busts, cherubs, books, and attendants in a veritable marble wedding cake. The inscription, in Italian rather than Latin, reads, "La Fortuna divide troc uguali la gloria dei due chirurghi" (Fate divides all too equally the glory of these two surgeons).

You can complete your visit by going out to the cloisters, to the right of the main altar. In the first courtyard, on the wall to your right, is a small black plaque showing where the entrails of **Thomas Howard** (1586–1646) have been left behind. Howard, the earl of Arundel, is considered the first great English art collector. He collected a number of ancient Roman statues, which were later doznated to Oxford University and are known as the Arundel Marbles. Married to a goddaughter of Queen Elizabeth I, he maintained close ties with the court.

In the alcove to Howard's right is the oldest sarcophagus in the basilica, that of **Guido da Lozzo** (d. 1295) and his niece, **Constanza d'Este** (d. 1297). The monument shows two stylized plants flanking an eaglelike bird standing on a wreath.

In the second cloister is the memorial bust of **Giuseppe Tartini** (1692–1770). Here we see, bewigged and appropriately frilled, the composer and the greatest violinist of his day, holding his instrument of choice. The monument was actually executed in 1924 by Liugi Soressi.

Tartini wrote about 150 concertos and 200 violin sonatas, including the "Devil's Trill," which was inspired by a dream wherein the Devil himself played the piece for the composer. He was best known for redesigning the bow and for his *Treatise on Ornamentation* (ca. 1750), which significantly advanced bowing technique.

DIRECTIONS AND HOURS: If you are driving, follow the yellow signs for the basilica or the centro and leave your car in the parking area at Prato Della Valle. If you arrive by train, take the no. 3, 8, or 18 bus going to Riviera Businello. The basilica is open daily 6:30 A.M. to 7:00 P.M.

CHAPTER 14

VENICE
San Zanipolo and
Chiesa di San Lorenzo

▲   ▲   ▲

SANTI GIOVANNI E PAOLO
(SAN ZANIPOLO)

The Basilica of Saints Giovanni and Paolo is not named for the well-known New Testament figures, as you might expect, but for two brothers, John and Paul, who were martyred in Rome during the fourth century. Unfortunately, nothing else about them survives. The building of the basilica commenced around 1246 after Doge Jacopo Tiepolo convinced the Senate that he had had a dream about doves with gold crosses on their heads, talking angels, and a voice proclaiming, "This place I have chosen for my preachers"—referring to the Dominicans, whom Tiepolo hoped to anchor permanently in Venice.

Once built, the basilica was added to and subtracted from until 1806, when the Dominicans were brutally ejected under Napoleon and the building was turned into a military hospital. It was partially consumed by fire in 1867 (destroying paintings by Tintoretto, Bellini, and Titian) and bombed during World War I; the last restoration was not completed until 1959.

Legend asserts that the sheer size of San Zanipolo, as it is traditionally known, alarmed Venetian rulers, who felt that no church should be larger than the state chapel, San Marco. It was finally agreed that Zanipolo would become a political adjunct by hosting the funeral services of the doges. Twenty-five doges are buried here.

The elaborate system of electing a doge appears to have

Opposite: San Zanipolo

ZANIPOLO

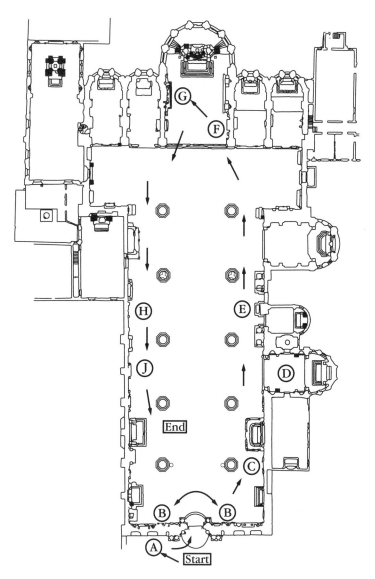

A Jacopo Tiepolo
B Mocenigo Family
C Marcantino Bragadin
D Giacomo Salomoni
E Valier Family

F Michele Morosini
G Andrea Vendramin
H Tommaso Mocenigo
J Nicolò Marcello

been imported from nearby Byzantium. According to novelist and travel writer Mary McCarthy, "Out of the Great Council . . . nine were picked by lot to elect 40 electors, who had to be chosen by a majority of at least 7. The forty drew lots to see which 12 would elect 25 more by a majority of at least 7. These twenty-five then drew lots to see which 9 would elect 45 by a majority of at least 7. Finally, these 45 drew lots to choose 11, who would vote for 41 electors, who would elect the doge by a majority of at least 25." A cynic might argue that the result would have been the same had the Great Council just voted en masse in the first place.

Before you enter San Zanipolo, stop and look under the pointed arches flanking the portal. The arch in the center contains the sarcophagus of **Jacopo Tiepolo** (d. 1249), the doge who dreamed the basilica into existence. With binoculars you can see the carved doves with crosses on their heads, and flowers. The two angels from the dream are on the sarcophagus. Jacopo's son, Doge **Lorenzo Tiepolo** (d. 1275), is in the sarcophagus to his right.

As you enter the church, turn around. The entire back wall is a monument to members of the Mocenigo family. The monument of Doge **Giovanni Mocenigo** (d. 1485), carved by Tullio Lombardo, shows him recumbent above a sarcophagus on which are low reliefs of towers; it has been suggested that these represent cities around the Po River conquered by the Venetians. From a distance the mannered carving of his robes gives the doge the look of a dirigible.

Despite his military victories, Giovanni's was a melancholy reign, overshadowed by the threat of national bankruptcy and war. Pope Sixtus IV had placed an interdict on the city, and, even worse, a candle left burning had destroyed part of the Doges' Palace and many priceless works of art.

The monument to **Pietro Mocenigo** (d. 1476), the work of Pietro Lombardo (Tullio's father), shows the doge standing in battle regalia, flanked by an honor guard of Roman soldiers. The three warriors holding up his tomb represent youth, middle age, and old age. On the sarcophagus itself are bas-reliefs of Pietro's victory over the Turks in Scutari and Famagusta. Demonstrating the Venetian preoccupation with money as well as war, there is the statement "*Ex hostium manibus*"—assuring the viewer that the tomb was fully paid for by the spoils from Turkey. When Mocenigo died, it was suggested that he had been worn out by another kind of spoils: the 10 beautiful Turkish concubines he had brought home with him.

Against the right wall is the bust of **Marcantonio Bragadin** (d. 1571), one of the city's most glorious warriors, who spent two years attempting to defend Venetian forces on Cyprus against the Turks. The Venetians finally surrendered and were given surprisingly humane terms, which included safe passage out of the area and any assistance they might require. The victorious general, Pasha Mustafa, even sent a letter complimenting Bragadin and his commander in chief, Astorre Baglioni, on their courage.

Thinking to return the favor, Bragadin proposed to meet with Mustafa and turn over the keys to the city. But during the evening the mood turned shockingly ugly. Whipping out a knife, Mustafa cut off Bragadin's nose and ears and ordered his guards to behead Baglioni. Any Christians within reach were fair game, and the death toll leaped to 350. Held in prison for nearly two weeks, his wounds festering, Bragadin was tortured and, maintaining a stoic silence through it all, died while being skinned alive. His skin was then tanned, stuffed with straw, and paraded through the streets.

In 1580 the skin was retrieved from the Arsenal of Constantinople and eventually placed here in a lead casket behind his somber bust. A group of scholars led by one of Bragadin's descendants, Maria Grazia Siliato, opened the casket in 1961 and found several pieces of tanned human skin inside.

In the next chapel is the startling sight of the mortal

remains of **Giacomo Salomoni** (1231–1314) in a glass coffin. Salomoni entered the convent next door when he was 17. Later, he was beatified for his work with the poor and the sick.

Outside the chapel on the wall is the massive monument of the Valier family, showing Doge **Bertucci Valier** (1597–1658) in the center, his son, Doge **Silvestro Valier** (d. 1700), on the left, and Silvestro's wife, **Elisabetta Querini** (d. 1708), on the right. They are standing in front of a large marble curtain, their hands outstretched as if taking a final bow. Bertucci Valier, though young for a doge when he was elected at 59, soon became an invalid and died within two years. His son Silvestro, more energetic and capable, had a longer run of six years but died of apoplexy after an argument with his wife. Perhaps remorse prompted her to commission this grand memorial from Andrea Tirali.

Timid visitors may be shocked to come upon the foot of St. Catherine of Siena outside the next chapel. It looks small and desiccated, displayed inside an ornate gold and glass reliquary. Her body is buried in Santa Maria sopra Minerva in Rome.

At this point you may be feeling doged out. But take a moment to look at two more monuments in the apse. The one of Doge **Michele Morosini** (d. 1382) has a lovely mosaic background. It is speculated that the scrupulous and capable Morosini would have made an excellent ruler had he not died of the plague four months after taking office. Worse, he has been maligned by one misquoted word. The wealthy Morosini bought up property during one of the city's worst financial crises to help keep up values and restore confidence. When asked why, he replied, "If this land comes to grief, I do not wish to prosper." Sanudo's *Lives of the Doges* (c. 1508) has him answering, ". . . I wish to do well out of it."

The tomb of Doge **Andrea Vendramin** (d. 1478) is wonderfully detailed. With his incredibly homely nose and pouchy cheeks, Vendramin resembles someone you might meet in any bar. His warriors are also interesting for their armor, which includes the lions of Venice and tiny, lifelike heads of the Roman emperors.

Along the left wall are the final collection of doges, two of them particularly noteworthy. The tomb of Doge **Tommaso Mocenigo** (1343–1423) is important because of the man himself. The monument, with its 16 attendant statues of saints and personified virtues, has a Gothic look that carries over to the doge's elongated features. On his deathbed Mocenigo summed up his nine-year rule by pointing out that he had reduced the national debt, increased Venice's trade surplus, and set the population on the road to prosperity—achievements that any current politician would be happy to emulate.

The nearby monument to Doge **Nicolò Marcello** (d. 1474), created by Pietro Lombardo, has a simpler, softer look, perhaps because it is home to the four feminine cardinal virtues. Marcello reigned for just a year.

Within the walls of an adjoining building, the Scuola of St. Orsola where the Dominican fathers still live, are buried **Gentile Bellini** (1429–1507) and **Giovanni Bellini** (1430–1516). There is not even a small marker to commemorate these artistic brothers.

For nearly 100 years there was a Bellini bringing glory to Venice. The patriarch, Jacopo, was also the father-in-law of painter Andrea Mantegna. Unfortunately, except for two books of his vivid drawings in the British Museum and the Louvre, most of Jacopo's work has disappeared. Thus his most important legacy is his sons.

Gentile Bellini was primarily concerned with the outward spectacle, with costumes and architectural details rather than psychological depth or the physics of motion. Nevertheless, his paintings have real charm. In the *Miracle of the True Cross*, now in the Accademia, a reliquary falls into a Venetian canal during a religious procession and a monk dives in to retrieve it. As art critic John Canaday describes it, buoyed up by the heavy golden casket "the happy monk . . . seems less the subject of divine intervention than a water sportsman enjoying a spin with a new form of outboard motor." Eminent Venetians of the day look on in appreciation.

At 50, Gentile was loaned to the sultan's court at Constantinople, where he created art and collected anecdotes. On one occasion he showed Sultan Mahomet II a painting of the beheaded John the Baptist. The sultan, finding it unrealistic, called in two slaves, one a swordsman. "This," he said a moment later, "is how a freshly severed head should look!" Gentile did not stay in Constantinople.

Giovanni Bellini, the most talented of the trio, is also the most mysterious. There is confusion surrounding his birth; documents indicate he was illegitimate, either because his parents were not yet married or because his father brought him into the family by adoption. There is also a mystery about his painting materials; he was involved in the changeover from tempera to oil paint, learning much about oils from Sicilian Antonello da Messina, whom he greatly admired. But he also used glazes, making exact identification of his medium difficult.

His poetic paintings increasingly reflect the soft sea light of Venice. Giovanni's early work is muted, full of emotion. In *Madonna and Child* (ca. 1465–1470) Mary looks down sadly on her recumbent, sleeping baby as if she knew how the story would end. As the artist matured, his work showed more warmth, color, and a rich and fluid atmosphere; a certain earlier poignancy gave way to a sense of well-being. *St. Francis in Ecstasy* (ca. 1485) shows a sunlit day and a calm countryside; the saint himself, arms spread, appears ready to burst into song.

Appointed the official painter of the Venetian republic in 1483, Giovanni was responsible for painting the doges' portraits and creating numerous altarpieces and votive works. Many of his best works were interpretations of Mary and Baby Jesus, such as *The Madonna with the Greek Inscription* (ca. 1470) and *The Madonna of the Trees* (1487). Although his most famous students, Giorgione and Titian, were continuing the tradition of his

sumptuous colors and fluid landscapes, in his eighties the master was still going strong. Two secular works, *Venus with Mirror* (1515) and *Feast of the Gods* (1514–1516), were his final gift.

DIRECTIONS AND HOURS: Take a no. 23 or 52 vaporetto to the Fondamente Nuova stop and make your way along the Rio del Mendicanti until you reach the basilica. It is open 8:30 A.M. to noon and 3:00 to 6:00 P.M.

SAN LORENZO

Nearby is a small church worthy of mention. San Lorenzo is important if only because it managed to lose the sarcophagus of its only notable burial, Marco Polo, when the church was rebuilt in 1592. Looking more like a warehouse than a church, it has an unfinished facade that is not one of the architectural glories of Venice. San Lorenzo is open only at odd times.

MARCO POLO *b. 1254, Venice; d. 1324, Venice.* Let us get it out of the way at the start. Marco Polo did not present pasta to Italy. What he did introduce was a wonderful travel book containing numerous accounts of lives, customs, and legends of exotic, faraway people and places. Indeed, to his readers his tales seemed so tall and outlandish that many doubted his credibility. *The Travels of Marco Polo* is a tribute to what must have been a photographic memory, for the details are rich and visual and were retained over the 24 years that he was away.

Yes, there are exaggerations. Marco was prone to superlative enthusiasms that overspiced his descriptions into blandness: "silken fabrics and cloth-of-gold . . . the finest ever seen," "the best goshawks in the world," "the best falcons in the world." An excusable trait in a parochial youth whose eyes were wide with wonder and excitement, but suspicious in the seasoned traveler. His accounts had an element of hucksterism, of self-promotion.

But it is a benign element, and he can be excused. For how many others had risked their lives in such travel, had spent 24 years away from home, and had become the honored guest of the great Kublai Khan? The trip was a response to the recent journey that Marco's father and uncle, Niccolò and Maffeo, had just completed. Traveling in the 1260s, they had reached the court of Kublai Khan. Before returning from that rotund, intellectually curious, enlightened despot, they were charged by him to come back with 100 learned Christians and a quantity of the oil that burned in the Church of the Holy Sepulchre in Jerusalem, for the khan wanted proof of the efficacy of the Christian faith.

The khan was more than just an exotic emperor, for the Tartars had conquered west to Poland, Germany, Persia, and Syria, and east to China, Korea, and down to Hanoi. Pope Alexander IV had issued a panicked warning, but where he saw apocalypse, evangelists and merchants saw fertile new territory. So in 1271, with Marco now 17, the three Polos set out for Karakorum carrying the holy oil and accompanied by just two learned brothers, directly appointed by the pope. Fearing the warring Mamluks more than papal wrath, these brothers deserted before the party left Syria.

Avoiding the Mamluks and bandits, the Polos made their way through Persia and central Asia, across the Gobi Desert, and on to Shang-tu, Cathay, the summer home of the great khan. Prostrating themselves, they were greeted as honored guests. The journey had taken three and a half years. They did not know they would remain another eighteen.

Marco became a favorite of the khan, who assigned him to be in charge of trips to Indonesia and also to India (where, as ordered, he purchased the teeth and begging bowl of Buddha). Upon his return, the admiring Marco entertained the khan with stories of his travels. Intelligent and observant though he was, he was naive, even gullible. He truthfully related that he saw fireproof cloth (made from asbestos) but also told stories of griffin-birds of the Indian islands which carried elephants high aloft in their talons and dropped them as a seagull does a clam in order to open it.

The Polos were not recognized immediately upon their return in 1295. Taken for strangely dressed beggars, they had to shake jewels and gold from their robes to gain credence. They had brought with them wealth and thus fame. Marco's book had to wait until he was captured by the Genoese in a naval battle. During his brief stay in a Genoese jail he was visited by a Pisan, Rustichello, who collaborated with Marco to write his book. It was published in 1299.

Little else is known about the remainder of his life other than that he married and had three daughters. His deathbed scene is a most fitting apocrypha. Urged by friends to recant his most blatant tall tales lest he die a sinner in the eyes of God, Marco whispered with exaggerated truth, "I never told the half of what I saw."

DIRECTIONS: Take the no. 14 vaporetto to the Riva degli Schiavoni stop and make your way back to San Lorenzo.

VENICE
The Frari, Madonna dell'Orto, and St. Lio

▲ ▲ ▲

THE FRARI

In keeping with its beginnings as a church built by followers of St. Francis, the Frari is of simple brown brick with a ground-level entrance. Named after the Fra[ti Mino]ri, the building was begun in 1330 and finished sometime after 1443. Given its humble intentions, you may be surprised to enter and find yourself in the midst of massive and ornate tombs, each group of mourners involved in its own private drama.

Inside and to the right hangs the *Pesaro Madonna* by Titian. In one of those odd juxtapositions of time that Renaissance artists enjoyed, the painting is of **Jacopo Pesaro** being presented by St. Peter to Mary and the Baby Jesus. Behind Pesaro, wearing a turban, is one of the prisoners he took in a battle against the Turks in 1503, a struggle in which he commanded 20 papal galleys. Pesaro, who later became a bishop, commissioned brothers Tullio and Antonio Lombardo to sculpt his funeral monument. It shows him reclining on his sarcophagus.

A descendant is commemorated in the next chapel. The monument to Doge **Giovanni Pesaro** (1589–1659) has everything you would want in a baroque tomb: writhing monsters, skeletons, Moors as support columns, figures representing the virtues. The doge himself is "in the act of haranguing the crowds," according to the basilica guidebook. Unfortunately, he did not get a chance to harangue them very long, dying 17 months after his election.

Opposite: The Frari

ANTONIO CANOVA *b. 1757; d. 1822.* Next door, the monument to sculptor Canova is simple by comparison, a design that he actually created to commemorate Titian, but which was never built. Against a huge pyramid, two angels hold up Canova's cameo. The figures of Sculpture, Painting, and Architecture mourn the artist, joined by an unhappy Lion of Venice and a winged figure representing Canova's genius. The children with torches are there to demonstrate that the light of art is never extinguished.

The remains of Antonio Canova are spread all over Italy. The hand that sculpted the marble is in the Accademia, his body is buried in a church in Possagno, and his heart is here in the Frari. This scrambling for relics is more understandable when you realize that he was considered the greatest sculptor of his time. In defiance of Austrian edicts against displays of Italian nationalism he was given the patriotic funeral of a hero.

Canova was born in the Venetian outpost of Possagno. By the time he was five, his father had died and his mother had remarried and moved away, leaving him in the care of his stonecutter grandfather. He was apprenticed to a garden statue workshop in Venice and, with his grandfather's help, established his own studio at the age of 18. The sale of his first notable work, *Daedalus and Icarus* (1777–1779), financed a trip to Rome. Thus exposed to antiquity, Canova moved from the baroque to neoclassicism.

After he successfully completed the tombs of Pope Clement XIV in Santi Apostoli and Pope Clement XIII in St. Peter's, he received commissions from all over the world. The work that resulted ranged from magnificent,

such as the tomb of Maria Cristina in Austria, to questionable, such as the statue of George Washington made for the capitol at Raleigh, North Carolina. First portrayed in the nude, then more modestly as a Roman senator, Washington's likeness was mercifully destroyed by fire shortly after its installation.

Perhaps because of the abandonments of his early years, Canova poured his emotional energy into his work. He supported a younger half brother who complained loudly of Canova's generosity to various charities, but he otherwise lived with austere simplicity, making his art his life. It was his art that finally killed him. Years of pressing a running drill against the marble with his chest had greatly deformed his ribs, leading to severe abdominal pain, then death.

Directly across from Canova is the monument to Titian. His wish to be buried at the foot of this altar was granted despite the fact that he was a plague victim, but it took nearly 300 years for him to have a proper memorial. Luigi Zandomeneghi and other disciples of Canova created this ambitious confection. Titian is flanked by Universal Nature and the Genius of Knowledge, as well as statues representing the graphic arts. Behind him, in bas-relief, are five of his greatest works.

TITIAN (TIZIANO VECELLIO) *b. ca. 1488, Pieve di Cadore; d. August 27, 1576, Venice.* Though he came from the mountains at age 9 or 10 to study art in Venice, Titian never lost a simple peasant's view of life. The ability to make a living seemed a precarious, season-to-season undertaking; he considered his paintings as much of a commodity as the lumber of his native Cadore. It is a gift to the world that despite his obsession with financial security, he also painted wonderfully and lived an exceedingly long time.

After a brief apprenticeship under Sebastiano Zuccato, Titian headed for the ateliers of the Bellini brothers. He studied first with Gentile Bellini, who dismissed him with the comment that he painted too quickly and boldly and would never amount to much. Giovanni Bellini, the more talented of the brothers, was a better match. Greatly in demand for Madonnas, altarpieces, and portraits, Giovanni pioneered the use of luminous color and light, and well-modeled figures, characteristics which Titian would adapt to his own style.

He was also influenced by the poetic landscapes and brush techniques of Giorgione and particularly liked his associate's idea of painting directly on canvas without

THE FRARI

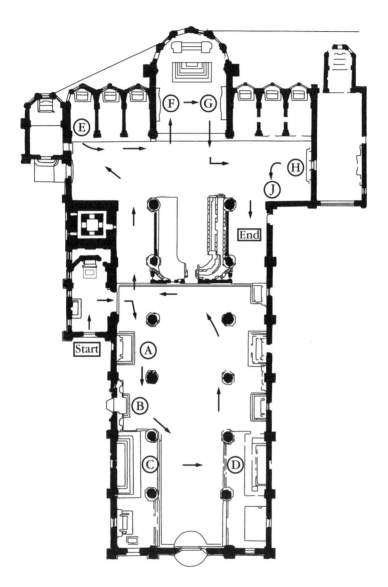

A Jacopo Pesaro   F Nicola Tron
B Giovanni Pesaro   G Francesco Foscari
C Antonio Canova   H Paolo Savelli
D Titian   J Jacopo Marcello
E Claudio Monteverdi

making preliminary sketches. When Giorgione died of plague in 1510, Titian was left to complete his unfinished commissions. There were differences of course, both in Titian's thicker, smoother application of paint, and his frankly voluptuous women; the models for *Sacred and Profane Love* (ca. 1515) were rumored to be courtesans. *Bacchanal of the Andrians* (1518–1519) and *Venus of Urbino* (ca. 1538) are replete with glowing flesh and sensuality.

After much conniving and many assurances to the Council of Ten that if he did not inherit the recently deceased Bellini's "broker's license" he would surely starve, it was awarded to him in 1517. The license provided a guaranteed income and tax exemptions, and also carried the responsibility of painting the doges' portraits and other commemorative scenes—a responsibility Titian tended to ignore in favor of more interesting (and lucrative) private commissions. Two such commissions were the wonderfully dramatic *Assumption of the Virgin* (1518) and the *Pesaro Madonna* (1519–1526), both here in the Frari.

In 1533 Emperor Charles V, delighted by his portrait by Titian, declared that he would no longer be painted by anyone else, and the Farneses, Strozzis, Medicis, and della Roveres lined up as well. These portraits, with their astonishing vitality and style, connect with the viewer to impart a sense of the sitter's dominant traits—or, at least, the traits that the subject wanted remembered. Titian, always insecure about money, would not paint anyone having a bad face day.

Since 1513, attempts had been made to lure Titian to Rome, but he had always resisted. In Venice were his close friends, the great wit and gossip Aretino, and the architect Sansovino, as well as his family. A Cadore girl, Cecilia, lived with him as housekeeper and mistress for five years and bore him two sons. When it appeared she would die in 1525, Titian married her. Good medicine it would seem, for she revived and lived five years more, presenting him with a daughter.

It was Titian's attempt to nail a promised benefice (yearly financial grant) from Pope Paul II for his older son, Pomponio, that finally lured the artist to Rome in 1545. Though he stayed for only a season before returning home and then heading to the court of Charles V in Augsburg, he admitted that his Roman sojourn had influenced his style. In his last years he relied on color and thicker brush strokes to suggest form, playing with light and shadow to evoke detail. Critics blamed it on failing eyesight and shaking hands, passing around a story that his assistants were so alarmed that he was altering his earlier paintings that they were mixing his colors with olive oil so they could later wipe off the damage. It took Tintoretto, Rembrandt, Rubens, Van Gogh, and Renoir to understand what he was doing and elaborate on the technique.

The elderly Titian offered a Pietà to the Franciscans in exchange for a burial place in the Frari. He was carried off by plague before he could finish the painting, but the kindly friars allowed him his spot anyway. What was not allowed was a funeral. The authorities, reeling from the epidemic that had carried off one in four Venetians, forbade any public gathering.

Walk around the choir to your left, passing two in-floor marble *gisants* of a bishop and a priest that are worn but still lovely. In the second chapel you will find the burial place of Claudio Monteverdi. He is remembered by a simple slab with his dates, and flowers tossed through the rails. On the right side is a recently done bronze bust of the musician.

CLAUDIO MONTEVERDI *b. May 1567, Cremona; d. November 29, 1643, Venice.* It is difficult to describe the personality of Claudio Monteverdi. Perhaps that is because the adjective that most easily leaps to mind is a bland one: *dutiful.* There is no evidence that he was a great wit or raconteur. Nor was he adventurous, violent, or given to sexual liaisons. Rather, he appeared to be serious, nervous, occasionally petulant, and lovingly devoted to his family. The high drama that was absent in his life flowed with great emotion from his music. Love, revenge, even battles were brought forth with a remarkable directness, which holds its power to this day. The inner passion of the man is found best in his music.

Monteverdi was an oddity in that he was both a prodigy and a late bloomer. It is likely that he was a choirboy at Cremona Cathedral and that he studied music at the church and the seminary, for the son of a doctor would not be apprenticed to a musician. By the age of 15, he had published a set of motets and a set of *madrigalli spirituali.* By 19, he had surpassed his teacher and was looking to leave the dead end of Cremona for more stimulating and lucrative work.

Monteverdi found the former but not the latter when, in about 1590, he entered the employ of Vincenzo I, duke of Mantua and member of the Gonzaga family—the same family that had employed Andrea Mantegna a century earlier and the same family that continued to pay modest wages with a haphazard carelessness. His early duties included playing and singing in addition to composing. Those duties he must have found pleasant enough, for he married a court singer, Claudia Cattaneo, in 1599.

Prestige came quickly and with it a desire for promotion to maestro di capella. His talent was in fact strong and original enough to attract not only praise but also the sharp criticism of the conservative critic and composer Giovanni Maria Artusi, who accused Monteverdi of deliberately perverting the noble rules of Renaissance polyphony.

The promotion Monteverdi sought was realized in 1602. While his continued output of madrigals secured his reputation, he turned also to opera, enjoying great success with the production of *Orfeo* for the carnival in 1607. But that same year his wife, Claudia, died in Cremona. Financially strapped and emotionally distraught, Monteverdi left the seclusion of his father's house to return to Mantua only at the beseeching of a close friend.

More success and grief awaited him. Another opera, *Arianna*, achieved wide acclaim, but during rehearsals the star singer, Caterinuccia Martinelli, only 18 years old and a close friend of Monteverdi's, died of smallpox in 1608. Like much of Monteverdi's music, the score to *Arianna* has been lost. All that remains is the beautiful and moving "Lament of Ariadne."

Monteverdi's grief and financial stress caused him to return to Cremona in a state of nervous exhaustion. He pleaded to be released from his duties, but it was not until 1612 that the newly installed Francesco Gonzaga dismissed him. A year later the maestro di capella of Venice

died, and the procurators of San Marco's invited Monteverdi for an interview. His sample rehearsal was so impressive that he was hired on the spot. Moving to Venice, he was robbed by highwaymen and arrived a pauper.

Everything else about Venice proved to be salutary for Monteverdi. The air, the intellectual stimulation, the work, and, finally, the money. He was paid 400 ducats a year, twice the salary of his predecessor. He was revived and resurrected.

In Venice Monteverdi assumed administrative duties in addition to composing and teaching. The musical forces in Venice were far larger than those in Mantua, possibly the largest in Italy. Forty festivals a year demanded the composition of much new music. Monteverdi received a lot of help, and despite his being a slow composer, madrigals, operas, and occasional pieces continued to flow forth. He even found time to compose on commission for patrons in Mantua. With a smug satisfaction bordering on contempt, he was able to reject two offers from Mantua to return to his old post.

His life became, if anything, too successful. As he relaxed into fame and old age, his music ceased to change and challenge. He was drifting, and it was only the tide of energy and innovation brought to Venice by two Roman composers, Francesco Manelli and Benedetto Ferrari, that renewed his energy. The first public opera house was opened in Venice with the production of a Manelli opera. Great success prompted the opening of other opera houses. Not to be outdone, Monteverdi once again produced inspired compositions and, at the age of 75, penned his masterpiece, *L'incoronazione di Poppea.*

In 1643 Monteverdi was given a six-month leave of absence to revisit his hometown of Cremona and whatever friends were still alive in Mantua. He returned to Venice and died of an unspecified illness. The most famous composer in Italy was buried with all the honors of the Venetian state. Fifty years later his music was all but forgotten. More than 350 years later the directness and power of its emotion ensure its survival.

Inside the main chapel, facing each other, are the monuments of two prominent doges. On the left is that of **Nicola Tron** (d. 1473), who donated his considerable fortune to the city during one of its financial crises. Despite the fact that the monument, which includes 22 figures, is considered a masterpiece of the Venetian Renaissance, it seems oddly lifeless. Tron himself was more coarse and colorful, a huge man with a stammer who amassed his wealth as a merchant in Rhodes.

The monument of Doge **Francesco Foscari** (1373–1457), across the way, is more appealing. It is done in rich gold tones with a unified focus: The doge is under a canopy on his deathbed, attended by Fortitude, Justice, Temperance, and Prudence.

Despite the fact that in the 34 years of his reign Foscari greatly expanded Venetian territory, he also depleted the treasury and in the end lost interest in government business, refusing to attend Senate and Council meetings. He was deposed a week before he died—a mild rebuke, considering that 19 earlier doges who had fallen from favor had been blinded by live coals or murdered.

Even so, the *signoria* felt guilty over his rapid decline, secretly worrying that they had killed him by breaking his heart. So Foscari was given a full state funeral as a doge and carried through the streets of Venice under a golden umbrella. His tomb holds a place of honor, though his portrait annoyed art critic John Ruskin, who described it as "a huge, gross, bony clown's face, with the peculiar sodden and sensual cunning in it which is seen so often in the countenances of the worst Romanist priests."

Two more monuments are worthy of notice as you come out of the main chapel and turn left. High on the back wall of the transept is the memorial to **Paolo Savelli** (d. 1405), the first tomb in Venice to show an equestrian statue. There is something engaging about the way he sits stiffly astride his wooden horse. A skilled military commander, he succumbed to the plague.

On the wall nearby, enclosed in an unusual oblong, is the monument of a sea captain, **Jacopo Marcello** (d. 1484). His occupation is cleverly hinted at in the sculpture. He stands on a sarcophagus with sides that slope in like a small boat's, then flare out again as if being seen in the water's reflection. The three distorted figures below also seem a reflection of the captain and his two pages, and the long thin staff he is holding resembles nothing as much as a fishing pole. It is impossible not to think that the sculptor, Pietro Lombardo, was enjoying his own game.

DIRECTIONS, HOURS, AND ADMISSION: Take the no. 1 vaporetto to the Campo S. Toma stop and work your way several blocks into the interior. The Frari is open daily 9:00 to 11:45 A.M. and 2:30 to 6:00 P.M. Admission is L 3,000.

MADONNA DELL'ORTO

Originally dedicated to St. Christopher, the patron saint of ferrymen and gondoliers as well as travelers, Madonna dell'Orto lies across the water from San Michele. A few years after the church was built, however, miracles began to be attributed to an unfinished statue of Mary in a nearby yard. The clergy, alarmed at the burgeoning cult, ordered the Madonna out of the *orto* (garden) and into the church. In 1377 the statue was purchased from the sculptor Giovanni de Santi and placed on the altar, where it remains today. Eyes lowered, the Madonna appears complacent about her role in ousting St. Christopher, who is hanging around on an outside portal.

Madonna dell'Orto, built around 1350, is a charming example of Venetian Gothic, though its interior has undergone many restorations—some of them disastrous. From our point of view the worst came in the 1860s when many historic and artistic memorial slabs were pried up and scrapped to make way for the red and white marble floor. A few, including that of **Giovanni de Santi** (d. 1392), were salvaged and are in the right-hand chapel near the front.

Fortunately, Tintoretto's ashes were kept safe. The remains of the artist, his daughter, **Marietta** (1560–1590?), and son, **Domenico** (1560?–1635)—who were also painters—rest in the chapel to the right of the altar, under a large marble slab. Tintoretto's terra-cotta bust is a recent addition, done by Napoleone Martinuzzi in 1937.

TINTORETTO (JACOPO ROBUSTI) *b. 1519, Venice; d. May 31, 1594, Venice.* Jacopo Robusti's more famous name derived from his father's occupation, that of a dyer (*tintore*) of silk fabric. Of his early life there is only an apocryphal story that he was apprenticed to Titian. The older man, it is said, was so threatened upon spotting Tintoretto's obvious genius that he dismissed him after only 10 days. More to the truth is that Titian, official painter of the doges, a man with all the right contacts, did not encourage Tintoretto or offer him easy access to the wealthy and powerful for commissions.

Titian nevertheless influenced him. Tintoretto's formal studies may have been rather meager, but his strongest early influences were the painters of the Roman and Florentine schools. He developed a style that was highly original, theatrical and improvisatory in appearance; a style derided by the traditionalists as "hasty" and "a farce." He had his defenders, first and foremost himself. Though slight of build, the young man acquired a historical reputa-

tion as brash, coarse, determined, and ready to push his way in where he was not wanted.

Support came from friends as well. The writer Andrea Calmo proclaimed him "a 'grain of pepper' that 'confounds, beats, and puts to rout ten bunches of (sleep-producing) poppies.' " An irritant he was. Through boldness and the connections of his wife, Faustina, he gained admission into the prestigious confraternity of San Rocco, an achievement met with prolonged and vocal resistance within the organization. One member even refused to pay for any of Tintoretto's work.

Tintoretto's reputation became established with his large-scale painting of *St. Marco Freeing the Slave* (1547–1548). Here he displayed his characteristic use of theatricality, of dramatic foreshortening, of crowds with the chief participants engaged in fevered, impassioned activity. His use of light is highly dramatic. For him, light was an element, another character, rather than just an effect. At times his work borders on and even lapses into melodrama, but even then it retains a power that holds the viewer. Though too early for the genre, it is easy to imagine Tintoretto being a stage designer for grand opera.

Tintoretto studied the dramatic effects of lighting by creating in his studio a small model stage that he populated with wax figures and illuminated by lamps placed at various angles and altitudes. From this model, he would carefully study and draw the effects of light and shadow.

Tintoretto employed several styles and techniques. His portraits are exquisitely painted and are absent the drama of his larger works. These owe an obvious debt to Titian, as other works do to Michelangelo, but none are mere copies. Nor was he without influence, for El Greco clearly borrowed from his sensibilities. His treatment of biblical and mythic scenes could portray an endearing look at human foibles: the dirty old elders peeping at the naked Susanna, or Mars hiding under a chest so as not to be caught by Vulcan in Venus's bedroom.

In the *Crucifixion* (1565), done for his confraternity, a huge canvas some 40 feet long, Tintoretto shows the crucified Christ in the top center. Mounted soldiers flank the scene, overseeing the efforts of workmen who are busy preparing and raising the crosses of the thieves. Neither in awe nor in grief, the men are caught up in their work. Christ on the cross rises above all, his forsakenness and sorrow accentuated by the humdrum activity about him. For the supremely religious Tintoretto, this is the climactic moment of history—a moment ignored and lost on all present except the small group of mourners gathered at the foot of the cross. This is an amazingly modern conception. Absent the usual piety, it draws instead on the varied responses of the individuals.

Tintoretto's vigor did not flag with age. His vision remained as charged as ever, though the size of some of the paintings demanded that assistants from his studio participate in their execution. The *Last Supper* (1592–1594), lit only by a hanging lamp and Christ's halo, combines the intimate interaction of the disciples, ghostly cherubim, the service of food, and the curiosity of a cat and a dog. Split diagonally, it runs the gamut from the sublime to the everyday, all in healthy, busy juxtaposition. It is Tintoretto's world: spiritual, dramatic, and human.

One benefit of visiting artists buried in church, of course, is being able to see some of their works. There are a number of important paintings by Tintoretto here, including the *Presentation of the Virgin in the Temple* (1552–1556) and *St. Peter's Vision of the Cross* (1555–1556). In the chancel, facing each other, are the *Last Judgment* (c. 1560) and the *Making of the Golden Calf* (c. 1560). No doubt having some fun, Tintoretto painted

Giorgione, Titian, and Veronese as the bearers of the idolatrous calf.

DIRECTIONS AND HOURS: Take the no. 5 vaporetto to the Madonna dell'Orto stop. The interior is open daily 9:30 A.M. to noon and 3:30 to 5:30 P.M.

ST. LIO

St. Lio is a tiny square of a church, bright with painted surfaces and candles. As the name suggests, the *chiesa* honors Pope Leo X, who sided with Venice against the Holy Roman Empire during one of their frequent feuds; a ceiling fresco by Giandomenico Tiepolo places St. Leo among the angels.

The importance of St. Lio's, outside of its possession of Titian's painting of St. James, is that it is the final resting place of another of Venice's foremost artists, **Antonio Canaletto** (1697–1768). His tomb in the right-hand front chapel is modest in the extreme. There is a bas-relief of a Pietà, but otherwise only a worn stone indicates his remains.

Although his paintings appear to have the accuracy of photographs, in actuality Canaletto placed himself at impossible vantage points and readjusted buildings to suit his artistic goals. It was his mastery of light on water and stone that makes you believe, riding down the Grand Canal, that you are seeing Venice exactly as he painted it. Two wonderful examples of his use of light are *Grand Canal: From Santa Maria della Carita to the Bacino* (1726) and *Grand Canal: The Stonemason's Yard* (ca. 1728).

That those paintings are now in Montreal and London is not accidental. Finding himself especially popular with English tourists, Canaletto soon learned that studies of Venetian back alleyways were not the souvenirs they wanted to take home; he turned his attention to the San Marco basin and more commercial scenes. An Englishman living in Venice, Joseph Smith, formalized the British connection by acting as a procurer of Canalettos for wealthy patrons, making sure that the works were authentic and safely shipped.

Relatively little is known about Canaletto the man. He never married and in 1768 died of an inflammation of the bladder, leaving his bed, his old clothes, and 28 unsold paintings to his sisters.

DIRECTIONS AND HOURS: Take the no. 1 or 2 vaporetto to the Rialto stop and work your way straight back from the Rialto bridge. St. Lio's is open daily but is closed between noon and 3:00 P.M.

VENICE
Buried on Water

▲   ▲   ▲

SAN MICHELE

By the early 19th century, skeletons were erupting from overcrowded churchyards all over Europe, stretching out bony arms as if fighting for air. Venice was no exception. With plague always a danger, Napoleon, who had seen similar conditions in Paris, ordered the churchyards closed to further burials. In 1810 the island of San Michele across the lagoon was selected as the city's new cemetery.

Here, as with Père Lachaise in Paris, there was a difference between buyers and renters. If you could not afford to endow a gravesite in perpetuity, your lease would be up in 12 years, your bones transferred to the remote island of Sant'Ariano. The practice still holds, but now nearby ossuaries are used for the evicted.

Although a certain Horatio F. Brown, practicing tabloid journalism in *Life on the Lagoons*, found San Michele "terrible and sinister . . . where the dead lie buried in the ooze of the lagoon-island," such a description is no longer true. When the sun shines on its gardens, San Michele is a pleasant cemetery indeed.

After a short vaporetto ride you will disembark and pass through the cloister. The church, San Michele in Isola, was built between 1469 and 1478, and is the earliest Renaissance church in Venice. Inside, a marble slab in the floor marks the burial place of Paolo Sarpi.

PAOLO SARPI *b. 1552, Venice; d. January 16, 1623, Venice.* Paolo Sarpi, a Servite friar from the age of 14, is by general agreement the only great intellect that Venice produced, for the power and concentration of Venice lay in commerce. Venetians held a distrust of individual power.

(Unidentified tomb)

Doges were beholden to the Council of Ten, and victorious military heroes were showered with dimmed and wary adulation by the grateful leaders and populace. The prepotent individual was not allowed to emerge. Power lay with committees and blocs, with group allegiances.

From out of this foggy conglomorate morass emerged the thin figure of Sarpi, a scientist, theologian, philosopher, historian, and polemicist. As a scientist, he is credited with discovering the contraction of the iris, the circulation of the blood, the valves in the veins, and with helping Galileo build his telescope. As a philosopher, he is argued to have preceded Locke in the theory of modes of knowledge.

In 1606, for the fourth time in its history, Venice fell under papal excommunication and interdict. The dispute centered on Paul V's challenge of the city's right to try two "criminous clerics" under Venetian control for civil offenses. There was no mistaking the stance of Venice. The priests were charged with temporal sins, and that was the jurisdiction of the state: the priests would remain under Venetian authority.

Venice turned to Sarpi as its chief defender. He wrote with logical conciseness and a directness that bordered on insolence. In his thought and writings he displayed the practicality of Venetian diplomacy: "I never, never tell a lie, but the truth not to everybody."

As for the interdict, the Venetians simply ignored it. Preempting the pope, they ordered their priests to continue with mass and confession. One priest who expressed doubts as to this policy found a gibbet erected outside his door. He took the hint. Another priest declared that he would turn over certain correspondence from Rome when the Holy Spirit moved him. Promptly advised that the Ten had already been moved by the Spirit to hang anyone who disobeyed, he too saw the light of Venetian logic.

The interdict lasted a year. Sir Henry Wooten, the British ambassador to Venice who had been none too subtly distributing Protestant Bibles, anticipated a Venetian break from Rome. Sarpi was not altogether unsympathetic to such an idea. Indeed, he wrestled mightily with the issue. The Venetians, holding the upper hand in their arrogant defiance, eventually turned the priests over but without prejudice to their rights. In return they gained property and relief on taxation. Venice stayed Catholic, and Sarpi, disillusioned with the concession, considered Lutheranism.

Wooten described Sarpi in his monastery cell "fenced with a castle of paper about his chair and over his head when he was either reading or writing alone, for he was of our Lord St. Albans' opinion that all air is predatory, and especially hurtful when the spirits are most employed." Often ill, Sarpi resorted to peasant cures and held a warmed piece of iron in his hands to relieve the chill. For sleep, he eschewed his bed for the top of a book box.

Sarpi's fame put his life in danger from assassins hired by Rome. Three attempts were made. One, on the steps of S. Fosca bridge, left him with a dagger embedded by his right cheekbone. Severely weakened, he was still able to pun in Latin that he recognized the style (in Latin *stilus* means both "style" and "dagger") of Rome. He later hung the dagger in his monastery as an ex-voto.

Refusing to turn over many papal documents, Sarpi got some measure of revenge in his *History of the Council of Trent* (1619), which painted an accurate and unflattering picture of papal power. He died in his bed under a painting depicting *The Agony in the Garden*, Jesus' own hour of indecision. For Sarpi, the hold of Venice had remained strong: His dying words were *"Esto perpetua"* (May she endure forever).

Outside in the cemetery of San Michele, you will see arrows pointing to the gravesite of Ezra Pound. Follow them to the Reparto Evangelico (Evangelical or non-Catholic section). If you have been traveling in Italy for a while, it may come as a shock to suddenly see epitaphs in English, French, and German. But this is the place to which foreigners have been relegated.

With unconscious humor, someone has erected a stone to "Frank Justice Stainer of Staffordshire, Who Left Us in Peace, Feb. 2nd, 1910." Another odd epitaph appears on

SAN MICHELE

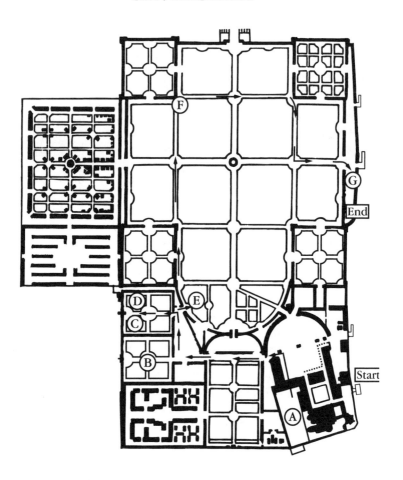

A Paolo Sarpi   E Petrus Penzo
B Ezra Pound   F Pallillo Family
C Sergei Diaghilev   G Frederick Rolfe (Baron Corvo)
D Igor Stravinsky

the monument of a Swiss artist, **Leopold Robert** (1794–1835), who killed himself exactly 10 years after his brother committed suicide. According to the inscription Robert, a painter of Italian folk scenes, took his life in a fit of weakness: "Whereas Michelangelo would have overcome it," his memorialist chides, "Leopold Robert succumbed."

What Robert succumbed to were the frustrations of love. After a night of drinking, the artist, who was infatuated with Napoleon's niece, Charlotte Bonaparte, announced that since she would not give herself to him, life was useless. Then he slit his throat with a razor and bled to death on his studio floor in front of horrified friends, who were unable to save him.

Not far from the entrance to this section, Ezra Pound lies beneath a holly tree. The masses of ivy and other plantings are so thick that you can barely see the slab with his name.

EZRA LOOMIS POUND *b. October 30, 1885, Hailey, Idaho; d. November 1, 1972, Venice.* Ezra Pound was arguably the greatest literary figure of the 20th century. Ironically, his own poetry, while much admired in part, too often sails into the fog of obscuration, and so his great influence is most readily seen in his impact on the works of others: William Carlos Williams, Hilda Doolittle, W. B. Yeats, Ernest Hemingway, T. S. Eliot, Wyndham Lewis, James Joyce, Louis Zukofsky, and Charles Olson. Pound's mind was intellectually fertile and endlessly inquisitive. Erudite and intuitive, he was the preeminent critic of his day. He tirelessly reviewed, critiqued, and promoted the works of others. He was audacious and alive. What he was not was revealing of himself. What he became was virulently anti-Semitic.

Fond of but unimpressed by his parents (his father, "the naivest man who ever possessed good sense"; his mother, "a peacock Presbyterian"), Pound identified with the West of his birth, while despising the suburbia of his Pennsylvania childhood. Throughout his life, with a perverse pride, he made deliberate use of backwoods speech and spelling, a punning patois similar to that of George Herriman's contemporaneous Krazy Kat. Pound's roots lay in the populism of his grandfather and his long American lineage. Confirming the ease with which populism can be converted into bigotry and xenophobia, Pound was later to blame his grandfather's lost fortune on devious foreigners; he declared that World War II, "fighting the kikefied usurers," was a vindication of his grandfather's loss.

When, as an unknown American, Pound sailed into London in 1908, to "meet Bill Yeats," the eccentric egoist quickly made his presence felt. By hawking his poems he gained entrée to literary circles. Then, following the tradition of Whistler and Wilde, he used dominating conversation, affected airs, and stinging wit to assert his supremacy in London. He not only met Yeats but, by force of personality, took over his "Monday evenings" where the literati gathered for talk and wine. Similarly, he gained influence over Ford Maddox Ford and the *English Review*.

Pound involved himself with Imagism and then Vorticism and its periodical, *BLAST*. In 1914 Pound married Dorothy Shakespear, a quiet, talented painter, "a beautiful picture that never came alive." Indeed, who could grow under his continual shadow? In 1922, now living in Paris, he met the violinist Olga Rudge, who became his lifelong mistress and bore him his daughter, Maria.

Over the next few years Pound critiqued and promoted Joyce's *Ulysses*. It was his strong suggestions to Eliot that resulted in the leaner and more focused final version of *The Waste Land*, which was dedicated to Pound. He also published his own poetry, including *Hugh Selwyn Mauberley*, wrote an opera, and began work on his *Cantos* and various translations. The *Cantos* were to be nothing less than a history of humankind, "the tale of the tribe," drawn from numerous cultures, languages, philosophies, and aesthetics.

As the 1920s progressed, Pound's position as a star on the Paris scene was being usurped by younger artists and newer ideas. By 1924 he and Dorothy had moved to Italy with Olga in pursuit. Pound's vast ego was forced into an interior retreat, a withdrawn and uncomfortable lair. His personal inscrutability denied the access of friends, and he latched on to the philosophy of social credit and to fascism for his rationale. Oddly, he still gave his time and effort to young poets, including individual Jews, like Louis Zukofsky.

World War II found Pound lost in his cause and delivering venomous tirades over Italian radio, urging the defeat of the Allies and the Jews. Upon the Allied liberation of Italy, Pound was charged with treason and kept in a holding cage (10 × 10 × 7 feet) at a POW camp in Pisa. He suffered a breakdown and while recovering wrote his last great poetry, the *Pisan Cantos*. At war's end he was sent to St. Elizabeth's Hospital in Washington, D.C., where he was psychiatrically imprisoned until 1958.

With the help of his influential friends (e.g., Frost and MacLeish), charges of treason were dropped in 1958, and Pound returned to Italy. Ever the unrepentant showman, he proffered a fascist salute to reporters waiting for him dockside. Pound spent his last years in solitude, alternating between Dorothy and Olga. He retired to Venice. His solitude increased, and his health weakened. He told the poet Robert Lowell, "To begin with a swelled head and end with swelled feet." He had been a lion, a fighter, a defender, a caged brute, and looking every bit the old lion, he died peacefully in the city of lions.

Go into the Greek Orthodox *reparto* next door, where you will first come upon an angel pointedly looking the other way. The most interesting monuments line the left-hand wall, particularly a striking green-bronzed young woman who lies at the point of death. She is identified as **Sonia** (1885–1907). The nearby bust of **Romeo Suppancich** (dates unknown) is flanked by reliefs of a young woman and a piece of sheet music.

Against the back wall, its curved Russian dome supported by four pillars, is the monument of Sergei Diaghilev.

SERGEI PAVLOVITCH DIAGHILEV *b. March 19, 1872, Novgorod, Russia; d. August 19, 1929, Venice.* "I am firstly

a charlatan, though a rather brilliant one; secondly a great charmer; third, frightened of nobody; fourth, a man with plenty of logic and very few scruples; fifth, I seem to have no real talent. Nonetheless, I believe I have found my true vocation—to be a Maecenas [a patron of the arts]. I have everything necessary except the money—but that will come." Diaghilev wrote his self-assessment at 23. It was a prediction that largely came true.

He appeared to people to have sprung full-blown, a fleshy man with a tiny black mustache, bulldog chins, and a monocle. Because of his large head size, his mother had a difficult labor, and she died soon afterward. His step-mother, who entered his life when he was two years old, was a warmhearted woman who immersed Sergei in ama-teur musicales and concerts. He was also fascinated by his wealthy grandfather's collection of art books.

Yet when he went to the university at St. Petersburg it was to study law, a subject in which he had little interest. He studied music composition with Rimsky-Korsakov until the composer finally had to inform him that he showed no talent. The most productive influences in his life were his artistic circle of friends and his summer trips to Eu-rope. Posing as a Russian nobleman, he toured artists' stu-dios and wangled introductions to—and autographed photographs from—Zola, Gounod, and Saint-Saëns.

Art seemed the way for him to go. He mounted exhibi-tions in St. Petersburg and in 1899 helped to found a monthly magazine, *World of Art*. The periodical, which of-fended almost everyone, promoted art for art's sake: Saucy nudes, impressionists, and postimpressionists gam-boled through its large-format pages. Its success led to Diaghilev's appointment to the staff of the Imperial The-ater. He was delighted, but in his enthusiasm for his own vision he treated the staff badly. He also flaunted his ho-mosexuality. Yet it was a terrible shock to Diaghilev to open the newspaper in 1901 and read that he had been "dismissed without pension."

Taking his theatrical skills to Paris, he worked to arrange exhibits of Russian art and music. In 1908 he was success-ful with *Boris Godunov*, starring Fyodor Chaliapin, and the next year imported the Russian Ballet. He oversaw all as-pects, from the redecoration of the theater to the stage sets and the selection of the first-night audience (Rodin, Ravel, Isadora Duncan, Jean Cocteau, and the nobility). He spared no expense with other people's money.

By 1911 the bulk of the Russian ballet company, includ-ing Nijinsky, Karsavina, and Fokine, belonged solely to him as his Ballets Russes. The company was not without turmoil. Many old friends departed in anger, and in 1913, when the exotic, childlike Nijinsky, long Diaghilev's lover, was captured in marriage by Romola Pulska, the impresario wept, raged, and fired his star. History repeated itself in 1921 when his lead dancer, Leonid Massine, was dismissed for his romance with a company ballerina. As Diaghilev insisted, "There is nobody indispensable in this world."

Yet he had a talent for acquiring the almost indispensable, whether it was Stravinsky writing *The Firebird* and *The Rite of Spring* for him; Prokofiev composing *The Prodigal Son*; Ravel, *Daphnis and Chloe*; or Debussy, *Afternoon of a Faun*. He commissioned Picasso, Chagall, Roualt, André Derain, and others to design stage sets and amazing, original costumes.

In all, Diaghilev staged 68 different ballets. He managed to keep his company together through the havoc of World War I by touring the United States, Switzerland, Spain, and South America. But toward the end of the 1920s his focus wavered, and he took to collecting rare Russian books, causing his lead dancer, Serge Lifar, to lament that 1929 would be the ballet's last year. Instead, it was the last year of Diaghilev; already in poor health, the newly diagnosed diabetic began to run a mysterious fever. When his temperature reached 105, the Venetian doctors turned away helplessly, and the jovial, booming voice was stilled. A black-draped gondola carried the impresario to San Michele.

On the other side of the chapel in the plainest of slabs (nos. 36 and 37) are Igor and Vera Stravinsky.

IGOR FYODOROVICH STRAVINSKY *b. June 17, 1882, Oranienbaum (now Lomonosov), Russia; d. April 6, 1971, New York.* "His is a poetry of exactitude, a theater of delicate adjustments and relentless march." Virgil Thomson on Igor Stravinsky. Taut, spiky, and intellectual, Stravinsky's music was the antithesis of romanticism. Melodic content was of distant consequence. Ever-changing rhythms propelled his music, and reedy, pungent orchestrations gave it an acerbic feel. Over and over he stated that music could not convey emotion or depict scenes. Music was abstract and, like faith, a thing unto itself.

Stravinsky's father was a talented opera singer, a bass with a flair for theatrics whose rages at home caused the boy to fear him. His mother was distant and unsupportive. His only affection came from his brother, Gury, and the servants, Simon and his beloved Bertha. At school, the diminutive Stravinsky was an outsider and an indifferent student. What he loved were the smells, colors, and sights of St. Petersburg and the peasant songs and dances that later found their way into works such as *Petrushka.*

Stravinsky, considered talented but not precocious, studied music and piano but never attended a conservatory. Forbidding him a career in music, his parents insisted on law instead. Four tedious years in law school bore an ironic twist, for there Stravinsky befriended the son of Rimsky-Korsakov. He inveigled an invitation to have the master evaluate his fledgling works. Though not bowled over, Rimsky did encourage him and a year later, in 1903, took on Stravinsky as a student.

Stravinsky's initial compositions were derivative and academic, but he became exposed to the music of French composers, most notably Debussy, whose expanded use of tonality had a profound effect. Stravinsky's *Fireworks* (1909) attracted the attention of Sergei Diaghilev. He commissioned Stravinsky to write a score based on the Russian folktale of the firebird for his newly formed and sensational Ballets Russes. Stravinsky quickly obliged, and the performance of *Firebird* on June 25, 1910, brought him instant fame. Rooted in the nationalism and romanticism of Rimsky-Korsakov, the music was nevertheless new and bold and was Stravinsky's own.

Another collaboration on another folktale, *Petrushka*, followed a year later. Though the work was boldly marked by polytonalities and jarring rhythms, the public loved it. Then, in 1913, came *The Rite of Spring* and the greatest scandal in musical history. No sooner had the bassoon finished its opening phrase than the catcalls started. And then escalated. Factions screamed at one another. Fights broke out. The music—exciting, savage, dissonant, nonmelodic, filled with primitive polyrhythms—became lost in the barbaric uproar. Diaghilev switched the houselights off and on in an effort to quell the riot, while Nijinsky, from the wings, ineffectually screamed the rhythms to the dancers. Stravinsky left the theater in a rage, demanding to know how "people who had not yet heard it wanted to protest in advance."

Stravinsky was now the center of all attention. But, perhaps in reaction, his aesthetic changed. Although his music retained some of its primitive feel, he now wrote for small ensembles and eschewed the color and drama of his symphonic works. Works like the jazzy and spiky *L'histoire du soldat* (1918) and his cantata, *Les noces* (1923), exemplify this style and form a transition to his neoclassical period. Here, beginning with his *Octet* (1923), Stravinsky resorted to traditional forms, as he did with works such as his *Symphony of Psalms* (1930). He also modernized works of the past, as with Pergolesi's music in *Pulcinella* (1919). The *Octet* served another purpose as well, for it was dedicated to Vera de Bosset, a young dancer with whom Stravinsky had fallen deeply in love. Though both were married at the time, the love affair persisted for 18 years. They married in 1939 after the death of Catherine, Stravinsky's first wife.

Stravinsky was the ultimate logician and organizer. His scores were marvels in clarity: ruled staves, inks of different hues each with its own purpose, mistakes erased. Nothing was left to chance. He performed, conducted, and recorded his own works with regularity the world over. He viewed interpreters as egomaniacs and willful distorters.

Through World War II, many critics considered Stravinsky to be the greatest composer of his age. He had long fallen out of favor with the majority of the concertgoing public and then later with the intellectual avant-garde led by Pierre Boulez. He went on to compose a full-scale opera (*The Rake's Progress*, 1951) and ballets in conjunction with Balanchine (e.g., *Orpheus* [1948] and *Agon* [1957]). He experimented with serialism but in the end reverted back to neoclassicism, rescoring Wolf and Bach. Bach—a logician rescoring a logician. A return to roots, a return home.

As you leave, stop and look at the impressive mausoleum of the *famiglia* **Messinis da Leucade**, noticing its solemn bas-relief angels and religious mosaics. Then walk straight across through the archway into the walled circular cemetery, a beautiful area of trees, flowers, and small dark lizards. This section is set aside for military burials and has some wonderful monuments. As you come in, look for the lions of **Petrus Alojsius Penzo** (d. 1928); he is pictured around the other side wearing his aviator's garb, his monument topped by four scowling eagles.

Near Penzo are three tall slabs. The first shows only a bronze wing, the second Icarus in flight with his eyes shut, and the third a figure mending a set of wings. All three aviators seem to have died in World War I.

If you have the energy, walk all the way to the back wall along the path between Sections B and E to the monument of the *famiglia* **Pallillo**. A girl in turn-of-the-century clothing with a wide smile like a young Eleanor Roosevelt is stepping out of a setting that includes her dog, who watches her anxiously, and an older couple in shallower bas-relief behind her. The even flatter background looks

like a classical villa. Though you may be curious to know her story, no information is given except for her name, Talia Guadio Speravi.

To conclude your visit, walk all the way to your right and right again until you get into the stacks of niches in Section VII. Halfway down on the *exterior* wall, in the highest compartment, lies what remains of Frederick Rolfe, a.k.a. Baron Corvo.

FREDERICK WILLIAM ROLFE (BARON CORVO) *b. July 22, 1860, London; d. October 25, 1913, Venice.* Whatever his other talents, Frederick Rolfe had the ability to drive people to madness. A romantic with a veneer of creativity and learning, Rolfe attracted patrons who admired his painting, writing, and photography and sympathetically tried to help him—until they suddenly found themselves the recipients of a deluge of colorfully written poison-pen letters or a lawsuit.

Rolfe's family, piano makers in decline, did not understand their oldest son, particularly when he decided he had a vocation as a Roman Catholic priest. In 1887, at the age of 27, he begged to enroll in a seminary; but once accepted he spent his time painting and learning photography instead. A slight, elegant figure with tonsured hair and metal-rimmed glasses, Rolfe developed a reputation for never paying his bills. By the following year he had been expelled. Expelled from a second seminary in Rome two years later, he refused to leave his bed, feigning illness—a ploy he would use many times during other evictions. He was finally picked up, mattress and all, and set down outside the college gates.

When Rolfe returned to England in 1890, he had a new title, Baron Corvo. He had been befriended by the elderly Duchess Sforza-Cessarini, who, he said, conferred the honor upon him; later he intimated to people that she was his grandmother. If she had done so, it is easy to see why. The baron was a charming houseguest who played the piano, sang Gilbert and Sullivan songs, and "had many small accomplishments of the kind that make a man or woman welcome in dull country houses," according to a friend of the time.

Inspired by his Italian stay, Rolfe wrote a number of folktales about the saints, which were published first in a quarterly, *The Yellow Book*, then collected as *Stories Toto Told Me* (1898) and *In His Own Image* (1901). During this time he was also experimenting with flashlight, underwater, and color photography, and trying unsuccessfully to attract investors. (Photography was also a way to get close to the young boys whom he photographed nude.) But he was not too busy to quarrel with a priest who had generously paid for his food and lodging for two years, attacking him in the press and complaining to his bishop until the well-meaning cleric was transferred to Malta.

Hadrian the Seventh (1904), the most admired of Rolfe's novels, gave him the chance to strike back at a hierarchy that he believed had kept him from the priesthood. In the book George Arthur Rose, begged by a cardinal and bishop to take Holy Orders to "right the great wrong" of 20 years earlier, eventually becomes Pope Hadrian. As pope, he settles many scores for Rolfe. The novel is written in a witty and visual style, with an illuminating view of the workings of the papacy. Unfortunately, it made no money for its author.

After a quarrel with the proposed dedicatee, Rolfe dedicated *In His Own Image* "to the Divine Friend, much desired." Pathetically, despite his propensity to take offense, he saw himself as softhearted and vulnerable, desperately wanting a soul mate. Several "divine friends" contacted him, and Rolfe began collaborations with them to write other books, including *The Weird of the Wanderer* (1912).

His "divine friends" soon became enemies, and a few months later Rolfe accepted an invitation to travel to Venice with a respected professor of archaeology, a man he would later characterize as "carroty, freckled" and with the voice of a "strangulated Punch." The professor soon extricated himself from Rolfe's extravagance by leaving him some money and retreating to Rome. Rolfe stayed on in Venice, sometimes finding another benefactor, sometimes living in a battered boat. The pederasty hinted at in *Stories Toto Told Me* flared openly, as if in revenge at a world he felt had let him down too many times. If his letters are to be believed, he gloried in deflowering as many young boys as he could find.

At the end Rolfe became a picturesque figure on the canals, reclining in his leopardskin-covered gondola while dressed in a naval officer–style blue suit. But life cheated him one more time; at 53, he was found dead of a heart attack in his apartment.

DIRECTIONS AND HOURS: Take the no. 5 vaporetto from the Fondamente Nuove one stop to San Michele. (Check the schedule for your return trip, since the vaporettos run only every half hour.) The cemetery is open daily 8:00 A.M. to 5:00 or 6:00 P.M.

PALAZZO VENIER DEI LEONI

The charm of visiting Peggy Guggenheim's grave is that you are able to see her art collection at the same time. Set back from the water, the approach to her *palazzo* is down a narrow, picturesque street and through welded iron gates inset with Murano glass. The works she collected are interesting not only for the artists who later became famous—Calder, Pollock, Ernst, Chagall—but also for those who did not, whose work would not otherwise be seen.

The sense of the woman is strong here; you can imagine her at the gate, enthusiastically collecting admission and keeping a running total of the take in her head. Continue along the garden path instead of turning in at the villa, and you will come to her plaque on the wall:

Here Rests Peggy Guggenheim
1898–1979

But she does not rest here alone. Seeing the attendant inscription, "Here Lie My Beloved Babies," may be startling until you realize that Emily (1945–1960), Cappuccino

(1949–1953), and Madame Butterfly (1954–1958) were her Lhasa apsos. There are 14 Beloved Babies in all.

PEGGY GUGGENHEIM *b. August 26, 1898, New York; d. December 25, 1979, Venice.* When Peggy Guggenheim was born, she inherited stinginess and a death wish from her mother's family. From the Guggenheims came her renowned sexuality, her interest in art, and a bulbous "potato" nose. That nose, coupled with dyed black hair, crookedly drawn-on red lips, and miniature Calder mobile earrings, made Peggy a work of art herself.

The marriage of her parents, Benjamin Guggenheim and Florette Seligsman, was a merger of two mining fortunes. Florette, whose repetition of phrases made her sound like a Gertrude Stein poem, was at least more normal than her brother, Washington, whose teeth and tongue were blackened from eating only charcoal. Washington and another brother, Jesse, committed suicide, Jesse taking his young wife along.

Peggy's gentle, handsome father, returning to his family in 1912 after nearly a year in Europe with his mistress, made the courageous decision to go down with the *Ti-*

tanic, giving his place in the lifeboats to others. But his death was an emotional and financial disaster for his family. A poor businessman, he left Peggy only a trust fund of $450,000, making her feel she was "not a real Guggenheim." After high school she liberated herself from the family by moving to Europe.

In Paris Peggy met artists and intellectuals. Her marriage to golden-haired bohemian Laurence Vail gave her two children, Sinbad and Pegeen, but ended in discord. Complaining that when he was drunk Laurence would stomp on her stomach and rub jam in her hair, she used her money to fight back. She imposed absurd economies on Laurence and the rest of the household, once docking a butler's pay for eating an extra apple.

Approaching 40, Peggy cast around for something meaningful to do. By then her mother and her beloved older sister, Benita, had died, and her two small nephews had mysteriously plunged to their deaths from a Manhattan rooftop while in the care of her other sister, Hazel. A friend suggested that Peggy open an art gallery, and with the assistance of Marcel Duchamp she launched Guggenheim Jeune in London in 1938, with a show by Jean Cocteau. She went on to exhibit such "unknowns" as Wassily Kandinsky, Yves Tanguy, and Henry Moore before closing in the red.

The hot breath of World War II was threatening to blow Peggy back to New York—but not before she stopped in Paris and picked up works by Brancusi, Léger, Giacometti, and Dalí at bargain prices. She paid the fare for Max Ernst and André Breton to come to the United States and ended up marrying Ernst, who was German and feared deportation or internment. It was an unfortunate re-creation of her parents' union. Max, handsome and cultured, treated her coldly and made no secret of his romantic affairs.

Peggy again used money as a weapon, this time making a detailed list of their living expenses and taking out his share in paintings. Still unhappy, she returned to her practice of casual sex. According to a friend, she bought all her lovers the same cheap knit vest; when Max and Yves Tanguy encountered each other wearing the same sleeveless sweater, they cried, *"C'est pas possible!"* But it was.

New York gave Peggy a new artist to subsidize, Jackson Pollock, and a new gallery with which to create a sensation. Art of This Century opened in October 1942 with a strong emphasis on surrealism and abstract art. It stayed open until 1947, when Peggy decided to move back to Europe. Her parting gift to America was a book of memoirs, *Out of This Century* (1946), a tell-all exposé that was allegedly renamed *Out of Her Mind* by scandalized Guggenheims.

Peggy bought the Palazzo Venier dei Leoni in 1948. Opened to the public as a museum in 1951, it does not easily yield up its past. The room of childlike primitives by Peggy's daughter, Pegeen, does not hint at her marital unhappiness or her death from an overdose of alcohol and sleeping pills. The sedately hung Ernsts, Duchamps, and Pollocks do not reveal Peggy's often stormy relationships with those artists. No more unhousebroken Lhasa apsos race through the *palazzo*, and Peggy can no longer be seen reclining like a queen in her gondola. After dying at 81 from the complications of a stroke, she was cremated on San Michele and brought home to rest beside her beloved dogs.

DIRECTIONS, HOURS, AND ADMISSION: Take the no. 1 vaporetto to the Salute stop and make your way to the right, following the signs to the collection. The collection is closed Tuesdays, open 11:00 A.M. to 6:00 P.M. Wednesday through Monday and until 9:00 P.M. on Saturdays. Admission is L 9,000.

BIBLIOGRAPHY

Andrea Mantegna. Edited by Jane Martineau. New York: Metropolitan Museum of Art; London: Royal Academy of Arts, Olivetti/Electa, 1992.

Angelico. John Pope-Hennessy. Florence, Italy: Scala Books, 1981.

The Appian Way, a Journey. Dora Jane Hamblin and Mary Jane Grunsfeld. New York: Random House, 1974.

Arthur Hugh Clough. Isobel Armstrong. London: Longmans Green, 1962.

Atlantic Brief Lives. Edited by Louis Kronenberger. Boston: Little, Brown, 1971.

Augustus. A. H. M. Jones. New York: Norton, 1970.

The Autobiography of Benvenuto Cellini. Edited and abridged by Charles Hope and Alessandro Nova. New York: St. Martin's Press, 1983.

The Bad Popes. E. R. Chamberlin. New York: Dial Press, 1969.

The Basic Works of Cicero. Edited by Moses Hadas. New York: Dial Press, 1969.

Bernini. Charles Scribner III. New York: Abrams, 1991.

Boccaccio. Francis MacManus. London: Sheed & Ward, 1947.

The Borgias. Marion Johnson. New York: Holt, Rinehart & Winston, 1981.

Canaletto. J. G. Links. Ithaca, N.Y.: Cornell University Press, 1982.

Canova. Fred Licht and David Finn. New York: Abbeville Press, 1983.

Caruso. Howard Greenfeld. New York: Da Capo Press, 1983.

The Cemetery Book. Tom Weil. New York: Hippocrene Books, 1992.

The Churches of Rome. Roloff Beny and Peter Gunn. New York: Simon & Schuster, 1981.

Cicero the Statesman. R. E. Smith. Cambridge: Cambridge University Press, 1966.

Complete Poems. Salvatore Quasimodo. Translated by Jack Bevan. New York: Schocken Books, 1983.

Dante. Frances Fergusson. New York: Macmillan, 1966.

Diaghilev. Richard Buckle. New York: Atheneum, 1979.

The Divine Comedy. Dante Alighieri. Translated by Mark Mesa. New York: Penguin, 1984.

Donatello. Bonnie A. Bennett and David G. Wilkens. Mt. Kisco, N.Y.: Moyer Bell, 1984.

Elizabeth Barrett Browning. Margaret Forster. New York: Doubleday, 1988.

Bibliography

Expatriates and Patriots. Ernest Earnest. Durham, N.C.: Duke University Press, 1968.

Ezra Pound. Peter Ackroyd. New York: Scribner's, 1980.

The Fall of the House of Savoy. Robert Katz. New York: Macmillan, 1971.

Famous and Curious Cemeteries. John Francis Marion. New York: Crown, 1977.

Fellini, a Life. Hollis Alpert. New York: Atheneum, 1986.

Filippo Brunelleschi. Eugenio Battisti. New York: Rizzoli, 1981.

Five Roman Emperors. Bernard W. Henderson. Reprint of 1927 edition. New York: Barnes & Noble, 1969.

The Fortunate Pilgrims. Paul R. Baker. Cambridge: Harvard University Press, 1964.

Francesco Petrarca, Poet and Humanist. Maud F. Jerrold. Port Washington, N.Y.: Kennikat Press, 1970.

Frederick Rolfe: Baron Corvo. Miriam J. Benkovitz. New York: Putnam, 1977.

Galileo. James Reston, Jr. New York: HarperCollins, 1994.

The Gentle Bonaparte. Owen Connelly. New York: Macmillan, 1968.

Giotto. Eugenio Battisti. Editions d'Art Albert Skira. Cleveland: World Publishing, 1960.

Giotto and Florentine Painting. Bruce Cole. New York: Harper & Row, 1976.

The Glorious Ones. Harold Schonberg. New York: Times Books, 1985.

The Great Conductors. Harold Schonberg. New York: Simon & Schuster, 1967.

Great Leaders in Human Progress. Edward Howard Griggs. Freeport, N.Y.: Books for Libraries Press, 1969.

The Guggenheims. John H. Davis. New York: Morrow, 1978.

Hadrian. Stewart Perowne. Westport, Conn.: Greenwood Press, 1960.

History of Italian Renaissance Art. Frederick Hartt. Third edition. Englewood Cliffs, N.J.: Prentice Hall; New York: Abrams, 1987.

A History of Venice. John Julius Norwich. New York: Knopf, 1982.

Horowitz. Glenn Plaskin. New York: Morrow, 1983.

The House of Medici, Its Rise and Fall. Christopher Hibbert. New York: Morrow, 1975.

Il Duce. Richard B. Lyttle. New York: Atheneum, 1987.

Italian Journeys. Jonathan Keates. London: Pan Macmillan, 1991.

The Italian Painters of the Renaissance. Bernard Berenson. London: Phaidon Press, 1952.

James. Peggy Miller. New York: St. Martin's Press, 1971.

John Keats. Robert Gittings. Boston: Little, Brown, 1968.

Keats and His World. Timothy Hilton. London: Thames & Hudson, 1971.

The Life, Manners, and Travels of Fanny Trollope. Johanna Johnston. New York: Hawthorn Books, 1978.

The Lives of the Great Composers. Harold C. Schonberg. New York: Norton, 1970.

Lives of the Most Eminent Painters. Giorgio Vasari. Translated by Mrs. Jonathan Foster. New York: Heritage Press, 1967.

The Lives of the Painters, Sculptors and Architects. Giorgio Vasari. Translated by A. B. Hinds. New York: Dutton, 1963.

Ludovico Ariosto. Robert Griffin. New York: Twayne, 1974.

Machiavelli. Edited by De Lamar Jensen. Boston: Heath, 1960.

Machiavelli. Giuseppe Prezzolini. New York: Farrar, Straus & Giroux, 1967.

Marco Polo. Richard Humble. New York: Putnam's, 1975.

The Medici, a Tale of Fifteen Generations. James Cleugh. New York: Doubleday, 1975.

Michelangelo. Howard Hibbard. New York: Harper & Row, 1974.

Mussolini: The Tragic Women in His Life. Vittorio Mussolini. New York: Dial Press, 1973.

The Norton Anthology of English Literature. Edited by M. H. Abrams. New York: Norton, 1962.

Oxford Dictionary of Popes. J. N. D. Kelly. Oxford: Oxford University Press, 1986.

Painting in Cinquecentro Venice: Titian, Veronese, Tintoretto. David Roand. New Haven, Conn.: Yale University Press, 1982.

Peggy, the Wayward Guggenheim. Jacqueline Bogard Weld. New York: Dutton, 1986.

The Penguin Dictionary of Saints. Donald Attwater. New York: Penguin, 1965.

The Poems of Virgil. Translated by James Rhodes. Chicago Encyclopaedia Britannica, 1952.

Puccini. Howard Greenfield. New York: Putnam's, 1980.

The Quest for Corvo. A. J. A. Symons. Harmondsworth, England: Penguin, 1966.

The Radical Tradition. Edited by Gilbert Markus. New York: Doubleday, 1993.

Ravenna Guide-Book. Giovanni Mesini. Ravenna, Italy: Longo, 1994.

The Roman Way. Edith Hamilton. New York: Norton, 1932.

Rossini. Herbert Weinstock. New York: Knopf, 1968.

Saint Francis of Assisi. Morris Bishop. Boston: Little, Brown, 1974.

Saint Peter. Michael Grant. New York: Scribner's, 1994.

Saint Watching. Phyllis McGinley. New York: Viking Press, 1969.

Saints Preserve Us! Sean Kelly and Rosemary Rogers. New York: Random House, 1993.

Sayonara, Michelangelo. Waldemaar Januszczak. Reading, Mass.: Addison-Wesley, 1990.

A Serious Character. Humphrey Carpenter. Boston: Houghton Mifflin, 1988.

Shelley, the Pursuit. Richard Holmes. New York: Dutton, 1975.

The Stones of Florence. Mary McCarthy. New York: Penguin, 1959.

Stravinsky. Eric Walter White. Berkeley: University of California Press, 1969.

Bibliography

A Summer in Italy. Sean O'Faolain. New York: Devon-Adair, 1951.

Theodoric's Mausoleum. Wanda Gaddoni. Bologna, Italy: University Press, undated.

Tintoretto. Francesco Valcanover and Rerisio Pignatti. New York: Abrams, 1985.

Toscanini. George Marek. New York: Atheneum, 1975.

Trajan's Column and the Dacian Wars. Lino Rossi. Ithaca, N.Y.: Cornell University Press, 1971.

A Traveler in Rome. H. V. Morton. New York: Dodd, Mead, 1957.

The Twelve Caesars. Michael Grant. New York: Scribner's, 1975.

The Twelve Caesars. Gaius Suetonius Tranquillus. Translated by Robert Graves. Revised by Michael Grant. New York: Penguin, 1980.

Understanding Toscanini. Joseph Horowitz. New York: Knopf, 1987.

Venice Observed. Mary McCarthy. New York: Penguin, 1961.

Verdi. Mary Jane Phillips-Matz. Oxford: Oxford University Press, 1993.

Virgil. Edited by Henry Steele Commager. Englewood Cliffs, N.J.: Prentice Hall, 1966.

Walter Savage Landor. Ernest Dilworth. New York: Twayne, 1971.

Women Artists, Women Exiles. Constance Fenimore Woolson. Edited by Joan Myers Weimer. New Brunswick, N.J.: Rutgers University Press, 1988.

The World of Serge Diaghilev. Charles Spencer. New York: Penguin, 1974.

The World of Venice. James Morris. New York: Pantheon, 1960.

INDEX

Accoramboni, Vittoria, 102
Adelaide, Archduchess of Austria, 30
Agrippa Postumus, 6
Agrippa, Marcus, 4, 25
Agrippina I (the elder), 3
Agrippina II (the younger, mother of Nero), 16
Ahenobarbus, Gnaeus Domitius (father of Nero), 16
Ahenobarbus, Lucius Domitius (see Nero)
Alexander IV, 194
Alexander VI (Cardinal Rodrigo Borgia), 14, 149, 150
Alexander VII, 22, 32, 58, 59, 61–62, 149
Alexandro VII, 32, 37
Alfieri, Vittorio, 64, 118, 119
Amerighi family, 144
Angelico, Fra, 33–35, 37, 98
Angelo, Fra, 86
Anicetus, Pope, 57
Anthony, Mark (Antonius), 4, 81
Appian Way (Appia Antica), 71–73
Aquino, Maria d', 90
Arena Chapel, 111
Ariosto, Ludivico, 39
Arminius, 6
Arnold, Matthew, 76
Arqua Petrarca, 177–79
Artusi, Giovanni Maria, 203
Assisi, 83–88
Attila the Hun, 154
Augustus Caesar, 1, 3–6, 7, 77, 78, 81

Bach, Johann Sebastian, 221
Baglioni, Astorre, 188, 189
Balanchine, George, 221
Bandinelli, Baccio, 140–41
Bar Kokhba, 10
Barberini, Maria, 148
Barezzi, Antonio, 166, 169
Barrett, Edward, Sr., 133, 134
Bartolini, Lorenzo, 124
Bathhurst, Rosa, 47, 53
Bayezid II, Sultan, 63

Beata Giulia, 92
Bell, John, 48
Bellarmine (Cardinal), 127
Bellini, Gentile, 191, 199
Bellini, Giovanni, 185, 191–93, 199, 201
Bellini, Jacopo, 191
Bembo, Pietro, 150
Benedict XIII, 33, 37
Benedict XIV, 59, 60
Benjamin, Dorothy Park, 75
Bernini, Gian Lorenzo, 13, 14, 15, 21–23, 25, 32, 33, 57, 58, 61, 62
Bibbiena, Maria, 29
Biraghi family, 176
Bisceglie, Alfonso di, 149–50
Bismark (prince), 26
Boccaccio, Giovanni, x, 89–91, 110
Boethius, 155
Boleyn, Anne, 132
Bologna, 147–48
Bonaparte, Charlotte, 119, 124, 215
Bonaparte, Joseph, 124
Bonaparte, Napoleon, 19, 124
Bonarelli, Constanza, 22
Bonelli family, 170
Boniface VIII, 152
Borghese, Camillo (See Paul V)
Borghese, Pauline Bonaparte, 19
Borgia, Cesare, 14, 120, 149, 150
Borgia, Giovanni, 14
Borgia, Giovanni (son of Cesare Borgia), 149
Borgia, Lucrezia, 14, 148–50
Borgia, Maria Enriquez, 14
Borgia, Rodrigo, 150
Borgia, Rodrigo (see Alexander VI)
Botticelli, Sandro, x, 108, 137–39
Boulez, Pierre, 221
Bragadin, Marcantonio, 186, 188–89
Bramante, Donato, 57
Brancusi, Constantin, 226
Brawne, Fanny, 45, 46
Bresci, Gaetano, 27
Breton, Andre, 226
Britannicus, 16
Brown, Charles, 45, 46

Index

Brown, Horatio F., 211
Browning, Elizabeth Barrett, x, 49, 129, 132–35
Browning, Robert, 49, 129, 132, 134, 135
Bruch, Max, 148
Brunelleschi, Filippo, x, 98, 100, 109, 111–13, 124
Brutus, Marcus, 1, 3
Buddha, 194
Bueri, Piccarda, 99
Byron, Lord George, 44, 52, 53

Caecilius, Marcus, 71
Caesar, Gaius Julius, 1–3, 4, 5, 9, 77, 79, 80, 81
Caffe Greco, 54
Calder, Alexander, 224, 225
Caligula, 6, 16
Calmo, Andrea, 207
Campus Martius, 1, 3
Canaccio, Bernard, 151
Canaday, John, 191
Canaletto, Antonio, 209
Canova, Antonio, 19, 60, 64, 65, 118, 198–99, 200
Capelle Medicee, 102–9
Capello, Bianca, 103, 104
Capi, Giuseppe, 148
Caravaggio, 13
Carducci, Giosue, 26, 147
Caruso, Enrico, x, 73–75
Casentini, Andrea di Mariano, 131
Castaldi, Maria, 74
Castel Sant'Angelo, 8–9, 11, 40
Catacombs of St. Calixtus, 69, 70, 72, 73
Catherine of Aragon, 40
Catiline, Lucius, 79, 80
Cattanei, Vannozza, 14, 149
Cattaneo, Carlo, 166
Cattaneo, Claudia, 203
Cattani, Jean-Louis, 53
Cavalcanti, Andrea (Il Buggiano), 113
Cavalieri, Tommaso de', 117
Cavour, Camillo, 30
Cellini, Benvenuto, 141, 142–44
Cenci, Beatrice, 9, 52, 71
Certaldo, 88–92
Certosa, 147–48
Cestius, Caius, 54
Chagall, Marc, 219, 224
Chaliapin, Fyodor, 218
Charlemagne, 61, 97
Charles (King of Spain), 40
Charles Albert (King of Sardinia), 30
Charles V, 38, 201
Charles VIII, 120
Chaucer, Geoffrey, 89
Cherubini, Luigi, 115

Chigi, Agostino, 14–15
Christina, Queen of Sweden, 57–58, 59
Christine of Lorraine, 105
Churchill, Sir Winston, 80
Ciano, Gaetano, 159
Ciceri, Eduardo, 176
Cicero, 2, 4, 79–81
Cimabue, 109, 110
Cimitero Monumentale, 165–76
Cinna, 2
Clairmont, Claire, 51, 52
Clark, Charles Cowden, 45
Clary, Julie Bonaparte, 119, 124
Claudius, 6, 16
Clement VII (Giulio de' Medici), 29, 38, 39–41, 141, 143
Clement VIII, 18, 19, 71
Clement XIII, 59, 60, 198
Clement XIV, 198
Clench, Claude Shakespeare, 130
Cleopatra, 3, 4
Cocteau, Jean, 218, 226
Cody, William "Buffalo Bill," 54
Colbran, Isabella, 123
Colonna family, 3
Colonna, Giovanni (Cardinal), 178
Comini, Giovanni, 182
Constantine, 57
Contarini, Alessandro, 180
Coolidge, Calvin, 27
Copernicus, 40, 127
Copley, John Singleton, 129
Cornelia (wife of Julius Caesar), 2
Corvo, Baron (see Rolfe, Fred.)
Coscia, Niccolò, 33
Crassus, 2, 3
Crespi, Pasquale, 168, 170

D'Aquino, Maria, 90
Dalí, Salvador, 226
Dante Alighieri, x, 76, 89, 109, 113, 115, 118, 150, 151–53, 176
Debussy, Claude, 95, 219, 220
Delisser family, 131
Derain, André, 219
Descartes, René, 58
Diaghilev, Sergei Pavlovitch, x, 214, 217–19, 220
Dickens, Charles, 165
Dio Cassius, ix
Diocletian, 57
Diogenes, 132
Donatello, 98, 100–102, 181, 182
Donati, Gemma di Manetto, 152
Doolittle, Hilda, 215
Dryden, John, 76
Duchamp, Marcel, 226, 227
Duncan, Isadora, 218
Duomo (See Santa Maria del Fiore)

Durante, Jimmy, 152
Dürer, Albrecht, 142

El Greco, 208
Eliot, T. S., 215, 216
Elizabeth I, 20, 182
English Cemetery (Florence),
    129–35
Enriquez, Maria, 14
Erasmus, 39
Ernst, Max, 224, 226, 227
Este, Alfonso d', 150
Este, Constanza d', 182
Eugenius IV, 83

Fabris, Giuseppe, 29
Farrar, Geraldine, 75
Favarone, Beatrice di, 88
Favarone, Caterina di (Agnes), 88
Fellini, Federico, x, 160, 161–3
Ferrara, 148–50
Ferrari, Benedetto, 204
Florence, 97–145
Foggini, Giovanni, 125
Fokine, Michel, 218
Fombelle, John, 131
Ford, Ford Maddox, 216
Formia, 79–81
Foscari, Francesco, Doge, 200, 205
Foscolo, Ugo, 124
Fossati, Luigi, 170
Francis I (King of France), 40, 143
Franz Joseph, 26
Frari, 197–205
Frederick II, 88
Frost, Robert, 216
Furtwängler, Wilhelm, 173

Gaddi, Taddeo, 137
Gaius Caesar, 6
Gaius Cestius, Pyramid of 43, 47,
    54–55
Galileo, Galilei, x, 61, 105, 119, 125–
    27, 132, 212
Galla Placidia, ix, 153–54
Galli, Dina, 168, 171
Gamba, Marina, 126
Garibaldi, Giuseppe, 30
Gentile, Giovanni, 124
Geoghegan, Lewis, 54
Ghiberti, Lorenzo, 100, 112–13, 119,
    124–25
Ghirlandaio, Francesco, 108, 116,
    137
Giachetti, Ada, 74
Giacometti, Alberto, 226
Giambologna (Giovanni da Bolo-
    gna), 141
Gilbert, Sir W. S., 223
Ginestera, Alberto, 71
Giorgione, 192, 199, 201, 209

Giotto de Bondone, 109–111, 116
Gisleni, G. B., 15
Godwin, William, 51
Goethe, Johann Wolfgang von, 3
Gonzaga, Francesco, 150, 203
Gounod, Charles, 218
Gramsci, Antonio, 47, 54
Graves, Robert, 6
Gregory VII, 60
Gregory XI, 36
Gregory XVI, 27
Guerrazzi, Francesco, 71
Guggenheim, Benita, 226
Guggenheim, Benjamin, 225
Guggenheim, Florette, 225
Guggenheim, Hazel, 226
Guggenheim, Jesse, 225
Guggenheim, Peggy, x, 224–27
Guggenheim, Washington, 225

Hadrian, 7, 8–10, 15, 25
Hadrian's Villa, 10
Haseltine, William Stanley, 47, 54
Hawkwood, Sir John, 36
Hawthorne, Nathaniel, 49
Hemingway, Ernest, 215
Henry IV, 62
Henry VIII, 40, 61, 132
Herennius, 81
Herriman, George, 215
Hitler, Adolph, 158–59
Hobbes, Thomas, 127
Horace, 4, 77
Horowitz, Sonia, 175
Horowitz, Vladimir, x, 168, 174–76
Horowitz, Wanda Toscanini, 175
Hoving, Carl Isak Victor, 54
Howard, Thomas, 182
Hugo, Victor, 150
Humbert I, 25–27
Humbert II, 31
Hunt, Fanny Waugh, 135
Hunt, Holman, 135
Hunt, Leigh, 45, 51, 52

Indian Army War Cemetery, 156
Innocent II, 10
Innocent III, 85, 88
Innocent VI, 91
Innocent VIII, 59, 63–64, 109
Innocent XI, 59, 62–3

Jacopo e Filippo, Church of, 88–92
James, Henry, 43, 49
Jefferson, Thomas, 129
Joanna of Austria, 102–3
John the Baptist, 28, 191
John XXIII (antipope), 8
Jovian, 1
Joyce, James, 215, 216
Julia (daughter of Augustus), 3, 6

Index

Julia (daughter of Caesar), 2, 3
Julius II, 28, 29, 38, 117
Julius Caesar (see Caesar, Gaius Julius)

Kandinsky, Wassily, 226
Karsavina, Tamara, 218
Kat, Krazy, 215
Keats, John, x, 43, 44–48, 89
Koch, Kenneth, 35
Kublai Khan, 193–4

Landor, Arnold Savage, 128, 129–130
Landor, Julia, 132
Landor, Walter Savage, 130, 132
Latini, Brunetto, 153
Lazzati, Pietro, 165
Léger, Fernand, 226
Leo I (Leo the Great), 39, 61
Leo II, 61
Leo III, 39, 59, 61
Leo IV, 39, 61
Leo X (Giovanni di Lorenzo de' Medici), 19, 28, 38–39, 40, 107, 141, 151, 209
Leo XI, 59, 62
Leo XII, 61
Leonardo da Vinci, 28, 40, 115, 138
Leone, Fra, 86
Leopold II, 102
Lepidus, 4
Leucade, Messinis da, 221
Lewis, Wyndham, 215
Lifar, Serge, 219
Lippershey, Hans, 126
Lippi, Fra, 98, 138
Liszt, Franz, 174
Livia Drusilla (wife of Augustus), 6
Locke, John, 212
Lombardo, Antonio, 197
Lombardo, Pietro, 151, 187
Lombardo, Tullio, 187, 197
Lotto, Lorenzo, 15
Lowell, Robert, 217
Lozzo, Guido da, 182
Lucius Caesar, 6
Ludovica, Anna Maria, 103
Luther, Martin, 39, 40

Machiavelli, Niccolò, x, 39, 118–122
MacLeish, Archibald, 216
Maderno, Carlo, 57, 69, 72
Madonna dell'Orto, 206–09
Maecenas, 4, 77
Mahomet II, Sultan, 191
Manelli, Francesco, 204
Manetti, Antonio, 111
Manfredi, Doria, 94
Mantegna, Andrea, 191, 202

Manzoni, Alessandro, 165–66, 168, 169
Marcello, Jacopo, 200, 205
Marcello, Nicolò, Doge, 186, 191
Marchetti, Domenico, 182
Marchetti, Pietro, 182
Margherita, Queen of Italy, 25–27
Marguerite-Louise of Orleans, 105
Maria Cristina, 199
Marius, 2
Martelli family, 100
Martinelli, Caterinuccia, 203
Martinuzzi, Napoleone, 206
Masaccio, 116
Maserati, Ernesto, 148
Masina, Giulietta, 160, 161, 162, 163
Masseo, Fra, 86, 87
Massine, Leonid, 219
Matilda of Canossa, 58–60
Mausoleum of Augustus, 3–6, 11
Mazzini, Giuseppe, 166, 168
McCarthy, Mary, 129, 187
Medici, Cosimo de' (Cosimo the elder), 34, 98–99, 101
Medici, Cosimo de' (Cosimo II), 105
Medici, Cosimo de' (Cosimo III), 105–6
Medici, Cosimo di Giovanni de' (Cosimo I), 102, 103, 115, 143
Medici, Ferdinando de' (Ferdinando I), 104–5
Medici, Ferdinando de' (Ferdinando II), 105
Medici, Francesco di Cosimo de' (Francesco I), 103–4
Medici, Giovanni de', 99
Medici, Giovanni de Bicci de', 97–98, 99
Medici, Giovanni di Lorenzo de' (see Leo X)
Medici, Giuliano di Lorenzo de', 28, 107–8
Medici, Giuliano di Piero de', 40, 108
Medici, Giulio de' (see Clement VII)
Medici, Isabella di Cosimo de', 102
Medici, Lorenzo de' (Duke of Urbino), 107
Medici, Lorenzo de' (the Magnificent), 38, 40, 64, 108–9, 116, 138
Medici, Piero de' (the Gouty), 99, 101–2, 108
Melba, Nellie, 75
Messina, Antonello da, 192
Messina, Francesco, 58
Metella, Cecilia, 72
Michelangelo (Buonarroti), ix–x, 14, 21, 28, 29, 40, 57, 59, 61, 98, 106, 108, 115–18, 119, 143, 151, 208, 215
Milan, 165–176
Milstein, Nathan, 175

Milton, John, 76, 127, 132
Missiano, Eduardo, 74
Mocenigo family, 186
Mocenigo, Giovanni, Doge, 186, 187
Mocenigo, Pietro, Doge, 186, 187
Mocenigo, Tommaso, Doge, 186, 190–91
Modigliani, Amedeo, 175
Molière, Jean Baptiste, 89
Montale, Eugenio, 170
Montelupo, Raffaello da, 15
Monteverdi, Claudio, 200, 202–4
Moore, Henry, 226
Moravia, Alberto, 71
Morosini, Michele, Doge, 186, 190
Mussolini, Alessandro, 156
Mussolini, Benito, x, 31, 54, 124, 156, 157–60
Mussolini, Bruno, 156
Mussolini, Gina Ruperti, 156
Mussolini, Rachele, 156, 158
Mussolini, Rosa, 156
Mustafa Pasha, Lala, 188–89

Naples, 73–78
Napoleon III, 30
Napoleon, Louis, 124
Narni, Erasmus da (Gattamelata), 180–81
Narni, Giannantonio da, 180
Negri, Anna Maria Mussolini, 156–57
Nelli, Bartolomea, 118
Nero, 13, 15–17, 67
Niccolò, Bernardo di, 118
Nicholas V, 34
Nicomedes, King of Bithynia, 2
Nijinsky, Vaslav, 218, 219, 220
Noves, Laura de, 177, 178, 179

O'Donnell, Rory, 71
O'Faolain, Sean, 111
O'Neill, Hugh, 71
Octavia (sister of Augustus), 6
Octavius, Gaius; Octavian (see Augustus)
Odoacer, 155
Ognissanti, Church of the, 137–39
Olson, Charles, 215
Orsini, Clarice, 108
Orsini, Paolo, 102
Ovid, 4, 76

Pacifica, 87
Padua, 180–83
Page, Thomas Jefferson, 54
Palazzo Venier dei Leoni, 224–27
Pallillo family, 214, 221–22
Pantheon, 10, 25–27, 29, 31, 61
Parker, Theodore, 130
Paschal I, 69
Paschal II, 13

Paul II, 201
Paul III, 59, 60–61, 143
Paul V, 17–18, 19, 21, 212
Paul VI, 84
Penzo, Petrus Alojsius, 214, 221
Perugino, 27–28
Pesaro, Giovanni, Doge, 197, 200
Pesaro, Jacopo, 197, 200
Petacci, Clara, 159
Petrarca, Francesca, 179
Petrarca, Francesco, x, 89, 177–79
Petrarca, Giovanni, 179
Pharnaces, King, 2
Picasso, Pablo, 175, 219
Piccarda Bueri, 99
Pinelli, Tullio, 162
Piombo, Sebastian del, 28, 29, 70
Pisa, Isaia da, 35
Pius II, 98
Pius V, 19–20
Pius VI, 65
Pius IX, 30–31
Pius X, 59, 63
Pius XII, 58, 59, 87
Plantagenet, Devereux, 54
Platina, Bartolomeo, 19
Plato, 132
Pliny, 8
Plotina (wife of Trajan), 8
Plotina, Bartolomeo, 18
Poe, Edgar Allan, 165
Pogliani, Enrico, 165
Polli family, 171
Pollock, Jackson, 224, 226, 227
Polo, Maffeo, 193–94
Polo, Marco, 193–95
Polo, Niccolò, 193–94
Pompey, 2, 3, 80
Ponchielli, Amilcare, 94
Pontormo, Jacopo da, 141–42
Poppaea (wife of Nero), 16
Portinari, Beatrice, 152, 153
Pound, Ezra, x, 210, 213, 214, 215–17
Predappio, 156–60
Prokofiev, Sergei, 219
Protestant Cemetery (Rome), 43–55
Ptolemy, 127
Puccini, Elvira, 93, 94
Puccini, Giacomo, x, 74, 92–95
Pulska, Romola, 219

Quasimodo, Salvatore, 168, 169–70
Querini, Elisabetta, 190

Rabirii family, 72
Rabitti, Piera, 176
Rachmaninoff, Sergei, 174, 175
Raffaello da Montelupo, 15
Raphael (Raffaello Sanzio), ix, 14, 15, 27–29, 39, 40, 57, 70

Index

Ravel, Maurice, 218
Ravenna, 150–55
Redaelli family, 164, 165
Rembrandt van Rijn, 202
Renoir, Pierre Auguste, 175, 202
Respighi, Ottorino, 148
Ricordi family, 94
Rimini, 160–163
Rimsky-Korsakov, Nicolai, 148, 218, 220
Robbia, Luca della, 98
Robert, Leopold, 215
Robert of Anjou, 90
Robusti, Domenico, 206
Robusti, Faustina, 207
Robusti, Jacopo (see Tintoretto)
Robusti, Marietta, 206
Rodin, Auguste, 218
Rodriguez, Gonsalvo, 21
Rolfe, Frederick (Baron Corvo), x, 214, 222–24
Rome, 1–67
Roosevelt, Theodore, 63
Rossellini, Roberto, 161–62
Rossellino, Bernardo, 57
Rossini, Gioacchino, 119, 122–24
Rossini, Olympe Pelissier, 122, 123
Rota, Nino, 162
Rouault, Georges, 175, 219
Rovere, Vittoria della, 105
Rozzi family, 176
Rubens, Peter Paul, 202
Rudge, Olga, 216, 217
Rudolf II, 17
Rufino, Fra, 86
Ruggieri, Archbishop, 153
Ruskin, John, 21, 111, 205

Sabina (wife of Hadrian), 8, 10
St. Anthony, ix, 181–2
St. Augustine, 80, 139, 178
St. Barbara, 29
St. Calixtus, 72
St. Catherine of Sienna, ix, 35–38, 190
St. Cecilia, 69–70, 72
St. Cecilia in Trastevere, ix, 69–70, 71
St. Clare, 86, 87–88
St. Cosmas, 34
St. Damian, 34, 85
St. Felix, 181
St. Francis, ix, 83–86, 87, 88, 197
St. Francis of Xavier, 106
St. Genesius, 57
St. Giovanni, 185
St. James, 209
St. Jerome, 19, 20, 21
St. John, 36
St. Lawrence, 21, 34, 154
St. Lio, 209

St. Matthew, 21
St. Maximus, 70
St. Paolo, 185
St. Paul, 14, 36
St. Paula, 19
St. Peter, 7, 14, 22, 39, 57, 59, 65–67, 70, 148
St. Peter's Basilica, 22, 25, 28, 57–67, 148
St. Stephen, 34
St. Theresa, 21, 23
St. Tibertius, 70
St. Valerian, 70
Saint-Saëns, Camille, 218
Salomoni, Giacomo, 186, 190
Salzman, Gerda, 54
San Francisco, Basilica of, 83–87
San Lorenzo (Florence), 97–102
San Lorenzo (Venice), 193–95
San Michele, 211–24
San Pietro in Montorio, 69, 70–71
San Zanipolo, 185–93
Sansovino, Jacopo, 201
Sant'Antonio, Basilica of, 180–183
Santa Chiara, Basilica of, 87–88
Santa Croce, 115–127
Santa Maria del Fiore, 109–113
Santa Maria del Popolo, 13–17
Santa Maria Maggiore, 17–23
Santa Maria sopra Minerva, 32–41
Santi, Giovanni de, 206
Santissima Annunziata, 139–45
Sarpi, Paolo, x, 18, 211–13, 214
Sarto, Andrea del, 139–40
Sarto, Lucrezia del, 140
Satie, Erik, 123
Savelli, Paolo, 200, 205
Savonarola, Girolamo, 139
Scarlatti, Domenico, 174
Schumann, Robert, 174
Scott, Sir Walter, 165
Seneca, 16
Severn, Joseph, 43, 45, 46, 47, 48
Sforza, Giovanni, 149
Sforza-Cessarini, Duchess, 223
Shakespear, Dorothy, 216, 217
Shakespeare, Beatrice, 130
Shakespeare, William, 50, 89, 130
Shelley, Harriet Westbrook, 51
Shelley, Mary Wollstonecraft, 51–52, 53
Shelley, Percy Bysshe, x, 43, 47, 50–52, 53, 71
Siliato, Maria Grazia, 189
Siro the Epicurean, 76
Sixtus III, 17
Sixtus IV, 108, 187
Sixtus V, 20
Smith, Joseph, 209
Sobieski, Maria Clementina (wife of James Stuart), 64–65

Soderini, Pietro, 120
Spenser, Edmund, 45, 76
Speravi, Talia Guadio, 222
Stainer, Frank Justice, 213
Stein, Gertrude, 225
Stolberg, Luisa, 64
Story, Emelyn, 49
Story, Joseph, 49
Story, William W., 47, 49, 132
Stravinsky, Catherine, 221
Stravinsky, Igor, x, 214, 219–221
Stravinsky, Vera, 219, 221
Strepponi, Giuseppina, 169
Strozzi, Ferdinando, 144
Stuart, Charles (the Young Pretender), 59, 64
Stuart, Henry (cardinal Duke of York), 59, 64
Stuart, James (the Old Pretender), 59, 64, 65
Suetonius, ix, 3
Sulla, 2, 79
Sullivan, Sir Arthur, 223
Suppanich, Romeo, 217
Swinburne, Algernon, 132

Tacitus, ix, 6
Tanguy, Yves, 226
Tartini, Giuseppe, 183
Tchaikovsky, Peter, 175
Tennyson, Alfred, 76
Terentia, 79
Theocritus, 77
Theodoric, ix, 8, 150, 154–55
Theodoric's Mausoleum, 154–56
Theodosius, 154
Thomson, Virgil, 35, 219
Tiberius, 6
Tiepolo, Giandomenico, 209
Tiepolo, Jacopo, Doge, 185, 186, 187
Tiepolo, Lorenzo, Doge, 187
Tintoretto, x, 185, 202, 206–9
Tirali, Andrea, 190
Titian, x, 185, 192, 197, 198, 199–202, 206, 208, 209
Toledo, Eleonora da, 102
Tolstoy, Leo, 165
Torre del Lago, 92–95
Torrigiano, Pietro, 116
Toscanini, Arturo, x, 94, 95, 168, 171–74, 175
Toscanini, Carla, 172
"Toto," 75–76
Tournabuoni, Lucrezia, 99
Trajan, 8, 9, 10
Trajan's Column, 7–8, 11
Trambetta, Antonio, 180
Trelawney, Edward, 47, 50, 52–53
Trentini, Emma, 75
Trollope, Anthony, 131, 132

Trollope, Fanny, 131–32
Tron, Nicola, 200, 204–5
Tucca, 78

Ugolino, Count, 153
Ungaretti, Giuseppe, 170
Urban V, 35
Urban VI, 38
Urban VIII, 22, 25, 59, 60–61, 127, 148

Vail, Laurence, 226
Vail, Pegeen, 226, 227
Vail, Sinbad, 226
Valier, Bertucci, Doge, 186, 190
Valier, Elizabeth Querini, 186, 190
Valier, Silvestro, Doge, 186, 190
Valla, Lorenzo, 33
Van Gogh, Vincent, 202
Varius, 77, 78
Varus, P. Quinctilius, 6
Vasari, Giorgio, 29, 34, 110, 115, 139, 140, 142
Vecellio, Cecilia, 201
Vecellio, Tiziano (see Titian)
Vendramin, Andrea, Doge, 186, 190
Venice, 185–227
Vercellana, Rosa, 30
Verdi, Giuseppe, x, 93, 122, 165, 166–69, 173
Verdi, Margherita Barezzi, 167
Vergine, Giuglielmo, 74
Veronese, Paolo, 209
Verrocchio, 98, 108, 138
Vespucci, Amerigo, 137
Vespucci, Simonetta, 137, 138
Vettori, Francesco, 41
Victor Emmanuel II, 26, 29–31
Victor Emmanuel III, 31, 158–59
Vigevano, John, 32–33, 37
Vincenzo I (Duke of Mantua), 202
Vinci, Leonardo da, 28, 40, 115, 138
Virgil, 4, 76–78, 153
Visconti, Giangaleazo, 112
Volkoff, Georges, 54
Voltaire, 60

Wagner, Richard, 93, 123, 173
Walpole, Hugh, 60
Walter, Bruno, 173
Washington, George, 199
West, Benjamin, 129
Whistler, James, 216
Wilde, Oscar, 216
Williams, Edward and Jane, 52, 53
Williams, William Carlos, 215
Witfeldt, Berta Moltke, 99–100
Wolf, Hugo, 221
Woolson, Constance, 43, 47, 48–49
Wooten, Sir Henry, 213
Wordsworth, William, 48

Index

Yeats, William Butler, 215, 216

Zamoyska, Sofia, 119, 124
Zandomeneghi, Luigi, 199
Zanni, Zelio, 163

Zevio, Altichiero, 181
Zola, Emile, 218
Zuccato, Sebastiano, 199
Zukofsky, Louis, 215, 216